I0901371

THE HUMAN SPIRIT

Past and Present—Occult Fraternities and the Mystery of Golgotha

THE HUMAN SPIRIT

Past and Present—Occult Fraternities and the Mystery of Golgotha

Twelve lectures given in Berlin between 13 February and 30 May 1916

TRANSLATED BY MATTHEW BARTON

INTRODUCTION BY MATTHEW BARTON

RUDOLF STEINER

RUDOLF STEINER PRESS

CW 167

The publishers gratefully acknowledge the generous funding of this publication by the estate of Dr Eva Frommer MD (1927–2004) and the Anthroposophical Society in Great Britain

Rudolf Steiner Press
Hillside House, The Square
Forest Row, RH18 5ES

www.rudolfsteinerpress.com

Published by Rudolf Steiner Press 2015

Originally published in German under the title *Gegenwärtiges und Vergangenes im Menschengeiste* (volume 167 in the *Rudolf Steiner Gesamtausgabe* or Collected Works) by Rudolf Steiner Verlag, Dornach. Based on shorthand transcripts and notes that were not reviewed or revised by the speaker. This authorized translation is based on the latest available (second) edition (1962), edited by Robert Friedenthal and Wolfram Groddeck

Published by permission of the Rudolf Steiner Nachlassverwaltung, Dornach

A catalogue record for this book is available from the British Library

ISBN 978 1 85584 522 0

Cover by Mary Giddens
Typeset by DP Photosetting, Neath, West Glamorgan
Printed and bound by Gutenberg Press Ltd., Malta

CONTENTS

During the war years, Rudolf Steiner spoke the following memorial words before every lecture for members of the Anthroposophical Society that he gave in countries affected by the conflict.

My dear friends, we here remember the guardian spirits of those who stand on the great battlefields of current events:

Spirits, guardians of your souls,
May your wings bring
The petitioning love of our souls
To earthly human beings
Entrusted to your protection
So that, united with your power
Our plea shine out, bring help
To the souls it loving seeks.

And turning also to the guardian spirits of those who have already crossed the threshold of death during these dire events:

Spirits, guardians of your souls,
May your wings bring
The petitioning love of our souls
To human beings in the sphere
Entrusted to your protection
So that, united with your power
Our plea shine out, bring help
To the souls it loving seeks.

And the spirit whom for years we have sought to approach through our science of the spirit, the spirit who passed through the Mystery of Golgotha for the earth's redemption and for the freedom and progress of humanity, may he be with you in your arduous duties.

INTRODUCTION

The word 'truth' is used by all of us in all kinds of contexts and situations, and, it has to be said, often in a way that unconsciously serves our own less than comprehensive view of it. It is a word that figures frequently in this volume, and Steiner uses it, I feel, to challenge us in our often slapdash and partisan requisitioning of the word. For him, truth has to be continually sought, as if digging down through manifold strata of appearance to find a reality—another vital word for him—that underlies and encompasses all narrower perspectives. The 'truth' asserted by a partisan interest is invariably tinged with dishonesty, whether this be the outright mendacities of politicians and rulers (Steiner refers here to the machinations, in his day, of the British Empire, but similar intrigue clearly continues unabated) or equally—and often in collaboration with the former—the manipulative techniques of 'secret societies' intent on securing and shoring up their power.

In early 1916, when these lectures were given, the conflict of partisan interests had of course assumed very violent forms—entrenched positions all too aptly reflected in the actual trenches of the First World War. Truth, as we know, is the first casualty of war; but the machinations that had led to it (along with incompetence in high places) were not just untruth by omission but, in Steiner's view, intentional deceit that served hidden aims about which the public was mostly in the dark. By this time, however, the 'spirit of 1914', characterized by one Berlin professor at the time as a 'great single feeling of moral elevation, a soaring of religious sentiment, in short, the ascent of a whole people to the heights . . . ', must have started to pale as the horrors of the protracted war began to be felt by civilians too. It was in this year also that Steiner gave his lectures on 'the

Karma of Untruthfulness', speaking out against the frenzy, hatred and propaganda that were still ubiquitous, and trying to help his audiences to discern the spiritual struggle unfolding behind outer events.

Truth is never, it seems, easy, comfortable or superficial. 'Realities', says Steiner 'speed ahead of us while our knowledge hems them in like a dress too small and tight.' It can be sought therefore only by a willingness to review and revise our assumptions, to reappraise our fixed positions, whether these be unconscious habits of materialistic thought, with which our education has 'equipped' us, or our habitual efforts to (wrongfully) constrain and control others' thoughts and actions by insisting on the 'truth' of a limited point of view. In relation to the latter, Steiner highlights how, while we tend to reject overt authority in modern culture nowadays, we easily succumb to its more covert forms in the received wisdoms we adopt unthinkingly.

It is terribly difficult to be sure when we possess the truth, not least since the word 'possess' itself suggests an unwillingness to revise our purchase on it. But Steiner offers hints about how and when we can sense its presence in us: not just in our words themselves, or the views they express, but (and he reiterates this) the very way we use words, our tone, our tact in using them, and our apprehension of the scope and limits of language. Can we place words into a room of others, or a community of readers, in a way that does not insist too forcefully on one point of view but instead invites a free and mutually enlarging response? Another place where we can look for truth is in, say, art and architecture: in buildings whose inner purpose is reflected in their outer forms; or in painting that allows the spirit—rather than merely naturalistic reproduction of the world—to speak through it. These are also metaphors of our own congruency, of inner belief, intuitions or feeling corresponding to their outer expression. Utilitarian buildings and naturalistic art, made shallow in their echo of merely earthly imperatives, suppress non-material realities and, in Steiner's view, become part of our 'cultural illness': a disjuncture which divides us from ourselves and the deeper sources of our life and health.

In a key lecture in this volume Steiner shows that truth goes hand-in-hand with a sense of (perhaps unfashionable) gratitude for our place in the world—a realization of the interconnectedness of all things, of interdependence between all the realms both 'below' and 'above' us. This sense of humility clearly takes us further and deeper than mere economic exploitation of the earth's resources, and a limited view of ourselves as, primarily, 'Homo economicus'. Steiner thinks the partial truths of Darwinism ultimately need huge revision. Ideas of the 'selfish gene' (Dawkins) fail to recognize that, in the magnificently enlarged sense in which Steiner uses it, the 'I' upon which all evolution on earth is predicated signifies an *overcoming* of egotism, and the imaginative embrace of all other beings. The spiritual reality of the 'I' that descends to us from non-material worlds, and towards which we evolve through earthly lives, is the epitome of truth. 'To live in truth', says Steiner, 'to wish to be true in one's whole being, will be the watchword of the future'. But since to do this means facing ourselves with courage and unsparing honesty, we can be sure that it will be anything other than a comfortable undertaking.

Matthew Barton, October 2015

LECTURE 1

13 FEBRUARY 1916

We will hear a recitation of poems by Friedrich Lienhard and Wilhelm Jordan, and following this I would like to reflect on contemporary life from an anthroposophic and literary perspective. This will end the evening. First, though, I wish to say a few words by way of introduction.

Friedrich Lienhard[1] is a modern poet who, we can say, has to some degree come close to spiritual science through his own endeavour. On 4 October last year, 1915, Friedrich Lienhard celebrated his 50th birthday. In Dornach we joined our voices to the numerous good wishes from far and wide that were sent to this spirit-filled poet; and it is my belief that we have particular reasons to look a little more closely at the content and artistry, the poetic nature, of Friedrich Lienhard, who in some ways has affiliated himself with our movement, and regards it favourably. He himself says that he was born in French Alsace and that he experienced some difficulties in wrestling his way through to what he calls his world-view—which he increasingly sought to bring to the light of day, to develop and elaborate, from a central European, German quality. In his poems he really sought to unfold the authentic impetus of this central European, German nature. In this poet there lives something which he felt to have an intimate affinity with his being, and which, as I have tried to describe, he sought and strove for. An element lives in him whose value may perhaps only properly be understood from the artistic and spiritual perspective of spiritual science. In Lienhard's poems we have, above all, wonderful descriptions of nature: lyrical nature poems, but of a very distinctive kind. When he tries to write human utterances, though, these are also nature poetry. Here too there is something that emanates from human nature in an immediate and natural way, and reveals the spirit within natural existence. What is this due to? It originates in something that we may perhaps only properly heed in Friedrich Lienhard if we consider not only the content, the thoughts expressed in his work, but also the intrinsically artistic form they are embodied in. And this is true of all art, although nowadays it has vanished entirely from human awareness in respect of art, and poetry in particular. In the feelings, the thoughts that arise and develop, flare and fade, in this distinctive swelling of his soul experiences, as they come to expression in poetic language, we find something like the sway of an elemental spirituality, a sympathy of the poet's soul with what, as we see it, lives elementally in the etheric world in nature behind merely sensory existence, what lives in the etheric world when human nature comes to natural expression—as for instance in the utterances of a child's soul life. If we study the words of Friedrich Lienhard it really seems as if elemental spirits arise and move through them—these spirits who, as we know, stream and warm through all natural phenomena, live and weave within them. And this streaming and warming, this weaving life of elemental beings in nature, enters and lives in the words of such a poet, who truly understands how to live in harmony with the spirit of nature.

Furthermore, through his capacity to grasp contexts of great scope relating to humanity and the cosmos, with which he has a great, feeling affinity, he seeks—without ever lapsing into narrow nationalism—to encompass the driving, active powers and beings of national culture; yet he does so not by focusing on a randomly individual element, but by drawing on the whole sway and surge of the folk-soul principle, placing individual figures into the great, spiritual context of national life and culture. Thus Friedrich Lienhard can comprehend and portray a figure such as Father Oberlin[2] from

Steintal in Alsace, someone spiritualized by a kind of atavistic clairvoyance, and do so in a vividly three-dimensional and yet simultaneously intimate, soulful way. Out of this same impulse he knew how to re-invoke ancient figures of the gods and bring them back into the present. He does not do this, though, by simply taking the content of the old heroic sagas and legends but by really trying to find the means, in modern idiom, to reawaken the tide suffusing this ancient life, whose waves still lap at the shores of our own times. In a sense, therefore, Friedrich Lienhard is really one of our most elevated poets. Other modern poets have sought to distance themselves from all real art, from spirituality, by focusing on the naturalistic and realistic in their work, in what they see as a new style. The real poet does not seek to create something new by naturalistic means, though, but by grasping the eternal stream of beauty afresh, anew, in a way that allows art to remain art. And real art, therefore, can never be devoid of spirit.

No doubt it is due to this also that Friedrich Lienhard has come closer to what he calls 'Paths to Weimar'. For a long time he was the editor of a periodical called *Paths to Weimar* which appeared at irregular intervals, in which he tried to engage with the great ideas and artistic impulses of the great period at the end of the eighteenth and beginning of the nineteenth century, to discern, as we may find in our concluding reflections, what was of real worth in this era that has now been completely or at least largely forgotten. By this means he sought to deepen his own, later artistic culture, to make it more inward; and thus wonderfully inward poems eventually emerged from this endeavour, such as those about St Odile and other figures. He connects all such things in a genuine, authentic way with the Christian impulses that surge through humanity. And it is remarkable how he so finely and subtly approaches an element—not through the outward content of his poetry, but by drawing on elemental qualities and beings to sustain it—which seemed to have been lost entirely from German poetry. When you hear the recitation you will notice this in certain passages in the form of alliterative art, alliteration.

This alliteration, and its affinity with the whole nature of central European, German folk culture, leads him close to another poet who, partly by his own fault and yet chiefly by the fault of our era and its aberrations, has met with little understanding. The second part of the recitation will be devoted to this poet, Wilhelm Jordan,[3] who, through stave rhyme or alliteration, sought to renew what he calls the 'resonant stream of speech of ancient days'. It was intrinsic to his nature to reintroduce this form of ancient poetry into the modern era, seeking to raise it above the small scope of the everyday to encompass great and moving impulses. And it has to be said that it is a terrible shame—although Jordan himself was partly to blame for this—that a poem such as 'The Demiurge' has remained so neglected. It is a poem which truly attempts to connect the world-moving spirit principles with the life of humanity on earth. In the 1850s, partly due to Wilhelm Jordan himself, it remained neglected. He is partly at fault himself since he did adopt something of the naturalistic, scientific mode of looking at the world, and this spoiled a good part of his endeavours. In his poem 'Nibelungen' much was spoiled by the fact that he allowed naturalistic principles of inheritance to hold sway, the material powers of descent from one generation to the next, rather than what older eras saw as much deeper principles. He places too great an emphasis on what passes down through the blood instead of from soul to soul. By this means, certainly, Wilhelm Jordan paid his tribute to the modern naturalistic and scientific mode. But at the same time this deprived his works of what, in a former era, gave human artistic endeavours their great spiritual impulses, preventing them from sinking into inartistic barbarism, which later frequently came to replace former spiritual principles. Today we can see how Wilhelm Jordan's efforts are ridiculed. But we, for our part, should let great impulses work upon us, wherever they appear, for the time will come when such impulses will need to fulfil a certain mission in the whole, universal evolution of humanity.

Certainly, the poet Friedrich Lienhard meets with great and widespread acknowledgement. But what we, in our circles, can find in his work, and should seek to discover, will primarily be what carries his artistic endeavours forward into the future upon and along with the wave of spiritual-scientific endeavours. And now let us first hear Friedrich Lienhard's poems, and then some passages from Wilhelm Jordan's Nibelungen poem, the legend of Siegfried.

[Recitation by Frau Dr Steiner of the following poems by Friedrich Lienhard: 'Faith', 'Morning Wind', 'Forest Greeting', 'The Light Creative', 'Lonely Rock', 'Did you learn of it too?', 'All the delicate flower bells', 'Soul Migration', 'Elfen Dance', 'Summer Night'. Songs of St Odile: 'Autumn on Mont Saint Odile', 'Saint Odile'. Recitation from Wilhelm Jordan's 'Nibelungen Song'.[4]]

It is always good to experience the art of poetry, of this kind particularly. In Friedrich Lienhard we have a poet who tries still to bear into the present era soul experiences of a spiritual, idealistic nature, who is strong enough still to unite these with experiences of the natural world. Here we can still sense that in art *how* you say things is more important than what is said. How wonderfully he conjures a feeling of enchantment in the area surrounding Mont St Odile, and how beautifully he conveys an immediate, lyrical apprehension of the feeling which this patron saint emanates from the region and from the monastery there. The legend, according to which she was once persecuted by her cruel father, but, blinded by him, gained the mystical ability through this very fact to heal the blind and give them back their sight, forms the centre of this poem around which everything else revolves. Everything of a true, mystical nature that relates to this legend, lyrically interwoven with the natural world around Mont St Odile in Alsace, comes to expression in the poems by Friedrich Lienhard that you have just heard. But there are many, many more poems of such power, and at the same time of such intimacy and subtlety by this same poet. The elemental powers resonating from his works does, in turn, give us cause also to recall the much denigrated and neglected poet Wilhelm Jordan.

The small sample we heard today will have shown you how this poet tries to create the figures he places before us out of the great, spiritual weft of life and at the same time to combine this with all we meet in outward physical life: a union of the latter with what weaves and lives in the surging spirit world. It seems to me that in Wilhelm Jordan's work we can, particularly, discern, how the poet's soul unites with world-historical currents, so that artistic, poetic endeavour embodies for us a striving that infuses the spiritual streams of evolution.

The last time we were here together, last Tuesday,[5] I felt the need to ask what would happen to human evolution on earth if no spiritual influx could enter what is given us by purely external, physical existence. Not only in external fields of knowledge, of science, and in social existence and so forth, but also in the artistic realm, it becomes strikingly apparent that we are living in critical times: we are experiencing a crisis (a word connected with 'critical') though not in the sense used by the diminutive literature of today. If the living nature of spiritual science does not encompass human soul life, art, which cannot exist without spirit, will be lost to humanity, must fade from us, no longer resonating as it still does from figures such as Wilhelm Jordan, and as poets such as Friedrich Lienhard seek to invoke it. As yet, human beings do not recognize the threat of artistic decline, since in many respects, here also, the intoxication and somnambulistic dreaming I spoke of last Tuesday still hold sway. Much of this could be discerned if people had the organs of vision to perceive it. It would be an excellent thing if more and more people could, through a true feeling for the science of the spirit, gain insight into the significant fact that the art of acting—that really did survive until quite recently—is now sinking into a slough of despond in forms that are anything other than artistic. Rheinhardtian principles[6] prefigure what art will become if nothing remains but an increasingly pervasive self-encapsulation from all spiritual life and spiritual feeling. It is very sad to see today how great a number of people can still regard the spectacles of Rheinhardtism as any kind of art.

To see clearly in this field we do need a strong impulse that can emerge from an artistic sensibility kindled by spiritual science. Modernity in art, as it is called, is often nothing more than a confused delirium. If we really try to comprehend modern life, we can actually identify the place, if you like, where an existence entirely consumed by materialism collapses into the swamp of art or, seen from another perspective, into oblivion of everything that really constitutes art. You see, in order for a real sense of art to keep taking root in humanity's further evolution, what originated in the past and for example lives also in Lienhard's poems, a kind of nature pantheism and spirit pantheism, needs to develop more tangibly and specifically: people must learn to comprehend the multiplicity of life in a way that enables them to perceive the etheric, astral and spirit alongside and within sensory reality. Without such perception humanity will remain blind, especially in relation to art. And specifically in terms of artistic vision, the world will, one might say, come to expression only as the rough-hewn external reality of the senses; artists will look at this outer reality and describe it directly as it is.

But in fact you cannot give descriptions of this kind, echoes and reflections of sensory reality, without at the same time conveying something that clouds our sense of life with unclarity, offering dream states and befuddlement in which, basically, we never quite know what we are dealing with. Today this dizzy delirium in relation to the phenomena of life is frequently regarded as subtle psychology. It often pains me to see how few people have the capacity to feel things strongly enough in this domain, and in some way or other to resist it. The artist has to develop an eye for the deeper life of the world, to look at others with the soul organs which humanity's evolution has developed in us, and to be able to say: Here is a human being, with such and such a nature, and he experiences this or that—one person dwells more in his physical body, another more in the I, yet another more in his astral body. We need a living feeling for the different characters and characteristics of human beings, informed more by the physical, or the etheric, or the astral, or the I. And if people cannot develop this perception today, but try to describe human beings—in poetry say—all that emerges is the kind of delirium now widely regarded as art.

One must be able to get a hold of the essence of significant phenomena so that we awaken understanding of what actually is. Let us imagine that we meet four people who have some kind of karmic connection with each other. If four such people are brought together, we can understand how karma has involved them in certain relationships with each other, but also how the stream of karma flows through the course of evolution and how these people, due to their karma, have sought to place themselves into the world in a certain way. We can never understand anything from perspectives possible today if we are unable to perceive these karmic connections in the world.

Let us turn for a moment to the four brothers Dmitri, Ivan, Alyosha and Smerdyakov in Dostoyevsky's *The Brothers Karamazov*.[7] If we can see with an eye of soul then we find in these four brothers really four types whom one can only fully understand in terms of the karma that has brought them together. A current of karma brings four brothers into the world, making them the sons of a typical modern rascal amidst degenerate surroundings. They choose this karma, and are introduced into this environment as the four sons of this rogue. Yet side-by-side we see they are each different in nature. In fact we can only understand them if we know that in one of them, Dmitri Karamazov, the I predominates, while in a second, Alyosha, it is the astral body. In Ivan, the etheric body is predominant, while in the fourth, Smerdyakov, the physical body holds full sway. If we can consider the four brothers from this perspective, then their life is illumined for us. And now reflect how a poet with the gifts of Wilhelm Jordan, and with a spiritual world-view that would accord with our times, would place four such brothers alongside each other, how he would succeed in comprehending their spiritual foundations and underlying constitutions. What does Dostoyevsky comprehend? Nothing more than that these four brothers of his are simply the sons of a very typical, drunken layabout from a certain stratum of society. The mother of the first son, Dmitri, is a half-hysterical adventuress who, having had enough of the drunken old layabout Karamazov, can no longer endure him; she beats him then leaves him with this elder son, Dmitri. But everything is seen only in terms of physical heredity—he is simply the offspring of a wastrel and a walloper. All is described reductively, as if the author were a modern psychiatrist who only considers the coarsest principles of heredity and has no sense of spiritual factors at work. He presents us merely with the 'burdens of inheritance'. Then we have the two next sons, Ivan and Alyosha, born to a second wife since naturally these 'burdens of heredity' must act differently in these two figures. Their mother is not half but wholly hysterical, given to continual fits of sobbing and crying. Whereas the old drunkard's first wife often beat him, he now beats her. The fourth son, in whom everything of a physical nature predominates, is Smerdyakov, a kind of hybrid between wise humility and idiocy, of real stupidity and yet also great acuity. He too is the son of the typical layabout, but his mother is dumb, the village idiot named 'stinking Lisaveta' whom the old drunkard rapes and who dies giving birth. Naturally no one knows this is also his son. Smerdyakov stays at home, and now all the scenes between these figures unfold as the novel develops. Dmitri, due to the 'burden of heredity', naturally becomes a person in whom the subconscious I storms and rampages, driving him on through life so that he staggers about without direction. In the way he is described it is clear that he is not a healthy, spiritual figure but a sensualist and hysteric. But this derives also from inevitable modern developments, which militate against anything that can originate in a spiritual world-view: everything that does not really know what it wants, unclear instincts, which can equally well become either the loftiest mysticism or the worst, criminal excess. Indeed, fuelled by the unconscious, there is an easy transition from one to the other; and all this Dostoyevsky embodies in a sense in Dmitri Karamazov. He wants to describe a Russian, since invoking the true nature of Russians is always his aim.

Ivan, the next son, is a rationalist and more western-oriented. Dmitri knows nothing of the culture of the West but is rooted fully in Russian instincts. Ivan was in Paris, has studied widely, absorbed a western perspective and world-view, and, as Dostoyevsky portrays him, is filled with materialistic ideas which he discusses with everyone: ideas of western materialism but tinged with Russian musing and reflection. In his discussions with people, the fog of instincts is interwoven with all kinds of ideas about modern culture. Should one be an atheist or not, he wonders. Can one accept a God, or not? He concludes that one can, after all, accept the existence of God. Yes, he says, I accept God—that is his ultimate position, but he cannot accept the world. If he accepts God, then he cannot accept the world, since this world, as it is, as it appears, cannot have been created by God. I accept God but not the world, he says.

The third son, Alyosha, joins a monastery at a young age. The astral body predominates in him, and it is also apparent that all kinds of instincts are at work in him, develop in him, through mysticism too. It becomes clear that, like his elder brother Dmitri, he too has a potentially criminal nature and is in thrall to the same instincts, although in him these take a different form, making him into a mystic. Criminality is only a particular elaboration of the same instincts which, diverted in a different direction, can call forth fervent prayer and faith in the divine love pervading the world; both come from a lower realm, from the lower instincts of human nature, but develop in different ways.

Naturally there is absolutely no objection to portraying such characters artistically, for all reality can become a subject for art. But what counts is the manner of portraying it, not the content itself. These figures must be fully imbued with the living nature of the spirit. Due to the idiosyncratic circumstances I have often described here in relation to Russian culture, what comes to expression in Dostoyevsky, in particular, is the form human evolution must take if Russian life adheres to a spirituality that develops in merely natural ways. Recently I made a distinction between this and the development of spiritual conditions. From the very outset, Dostoyevsky was the embodiment of anti-German sentiment, and instinctively refused to allow anything of western European culture to flow into his soul. He sought to go no further than to grasp cosmic forms and figures in a kind of delirium, letting them pass him by, and carefully avoiding seeing anything spiritual in the physical throng of humanity that surged before his inner gaze. Instead of grasping his characters through profundities of soul, he brought them forth from the subterranean realms of purely physical nature, which in him was pathological. And this had its effect upon those who had forgotten their capacity to raise themselves to the spirit. A powerful effect was exerted upon them by the, let us call it, pathological bubbling and boiling that acts in human guts and innards which Dostoyevsky's nature was able to transform artistically, but to the exclusion of anything spiritual. This had its effect. Otherwise, of course, a mere description or characterization would be nothing but that, a straw blaze, a wooden portrayal. But since it emerged from a subconscious that was pathological, that acts hysterically, it became interesting—specifically by virtue of the paradox arising if one gives oneself up to purely physical existence without a spark of spiritual life, but does so with feeling; for that is something Dostoyevsky possesses to the highest degree.

And then we have interwoven into *The Brothers Karamazov* that remarkable episode about the Grand Inquisitor, before whom, as it is presented to us, the reincarnated Christ appears. This is presented as a novella by Ivan Karamazov incorporated into the book. The reincarnated Christ appears before the Grand Inquisitor—a worthy representative of orthodox Christianity, who is fully conversant with the nature of Christianity in his age. Picture this: a Christian, a true proponent of orthodox Christianity, faces the reincarnated Christ. He clearly has no other option, this Grand Inquisitor who represents 'proper' and 'lawful' Christianity, than to have the reincarnated Christ locked up! That is the first thing he does, for it is his task to hold inquisitions. It becomes apparent that the Grand Inquisitor, who represents due and lawful religion, knows what Christianity in our era requires. He sees that the Christ has come again and now stands before him. Yes, you are surely the Christ, he says to him—I am rendering this very roughly—but in the concerns of Christianity that we must represent, you have nothing to say, for you understand absolutely nothing about it. What you accomplished—did it do humankind any good, did it make human beings happy? It was left to us to make something proper out of the one-sided impracticality you brought us. If your form of Christianity alone had come amongst humankind, then people would never have found in it the salvation we have brought them. You see, to really bring human beings salvation one needs teachings that influence them. You thought that the teaching must be true, but such things get nowhere with humankind. The most important thing is that people should believe the doctrine they are taught, that it is given them in a way that compels them to believe. It is we who have established this authority.

Yes indeed: there was really nothing else to be done than to deliver up the reincarnated Christ to the Inquisition. In the Christianity that the Grand Inquisitor represents, you see, there is no room for the Christ if he should be so tactless as to reincarnate. The idea is grandiose, and executed in still more grandiose fashion. But it is interjected into a novel that is only a hysterical reflection of reality, offering nothing of the great impulses at work in the universe, offering no vision of anything spiritual in the author's mind but only an external counterfeit of Christ reincarnated and crushed by the Grand Inquisitor.

Such things relate to many other matters, and those who seek to comprehend the very pulse of spiritual science need to feel these affinities and not regard life too superficially. There are various things that can characterize the current state of our culture. We need only think, for instance, of two books[8] that appeared not long ago, one of which is called *Jesus, a Psycho-Pathological Study* and the other *Jesus Christ from a Psychiatric Perspective*. Here the message of the Gospels is, as it were, laid out on the psychiatrist's couch. Particular passages are subjected to an examination and diagnosed—in particular the words of Christ Jesus himself—to show the pathological state of this individual who stands at the beginning of modern evolution. The psyche of Christ Jesus is diagnosed as pathological. So here we have, already, the 'case' of Christ examined in line with the dictates of modern psychiatry.

But we must see such phenomena in a broader context. How many people really feel the full idiocy of a culture where such things surface, really feel all the ramifications of such ideas? Again and again, after all, we have witnessed a renowned psychiatrist to whom folk all run for treatment. He writes innovative works on psychiatry and is accorded great acclaim. There are pupils or colleagues of his who, still following closely on his heels, write psychopathological studies of Goethe, Schiller, Nietzsche and all sorts of other figures who have a place in history, write also about Christ Jesus himself. And as we cross the threshold of the psychiatrist or any other scientific observer with misplaced reverence, with unthinking faith in their authority, we are allowing ourselves to be conveyed upon a current that leads, in extreme, to caricature, to idiocy and distortion. To try to see living contexts clearly is no doubt something that many experience as uncomfortable and seek to avoid; yet it is necessary to kindle such efforts.

We really make no headway at all by gathering together here and, with a certain desire for sensation or mystical enthusiasm, simply allowing spiritual science to act upon us. We make progress instead when this spiritual science lives in us, and we learn to observe life in terms of the impulses this spiritual science can kindle in us. We are not yet practitioners of spiritual science because we allow words about elemental spirits or hierarchies and so forth to stream over us once a week like cold—or maybe warm, I have no idea—shivers down our back. We practise the science of the spirit, instead, by bringing these things to life within us, relating them to all aspects and details of life. Truly, in observing the quagmires of modern art we can feel a sense of distaste and disgust—or would do if we do not aspire, like theosophists, to let universal human love prevail, and therefore avoid calling these quagmires by their proper name.

It is curious how reluctant people are nowadays to really open their eyes. Naturally, individuals are not at fault as such—it is the fault of the whole of modern culture. It becomes extremely hard for an individual to see such things clearly, for state education often tries to conceal or ignore things such as those I have spoken of during this rather disconnected, episodic evening. People in a sense are drawn away from reality, blinded to it. In this respect we really live at present in one of the greatest eras of human schooling, and must not overlook what we are given to learn. Think for a moment of the lack of discrimination that exists about the ways in which people relate to each other. For instance, the principle that no differences exist should not lead us to try to erase and confuse all distinctions and nuances—as it led the director of the Theosophical Society when she sought to discount the differences between diverse religions, leaving Hinduism shining in especial glory. Otherwise she muddied the differences, employing a logic that I have often compared with someone saying that they should use all the condiments on the table indiscriminately. This way of treating all religions in the same way, seeing no differences between them, is more or less like saying that salt, sugar and pepper are all condiments and can be used indiscriminately. Just try putting pepper in your coffee, sugar in your soup or curry powder on your dessert, and you will find that there is a difference! But it is this logic, similarly, which blinds people to the real and specific nature of evolution.

Many things are muddled like this, so that people are persuaded into a nebulous, foggy kind of dream state. All too easily one is misunderstood when one says these things. And for this reason I will expressly state how greatly, as you know, I esteem Tolstoy.[9] But this does not mean we should forget that there lives in Tolstoy something, of course, that should not simply be equated with western European culture, painted in one uniform grey with it. In the past, in lectures on Tolstoy, I have often drawn attention to such distinctions. One can admire the greatness of a man like Tolstoy without overlooking aspects of his work that have been ignored. When Tolstoy was still widely read, in particular his first great works, people might—though only might—have seen in him a great spirit of the East, a great Russian author, who was however full of the bitterest hatred towards German culture, who disparaged it and disdained it. This was not remarked upon, because the early translators of Tolstoy into German left these passages out, or modified them. The unexpurgated translation by Raphael Loewenfeld[10] arrived too late in the day, and by that time German literature had adopted a falsified Tolstoy.

Either one should really be fully conversant with things or refrain from judgement! Judgement must be founded on real knowledge. There is no need to overestimate Tolstoy. Clear discernment will show that, besides his greatness as a writer, he was also very much rooted in his national culture, and emerged from this. We should not just follow the lead of modern small-minded journalists who, while acclaiming the greatness of, say, Goethe or Schiller, use the same words to rave about Dostoyevsky. They do so without any sense that, compared with *Wilhelm Meister* or *Elective Affinities*, or also the works of Lienhard, even a novel like *The Brothers Karamazov* is second-rate in terms of the aesthetic principles we have developed from a previous era. We can form clear, precise, tangible views and judgements when we gain insight into what is; and today we live at a time when we must hone our judgement, gain such insight. In our times, mutual hatred between nations is growing ever greater. If we wish to make judgements, we have to learn to see how this hatred can develop from what has long, long existed.

These things must be stated so that we develop amongst ourselves something of a feeling for the importance of spiritual-scientific endeavour. It is easy to feel rather bitter whenever some newspaper or journal or book prints disparaging and foolish words about theosophy, whereas it would be so important to really grasp the very fundamental efforts and endeavours of spiritual science—without being fanatical about it of course, but just to accord it its proper place in modern culture. We must recognize that people today cannot really embrace spiritual science, cannot love what it is seeking to achieve because they cannot even take the few simple steps needed to get beyond the most extreme frivolity which today pervades most of our cultural life. To engage in serious reflections in a serious time would seem a justified endeavour. Which moment of world history, after all, would be more suited for it than this, a moment in human evolution excessive in its dreadful, terrible nature, though naturally it presents us with great and necessary challenges and developmental opportunities. What moment would be better fitted than this hour of need? To bring this home to us we need only reflect that in just one large-scale battle in June or July last year, on the northern part of the western Front, as much ammunition was used as in the whole of the German-French war of 1870/71. Experts in such matters estimate that we will soon reach a point in these current conflicts when munitions expended will equal that of all previous wars since gunpowder was invented!

This is a grave time, and not one that can permit us to overlook the great spiritual crisis, too, through which humanity's evolution is now passing. The state of things is so dire that it would be unforgivable to avoid looking carefully at the whole importance of what human evolution requires, if we are able to do so by approaching these matters through the teachings of spiritual science.

Lecture 2

7 March 1916

Returning to various matters we have been speaking of recently, and have often spoken of in the past, I would like to expand on some of these things and, to begin with, make certain comments about the inner nature of the human being, our being of spirit and soul. As you know, we can identify an aspect of our inner life that we refer to, in abstract terms, as the etheric body. Whereas the human physical body can be perceived by the outer senses, by external science which is dependent on reason and sensory observation, the etheric body is supersensible in nature. Then we also speak of the next level of the human being as the astral body. We should recall here our frequent emphasis on the fact that our inner life is not something entirely unknown to us. In the physical world, within our corporeal existence, we also perceive our thinking, feeling and will. We experience them inwardly, and also experience them illumined and irradiated by the I. We can say that this thinking, feeling and will is something we inwardly perceive. But we cannot say—as you will gradually have become accustomed to thinking—that we actually perceive our astral body nor that we actually perceive our I. You see, this I of which we speak, as we showed in the course of our recent lectures, which returns to unconsciousness every time we fall asleep, is only a picture of the true, real I. In a sense, then, we can conclude that along with this I, our thinking, feeling and will are similarly only an expression, a manifestation of our true inner nature, just as the physical body is a manifestation or expression of the spiritual aspect we call the ether body. Naturally we are pleased when we can nicely compartmentalize any field of knowledge, box it up and store it away in neat categories. Many are happy to possess the really extremely phenomenological knowledge that the human being consists of physical body, ether body, astral body and I. But in fact—and I have often stressed this here—these four designations are not much more than words, verbal expressions. If we wish to proceed to real observation then in a sense we must always go beyond the confines that are so easily set by these terms.

Of course one can speak generally and say that thinking, feeling and will occur within the astral body. But this encompasses the reality of thinking only in a very one-sided, very abstract manner. As we stand, initially, within the physical world, the impulse for our thinking does indeed lie in the astral body, even in the I. But thinking develops as picturing capacity, as thought, only by virtue of our mobile etheric body. Here, as physical human beings, our whole thinking would remain unconscious for us if the astral body did not send its impulses of thinking into the etheric body, whose mobile character absorbs and incorporates them. And every thought, in turn, would simply fade without memory if we did not also have a physical body. We cannot say that the physical body is the bearer of memory; the etheric body is. But for us human beings in the physical body, the thinking that remains available to us in the etheric body would fade and disappear as dreams do if it could not inscribe itself into the physical matter of the physical body. In other words, it is only by virtue of our physical body that our thoughts can impinge upon this body.

So you can see what a complex process this thinking really is. Its impulses originate in the astral body, or even already in the I. And then these impulses communicate themselves to, and continue on into the etheric body, there calling forth thoughts, which in turn engrave or inscribe their traces into the physical body. By inscribing themselves in this way they can in turn be drawn forth again from memory during physical life.

Now let us once again consider something we have frequently addressed here—the actual nature of memory for us here in the physical body. We have experiences, don't we, and we process them; we move on from them, and a time may come when we know more or less nothing of them, hardly relate to them. But then a time comes again when we draw such experiences forth from ourselves, from our inner life; and then, in the form of memories, we become aware again of what we once experienced.

It is perfectly right to think, initially, that this memory process belongs to us, to our soul. When we walk along the road, gather in social groups, no one can see with outward, physical sense organs what experiences we have had and what memories we bear within us. We bear this within our soul. One can put it like this: the envelope of the physical body is like a cloak within which, in our soul, we store our concealed memories. They belong to us, and throughout our lives we work upon ourselves in this way. In a sense we make the outer world into our inner world. And then we bear this outer world with us through our lives in the form of memories. We bear these memories with us as our most intrinsic possession. But it would be a serious mistake to think that this bearing of our memories through life encompasses the whole process. That is not so. Darwin, for instance, was right to study whether creatures such as earthworms have a special task;[11] and he found that they do not exist only for the sake of it, but, in boring through the ground, have a vital part to play in soil fertility. Such things are acknowledged by science as a domain of certain knowledge. There is nothing to object to here, for it is good if science engages with specific phenomena. The problem comes when whole world-views are derived from such things. Naturally we must recall here the proverb about the man who digs eagerly for treasure but is happy merely to find earthworms.[12] Translated into spiritual terms, we can ask this: Is the human activity, by means of which we continually form experiences into thoughts and preserve them in memories, of no significance at all for the rest of the universe? Is this process of memory really only one that occurs within our own confines?

The materialist will inevitably say that this process of course occurs only within us. At death we lay our physical body in the grave, and everything we preserved as memory is then of course over, like a flame extinguished. I will not try to refute this materialistic assumption here—we have often done so in the past. I want to consider something else instead, asking this: Is it not possible that our process of thought and remembering is after all very, very different from what unfolds for us in our memory? While we think, while we form thoughts from our experiences and preserve them as memories, not only are we preoccupied with our thoughts but the whole world of the hierarchies—the third hierarchy, that of the Angeloi, Archangeloi and Archai—is also preoccupied with our thoughts. We do not think only for our own sakes, and preserve these thoughts within us, but in doing so at the same time we create a field of activity for the Angeloi, Archangeloi and Archai. We think that our thoughts live only within us, but in fact these three spiritual hierarchies are preoccupied with these thoughts of ours. The least important aspect of our thoughts is the one we are aware of. Even when we have forgotten our thoughts, they are still within us. And just as we on earth concern ourselves with our machines or with our eating and drinking, so the Angeloi, Archangeloi and Archai concern themselves with a fabric, a tissue spun and woven from our thoughts. They work continually upon our thoughts. In other words the aspect of thought activity we are aware of is only the side of it turned towards us. There is another, hidden aspect. This 'far side' of thinking, which we do not see, appears thus to spiritual vision: whereas we possess our thoughts within us, from without the spiritual beings I have spoken of are preoccupied with our thoughts and weave them in a way that can, when we recognize this, show us that our thinking process is certainly not something unnecessary to the cosmos. It is not for us alone but is embedded in the whole of cosmic evolution. It contributes to new substance continually being interwoven with world evolution. If we were not born as a separate person, if we had not developed thoughts and preserved memories, at our death the fabric that can be woven from our thoughts, that we do not weave ourselves, would be lost to cosmic evolution.

And when we cross the threshold of death—an elementary process that we have often described—we know that we lay aside our physical body, which is given up to the elements of the earth in one way or another. For a short while our etheric body remains with us. Initially it remains inner experience for us in the form of a great life tableau that it unfurls before us. Everything we otherwise remember through time is unrolled around us in a mighty panorama of our life. But then our etheric nature detaches from us, as if drawn out of us. Who accomplishes this? Yes, the beings of the three aforenamed spiritual hierarchies, and they slowly weave it into the cosmic ether. And thus, after our death, this weft of the cosmic ether consists of what we have embroidered in it, if you like, during our life between birth and death, and what the beings of the three next higher hierarchies have elaborated from this. Thus there is taken from us what we have additionally woven since our birth, that was not present before it; and this is inwoven into the whole cosmos. Every person gains knowledge of this after crossing the threshold of death. After we pass through the gate of death something occurs that we can only describe as follows. The human etheric body is detached from us, our etheric fabric is inwoven into the general cosmic ether; and so what we bore within us during our lifetime is now outside us. This is important. Knowing this we can describe it in a short phrase that we ought repeatedly to conjure in us meditatively, for it encapsulates an important, essential reality. Inner becomes outer—that is, what we have always felt to be within us, as our life of thought, becomes external to us, becomes outer surroundings. Just as rivers, mountains, trees, clouds and stars surround us here, so after our death what lived within us during our physical life becomes a part of the external world and we can therefore look upon it, observe it.

But now, apart from this etheric body, we also have the world of our astral body. The world of our astral body initially appears in our awareness as the sense or feeling we have of our thinking. But as I just characterized it, our thinking sends its impulses into the ether body and therefore thinking itself cannot become conscious in the astral body. Only feeling and will can become conscious in the astral body. We feel and will throughout our life. We harbour certain feelings about certain experiences. These are processes in our astral body. This also is a remarkable kind of weaving, but now not a weaving in thinking as I described before, but a weaving of feelings and will impulses, motivations to act. Higher hierarchies here likewise work upon our feelings and our will impulses during life. This too is a domain of activity for higher beings. Just as the beings of the third hierarchy work upon our thinking, so the beings of the second hierarchy, including the Thrones, work upon our feelings and impulses of will.

Imagine how we stand in the world if we know these things, how we feel ourselves embedded in the world of spirit. On the one hand we tell ourselves that we go through the world and have thoughts, but that this thinking reveals only one aspect to us, as inner activity. Yet at the same time what we think is substance for the work of the Angeloi, Archangeloi and Archai. And in our feelings and will, we also create substance for the Spirits of Form, the Spirits of Movement, the Spirits of Wisdom, and the Thrones or Spirits of Will. As human beings we dig over the earth and work or act upon it, but in doing this we are unaware that this is only one aspect and that vital processes are at work which are unavailable to our ordinary awareness. We think our feelings and will impulses are just our own. But they are also a field of activity for the work of the aforenamed beings of the higher hierarchy. Truly, we do not exist only as a physical body, nor is our physical body simply just connected with our surroundings, but we exist also as a being of soul and spirit, which is likewise connected and related to our surroundings. People usually overlook the fact that our physical body really belongs to our whole environment. But this is easy to picture. At any moment, if you picture your corporeal form, you know that you do not only have bones, blood and muscles and so on, but also that there is a current of air streaming in and out of you that you breathe in and out.

Breathing in, this belongs to us; but a moment previously it was outside us and in a moment it will be outside us again. Try to imagine yourself without this in-and-out flow of air. You can't, it belongs to you. It is senseless to think of the physical body as if it were only enclosed within your skin since it is dependent on a living interchange with the whole atmosphere outside us. But in the same way that our physical body lives as part of the atmosphere and temperature around us, so in our thoughts we live with the outer environment of the third hierarchy, and in our feelings and our will impulses we live with the beings of the second hierarchy and the Spirits of Will. That is how we stand within the cosmos.

If we apply this in turn to our passage over the threshold of death, we can say that after our etheric body has been taken from us and begins to be inwoven into the general cosmic ether, we pass through a reverse experience of our physical life during a period that is three times quicker than the period of our actual life between birth and death, at the same time perceiving the effects of this life. In other words, we do not perceive what we inwardly experienced during our physical life; we perceived that during our lifetime. If we insulted someone, then we experienced during our physical life the feeling which gave rise to the insult; that was the cause and is inscribed into our karma. But what we did not experience then was the impression which this insult made on the other person's soul. We do not experience anything at all of the effect of our actions and thoughts in the world around us. Here in physical life we do not experience this; but this is precisely what we experience in our reverse journey in the period between death back to birth. There we experience everything outside us, pass through it, not as we ourselves experienced it when alive but as the world around us experienced it. Really this is so: we experience everything which others experienced and felt as a result of our thoughts and words; and this is because what is outside must now become inside. In the case of our thoughts we saw how something inward becomes outward. In this life now, lived in reverse, things that were outside us, the effects of our thoughts and actions during our lifetime, become inward, become inward experience of the spiritual being we are after death. You see we now have to live our way into the world in which we live unconsciously during our lifetime by virtue of having an astral body upon which the spirits of the second hierarchy work; we must live our way into the world where our astral body gradually dissolves in the external environment, but this environment is one we now inwardly experience, really experience inwardly. We have to learn between death and rebirth to work in the sphere in which the spirits of the second hierarchy work, preparing what can then lead us to a new incarnation. And, after a while, as we know, the astral body dissolves into the outer world while the human being as such, with his intrinsic core, lives on in the period between death and rebirth.

Now if we wish to understand a little of this life between death and rebirth, we will always need to see things from many different perspectives. That is also our aim in general—not to be one-sided but to view things from many angles so that we can gradually develop a comprehensive understanding of these processes. In the same way that, at birth, we enter into natural processes occurring around us in the mineral, plant and animal realms, so at death we enter the world that surrounds us in the form of beings of the hierarchies I have spoken of. We are in a sense infolded into their activity, and what we bring with us is woven by them into the underlying substance of our next incarnation.

In this realm it is really very difficult to formulate concepts that modern people can grasp, for reasons I have often identified. Our modern era has the most distorted views of this domain. When someone is born and thus enters upon physical existence, he brings with him certain qualities. Modern outlooks see this in terms of inherited characteristics, meaning by this merely physically inherited traits. If a person displays a particular characteristic, it is said that the origin of this should be sought amongst his forebears. For instance, there is a very detailed book about Goethe that searches amongst his ancestors to discover traits and characteristics he displays—one quality from a great-grandfather, another from a great-grandmother and so on. Everything has been passed onto him through heredity, according to the author. Yet to say that a child displays characteristics of his parents is no wiser than to observe that you will get wet if you fall into water. A person acquires characteristics of his ancestors because he has guided his soul through them. There is no great wisdom in observing this. To attribute this fact to a narrow cause and to hail it as logical is in fact the most illogical way of proceeding. Attempting to prove that soul-spiritual qualities are physically inherited by showing that a genius like Goethe possessed the same qualities as his forefathers is no cleverer than to say we get wet when we fall into water. One might prove that genius and qualities of genius are connected with physical heredity if we could show that the descendants of a genius possess the same qualities. But people are not likely to do this. No one is likely to study Goethe's son to see how the qualities of genius of the father were transmitted to the son by heredity. Of course there may be cases where something like this is suggested. In Europe at present there is a statesman[13] whose father was also a statesman, so it could be said that the genius of the father was inherited by his statesman son. However, it is probably true to say that neither of them were geniuses!

A much, much deeper reality underlies these things. In our era, you see, people do not wish to acknowledge that external phenomena are merely the outer surface of processes that are at the same time inward, that flow from the spirit. Let us use the following hypothetical comparison to show what is meant by this. Let us imagine that there were beings who, while having certain rational powers, were unable to perceive human beings. Assume hypothetically that they could see everything else but not human beings. They would see clocks for instance. One of these beings might travel through Berlin and see no human beings anywhere but would observe that clocks spring up all over the place. This being would have to say to itself, these clocks arise by themselves. It is no cleverer than this to say that when people are born physically this occurs by itself through reproduction over generations, and there is no further need of explanation. People only think like this because they cannot see that what happens here in the physical world is only the outer expression for an activity that continually flows down from the world of spirit, just as the activity of clockmakers streams into the emergence of clocks. Moles for instance, if they developed a science and were intelligent enough to regard clocks as something created by intelligence, might form this view that clocks arise by themselves.

But what happens here on earth, of which human beings foolishly believe that it happens by itself and is only an outward, physical process, is in fact governed from the spiritual world in the same way that clockmakers govern their clock-making activity. And indeed, from the moment I referred to in the fourth Mystery Play as the midnight hour of existence,[14] from the moment that is poised halfway between death and rebirth, there begins an activity that inclines increasingly from the world of spirit towards the physical world, and which after centuries will guide the human being once more into physical existence. When a person crosses the threshold of death the activity that unfolds in the world of spirit is initially a processing and assimilation of what this person experienced and elaborated in his last life. This occurs in the first half of after-death existence. But from the midpoint between death and rebirth, preparation for the next incarnation begins. And we can picture it like this. Someone who is born has parents, who had parents likewise and so on. Picture the expanding scope of these preceding generations, back through 30 generations. But in passing backwards through these 30 generations you would find that many of these ancestors already display tendencies that will ultimately bring together a man A and woman B, who give their child new existence. And if the whole had not happened as it did through 30 generations, if marriages had not happened in such a way that ultimately A and B came together, then the twofold nature they embody, which a human soul can seek out as he descends again to physical incarnation, would not have developed and emerged. In this whole interplay and collaboration of many human beings, culminating eventually in the two who bear a child, the world of spirit is working in accordance with a specific individual's nature. And so, when we see that a son has qualities in common with his mother and father, and that these qualities in turn can be traced back to previous generations, to grandparents and great-grandparents and so forth, through 30 generations, this is because the individuality who will eventually be born after centuries has inclined for 30 generations towards his ancestors and has helped determine the way in which people find each other. All this plays its part. And inherited similarities are due to a power that seeks eventually to manifest in a particular individual, working down through 30 generations from the world of spirit. This power is at work in father, mother, grandfather, grandmother, great-grandmother and great-grandfather. This is always at work and ultimately gives us the qualities and attributes that need to emerge. Physical heredity does not act alone but in this way is incorporated into the spiritual stream. The very reverse of what external science asserts is therefore true. In order for Goethe to emerge, as the off-spring of Johann Kaspar Goethe and his wife Katharina Elisabeth, the beings of the second hierarchy brought his ancestors together through 30 generations in a way that could eventually allow Goethe to be born. Naturally this is not only true of the genius Goethe but of every single person. You may say that this is hard to imagine, and may also ask how this relates to human freedom if, 30 generations before we are born, how we are to be is already being determined. But the same was true for our father and grandfather too. And if it seems too complex to think this through, remember that this thinking, adapted to our normal earthly consciousness, may not encompass the nature of this whole process which unfolds in common endeavour with the Spirits of Form, with the Spirits of Movement and so on, and does so in a way that does not in the least impair human freedom. Naturally a higher wisdom is involved here, and corresponds to the nature of these hierarchies.

And thus what we can pass to the cosmic ether as thoughts is combined with expressions of feeling and will during our physical existence. Truly, spiritual science should not be only a sum of knowledge but should kindle in us a certain sensibility and mood of soul. I tried to indicate this mood of soul in the first scenes of the second Mystery Play,[15] in the meeting between Capesius and

Benedictus: to show how gods work together with gods, spirits with spirits in order for a human being to live here upon earth in his entirety; to show how the human being is the goal and purpose of these gods and spirits. This feeling of gratitude, as I would say, towards the spiritual universe, of knowing oneself to be embedded in the spiritual universe, is something that should also stream into our soul from spiritual science. This feeling must become as natural as it is natural for us to know our connection with the physical world. Normally we overlook this. But science has reached the point today where everyone is aware that he needs air and thus is not a self-enclosed entity but a part of his whole surroundings. When a person feels hunger or thirst of course he does recognize that his surroundings are necessary for his physical existence, and that basically he is part of a universal process, engaged with the outer world. But in the same way a person is also part of a spiritual process in the world of spirit, by virtue of his capacity to think he is connected with the Angeloi, Archangeloi and Archai, and, by virtue of his ability to feel and will, with the next higher spiritual hierarchy. Just as air and substance enter his physical body, so the activities of these hierarchies work into his soul.

We have often discussed the theoretical objections raised by modern proponents of materialism. These theoretical objections can be refuted by epistemological reflections and suchlike; but then the materialists often cite a pragmatic view which states that while a world of spirit may exist, it is of no help to us to know this, even if thinking, feeling and will are connected with these higher hierarchies. They say that we do not need to know about these hierarchies in order to think, that we can already think without resorting to this. Likewise, thank God, we breathe—for if we had to wait for precise theoretical knowledge of the breathing process before breathing, we would still not be able to breathe yet. Our physical, physiological knowledge of respiration would not yet be adequate to instruct us in how to do this. People say there is no need to indulge in 'eccentricities' since it is already possible to think without involving these hierarchies in the matter.

But we can reply to this with another question. Can we really think without their involvement? At present, you see, people are still depending on a past inheritance from olden times, working still really with what they have inherited; and drawing on this they have been able to invent many things, even machines complex enough to be used to kill others in warfare. But all this comes down to them from a former age. Naturally people are unwilling to acknowledge this dependency on the past. Rather curiously, many claim that the wonderful progress now apparent is only due to the realization that all thinking of past times was childish; that people have discovered how to think in an objective and sober rather than a childish way. This is of course nonsense, and can be proved to be so, even from a quite external viewpoint. Human beings have only possessed their present, prosaic form of thinking for a couple of hundred years.

Recently we were in Hamburg, and looked at a picture from the thirteenth or fourteenth century by Master Bertram.[16] I'd like to tell you the following about this picture. Let us go back for a moment to the biblical account of the Fall, which in spiritual science we call the luciferic temptation. A painter today who paints the Fall in our 'enlightened' times will paint Adam and Eve on either side of the tree, and then a snake curled around it. Depending on whether he is an Impressionist, Cubist, Expressionist or some other 'ist' he will paint this theme in a more or less hideous—sorry I mean of course 'lovely'—way. But he will paint a snake naturalistically, as a creature who slides through the grass. This is called realism, but is it actually realism? No, for in what way can it be realistic to think that this snake that crawls through the grass could ever have tempted Eve—however simple-minded she was (and she was not portrayed as being so). No woman, however simple, would be tempted by a naturalistic snake. It is inconceivable. So the whole thing cannot be conceived naturalistically. From our spiritual science we know that Lucifer is a being whose evolution stopped at the stage of ancient Moon. Lucifer therefore self-evidently cannot be seen with physical vision since during Moon evolution no one yet saw as we do during the Earth stage of evolution. This cannot be a snake as we see it with physical vision, but Lucifer must be seen inwardly.

If we study the human being in closer detail, as you can do by observing the skeleton, we find the latter already testifies to two parts: the skull with the spinal column attached, within which we have of course the brain and the spinal nerves. There is really no other way to describe it than 'attached'. And this—as we will examine in more detail on another occasion—is because the head we bear upon our shoulders is a very complex form, really a small cosmic sphere. We should be truly grateful that we human beings have no hand in our form at birth and that this head can arise. If we had to draw on our present understanding of anatomy or physiology to create this wondrous structure of the human head, this would produce some fine results! The head arises in a quite different way, arises because, during the time between death and rebirth, what is inscribed in our karma is inwoven into a mighty sphere that we can compare with the blue dome of the heavens, and a whole formation arises which, as the soul approaches incarnation again, becomes ever smaller and smaller and then unites with what comes from the mother. From the whole universe countless beings of many hierarchies weave what becomes our head, encompassing within it a wisdom of vast grandeur and enormous scope, formed from all the experiences gained in the passage through Saturn, Sun and Moon evolution. What is attached to this head is a product of the earth, of Earth evolution. Our head is an inheritance from Saturn, Sun and Moon. The earth with all its powers has only been able to give rise to what is attached to the head, which is, really, the Earth human being.

In trying to portray Lucifer, therefore, perceived in inward vision, how will we present a Moon being? We will depict it as a human head, with something snakelike hanging down from it, the as yet unossified spine. And this is how Master Bertram in the thirteenth/fourteenth century depicts Lucifer on the tree between Adam and Eve. You can see the picture in Hamburg Museum. If people today were able to think they would say that, at the time this was painted, a knowledge of the world of spirit was still alive, one which also encompassed insight into the nature of Lucifer.

So it is only a relatively short time ago that humankind lost its old, inherited, atavistic clairvoyance. But not much thinking happens nowadays. However, authority, acknowledgement of authority, is greatly disparaged as something a free human being should not bow to. Nowadays one reflects on everything and has one's own personal views. And yet having one's own view usually means no more than having forgotten which pamphlet, newspaper or journal one read the relevant opinion in. People forget where they read things that they repeat as their own opinions. If people really thought for themselves they would compare and contrast, would see from the way a painter of the thirteenth or fourteenth century painted Lucifer correctly what people still knew only a few centuries back, and how one might wrestle one's way through to such knowledge again.

But now I would like to look at the theme from another angle, examining the materialistic assertion that we do not need any influx from the world of spirit entering us, and informing our thinking and feeling in the same way as the air in breathing and the food that satisfies our hunger. If we wish to claim we do not need this, we might cite certain materialistic teachings that appear irrefutable. I have often quoted the important criminologist and anthropologist Benedikt,[17] the first to investigate the brains of criminals—after death of course. He dissected the brains of criminals to see whether he could discover any connection between brain structure and criminal attributes. Benedikt made a very important discovery here: that they all had a shared characteristic, a truncated occipital lobe that did not fully cover the cerebellum. So imagine that the shared trait of criminals' brains is a truncated occipital lobe—a feature also of apes—which does not cover the cerebellum. But self-evidently this is a characteristic of the physical body. Inevitably one must form the view that two kinds of people are born: those who have a properly formed occipital lobe that covers the cerebellum, and those who have a truncated occipital lobe. Those with a properly formed occipital lobe, it seems, do not become criminals, while those who do not inevitably become criminals. It seems they have no other choice.

In the face of these findings, to which no objection can be made since they are absolutely correct from a materialistic perspective, all our talk of morality becomes farcical, doesn't it? Is it right to punish people if they are unable to become anything other than criminals because of a truncated occipital lobe? This is the increasingly aberrant direction in which materialism takes us. Inevitably it extinguishes everything spiritual in the social, ethical and legal domain, or else it must continually subscribe to a lie. This fact I have quoted is right. That's how things are! And for anyone who does not acknowledge a spiritual world-view nothing more than this fact exists.

But how do we counter this point of view? Certainly, people are born with a properly developed occipital lobe but some also in whom it is truncated. But besides these physical factors we also possess an etheric body that can be developed in a very different way and is more mobile than the physical body. The occipital lobe of the etheric body corresponds to the same area of the physical body. People in future will need to learn to distinguish between children who have a truncated or long occipital lobe, and adjust their educational approach accordingly. They will need to know what characteristics come to expression in earliest infancy due to a truncated occipital lobe. The upbringing for such children will aim at strengthening the etheric lobe to counteract this. A strengthened etheric lobe will make it possible to prevent the damage caused by a truncated occipital lobe.

As yet the old legacy of the past has not faded entirely; but an era will dawn when it has. And if spiritual science cannot inform the sensibilities of people in the new age, then inevitably materialism will lay siege to all morality, all ethics, all jurisprudence, utterly extinguishing the spirit. This would be the logical outcome of it. We can only come to the insights we need if we are aware that just as we inhale air from the atmosphere so we need the collaboration of the spiritual hierarchies in the activity of our thinking and feeling. But along come our contemporaries, of course, and say, yes, we can think perfectly well already, thank you. Our thinking is excellent, and we do not believe that these hierarchies are labouring away in us as you say. Why shouldn't we think perfectly well without them? A modern scientist,[18] a very good one, who, however, has a weakness for writing all kinds of philosophical musings alongside his scientific research, unconsciously quotes Goethe's words about 'glorious advancements' in the conclusion to one of his lectures, without recalling the whole context of these words in *Faust*, and who speaks them. You see, people believe they can think perfectly well, and have no need of the spiritual world to make their thinking fruitful.

I could go on for a long time about this theme, but allow me perhaps to offer just a small instance. In my public lecture recently,[19] I referred to a forgotten thinker, Karl Christian Planck.[20] I certainly do not wish to dogmatically defend everything that Karl Christian Planck wrote. However I did draw attention to the fact that he worked out of a deeper, spiritual awareness, and produced what was, in a sense, a world-view that accords with the spirit. He died in 1880. No one really gave much attention to his books. A posthumous work by him appeared in 1912—a wonderful book entitled *Testament of a German*. It was written the year he died, 1880, and a first edition was published by Koestlin in 1881, then reissued in 1912. But it received little notice. I referred to Karl Christian Planck back in 1900 in the first edition of *Riddles of Philosophy*, in the essay 'Nineteenth-century world-views and outlooks'. But pointing to a world-view that accords with the spirit makes little headway today, since firstly people wonder what the point of it is and are loath to spend their money on it; and secondly they dismiss it since a world-view of this kind, which encompasses the spirit, is informed by the spiritual powers that render thinking fruitful. People who think materialistically believe that all such idealists and writers with a spiritual orientation are impractical and know nothing about reality. They think that to engage with such idealists would throw a spanner in the works of practical life, that one needs pragmatists to get anywhere. People who think like this have supped at the table of practical wisdom and do not dip their spoons in what they see as dreamy fantasies. Well, Planck was really an idealist, really someone who lived in a world of spirit and wished to draw on this realm of spirit in a way that actively engages with the world. I could cite many examples but as I said, I will give just one small illustration of what I mean in the shape of the work of this man, Karl Christian Planck. I did not mention this in my lecture here in Berlin since one cannot always mention everything, but I have mentioned it in public elsewhere. All the time you hear amateur diplomats, amateur politicians or even real diplomats and politicians saying it would be disastrous for political life if people listened to these idealists and their views of the world. But now let me read you a passage from Planck's *Testament of a German*, written back in 1880, where he speaks of the current war! That's right—this current conflict. And here he says the following:

> Given a merely national order, no political cleverness or love of peace on the part of Germany will be able to prevent this conflict occurring. The nature of the circumstances is more powerful than all cleverness, and already, despite the alliance between Germany and Austria, the mood of enmity from the Russian East is all the more apparent; and this is because it was impossible to give this region a free hand in everything. Inevitably constraints had to be placed upon it. When conflict breaks out, however much we must wage it for the sake of Europe, Europe will not stand with us. Just as we will have to fight in the East, so we will also simultaneously have to defend ourselves in the West and South. National jealousy will come to expression from all directions as enmity towards the new realm at the centre of Europe.

Let me ask you this: Did any of the 'practical' people in 1880 assess the situation that would arise in 1914, 1915, 1916 in such telling terms? How many of these pragmatists, and for how long, wished to know nothing whatever of the fact that conflict might also arise in the South for instance? This impractical idealist, one of those so disparaged for their lack of pragmatism, wrote words in 1880 that exactly describe what is happening today. We need the will to hearken to such realities. If we did, we would soon see that we are embedded in the world of spirit, would know that the world of spirit exists just as air exists for the physical body, and that this is something that renders thinking fit to properly judge reality.

This small example may perhaps show you that, even if people give no credence to the spiritual researcher, he is right to say this: Using their old legacy of thinking, people can still invent machines, but before 50 years have passed they will no longer be able to do so if they refuse to acknowledge the spiritual influences on their thinking. Everything that does not originate in the world of spirit but seeks to establish something in the physical world will fade and die. People can still invent machines today because of the old legacy that still exists. What is already happening to a great extent in other fields prefigures the degree to which spiritual capacities are declining—the ability to draw on the world of spirit to incorporate something new into the physical world. In many fields today, this inability is already, wrongly, called a 'greater ability'. No longer to be able to paint a proper face but just to make haphazard lines on the canvas and smear it with all sorts of stuff would, not so long ago, have been called 'daubing'. A real painter will still call it that. But nowadays there are schools of painting that call this 'higher art' while real art is passé, and thought outmoded. The same is true in all fields of human endeavour, every field.

The times demand that our endeavours are made fruitful by the world of spirit. And this can only happen if we grasp and comprehend spiritual realities as presented by spiritual science. Great universal tasks likewise can only be solved if our thinking is rendered fruitful in this way. Today we can observe infinitely sad phenomena, repeatedly seeing how, basically, all connection with the world of spirit is bankrupt. We are living at a time which, as has often been stressed, is moving towards a second coming of Christ on earth as it may be called: the etheric Christ being as second appearance of Christ on earth. But some preparation is needed for it so that this occurrence does not simply pass us by, or is even disparaged and ridiculed. And even the current events we are witnessing can only be undergone in the right way if there is some awareness that the terrible events happening around us are like a God-given sign that the human soul must be deepened. It would be the most terrible thing if materialistic human thinking survived these dire events, which are turning all society upside down. Yet it often seems that this will be the case. This would be the worst and most terrible thing. And those who belong to spiritual science must inscribe this in their souls as a fundamental truth, so that they really are strong enough to counter everything that comes flying at us from the modern world as opposition to the science of the spirit and a spiritual view of existence.

It is so difficult to impress such things on people in broader circles today. In some fields people seem wholly possessed by distorted thinking. Recently I gave a public lecture and spoke of how a faded and now inaudible tone still lives on in cultural life, a tone that is no longer heard but still exists in the cultural life of central Europe.[21] Two people came up to me afterwards and expressed their astonishment that anyone still speaks about circumstances in this way in our day. They had not expected that what they called theosophy would cause someone to speak as I had. They were pacifists and they regarded theosophy as something rather different. It is of course a fine thing to be a pacifist, isn't it, although one must be clear that since pacifism has arisen we have witnessed the greatest and bloodiest wars the world has ever seen—a fact I emphasized a decade ago in my Architektenhaus lectures.[22] But I wanted to point out something that is easily comprehensible. I said this to them: Does it not seem to you that all these circumstances, not just the warfare itself but the coming to light of such terrible deceitfulness as we can witness in the conflicting voices of nations, is an extreme, absurd form of everything that so-called culture has developed hitherto—that it is just the same things taken to absurdity? 'Yes,' said one of the gentlemen, 'this is certainly a sickness that must be healed.' Naturally we can agree with him. Well and good; it is a sickness. To speak trivially, the man was pleased as punch that he had formulated the right thought: that all this was a sickness. But he had no inkling that this 'right thought' led nowhere, and that it is not a matter of hammering home one's correct thought, but to see the whole context in which it belongs. For example, it did not occur to this gentleman that while it might certainly be correct to say we are plagued by sickness in society, we also have to ask what kind of sickness it is and what has caused it. The cause is a prior dysfunction! Illness, after all, is nature's resistance to dysfunction in order to make us healthy again, and unnatural circumstances always precede an illness. Sickness is an attempt to bring unhealthy conditions to light. You can say that it is a way of resisting the unnatural state that precedes an illness, that illness is this process of resistance. So when the gentleman states that current conditions are an illness, he shows that the illness was necessary because of unnatural circumstances, which we can sum up as being, in the most encompassing sense, the prevalent and ubiquitous materialism of our era. Naturally I mean materialism in its broadest sense, everything that leads to an impotent power of thinking, to the crushing and oppression of competent people who wish to act practically but who are trampled under the weight of all those who say they know what is really practical. Of course they know this, but in what sense?

Spiritual-scientific truths must enter us and act fruitfully in us in our feeling and sensibility. In our time there must be a number of people whose inner conviction enables them to keep faith with what emerges from spiritual science to further cosmic evolution. Then what needs to come about will come about; then Christ, in seeking to manifest in a new form, will find those he needs. And this is necessary. When he appears in his etheric form to one or another person, the times must not be such that this appearance of Christ is seen as lunacy. It must be seen as a destined call to humanity to advance, to find a forward impetus that consists, above all, in thoroughly overcoming materialism and all its consequences. This present century must not pass without human perceptions acquiring a fundamentally different form.

The significant and bloody events that now encompass us on all sides must be seen as a fiery sign of this, humanity's goal. Then the victims of this conflict will not have died or been terribly wounded in vain. Then everything that is now happening around us will contribute to humanity's ascent. This is vital. And therefore we must ever and again hold fast to the truth so often reiterated here:

From the courage of combatants
From the blood of slaughter
From the suffering of the bereaved
From the sacrificial deeds of the people
Spirit fruit will grow—
Will guide souls to awareness of the spirit,
To find their purpose in the spirit realm.

LECTURE 3

28 MARCH 1916

TODAY I have undertaken to discuss some aspects of history from a particular spiritual-scientific perspective. Here I must ask you to remember, since I can only give brief outlines of such matters on the passing wings, let us say, of the spirit, that only glimpses will be offered of this or that historical aspect. It will not be possible in this fleeting way to investigate immediate causes and effects as we are used to doing in mainstream history. The first thing to consider is, as we are aware through our science of the spirit, that behind everything that happens in the world spiritual powers, spiritual intentions, spiritual aims are at work.

If one studies history in an external way it naturally only affords us the outward historical mechanism in which the living reality of spiritual aims and intentions manifest. A trained seer is here largely aware of the direct spiritual streams and processes that underlie events. But in such accounts we must not think that the person giving them is seeking to make a tangible, specific connection between actual events and the realities he is describing. That is not the case. All that I will try to do, as I stated, is to offer a glimpse here and there of the deeper powers that remain unseen both in an outward study of material, historical facts, and likewise in an account of facts such as those I will present today. However, if we place underlying realities and historical facts alongside each other, we can gain a picture of what happens in the world.

Here I must mention someone with whom you are all familiar, H.P. Blavatsky.[23] As you all know, she was an especially psychically gifted individual living at the time that witnessed the high tide of materialism, and was involved in a very distinctive way in the spiritual movements of the second half of the nineteenth century. In her we find an eminently psychic individual engaged with what was otherwise very materially oriented activity, on which all science in the second half of the nineteenth century was more or less dependent. Now H.P. Blavatsky was not someone you would call a medium in the ordinary sense, but really a very, very remarkably psychic person in the profoundest sense. To fully understand her, at least to some degree, we have to study the milieu she emerged from. She was brought up in Russian surroundings, and the way in which her spirit and body interrelated was also characteristically Russian. This has to be seen as very unusual, abnormal. And here we have to discern the degree to which, due to national characteristics, the Russian people diverge from the people of western and central Europe. The inhabitants of western and central Europe have continued and in a certain sense creatively reconfigured the culture which emerged from the fourth post-Atlantean era, the Graeco-Roman. What once lived in the Graeco-Roman era continues and is furthered by central and western Europe. And this is due solely to the fact that in western and central Europe people's physical bodies developed into special instruments for, among other things, spiritual activity: for thinking, feeling and will. Western and central Europe were distinguished by the achievements of thinking, feeling and will mediated by the body. The Slavic people of eastern Europe, and the Russian people in particular, are different in this respect. Thorough mechanization of the physical body as in western and central Europe simply cannot occur in the Russian people if they retain their national characteristics. One cannot understand the Russian people with western European forms of thought. It is only possible to understand them if we know about the human etheric body. You see, the most salient expressions of Russian life do not enter the physical body as in western and central Europe but unfold more in the etheric body rather than penetrating the physical body. In the Russian people the etheric body has a much, much greater importance than it still has for the people of western and central Europe, and also for the American people—the latter quite especially. And this is why a direct, strong I can never develop in the Russian people—the people, mind you, not the ruling circles—to the same degree as in western and central Europe. Their I will always possess a dreamy inflorescence, a dreamlike quality. The way in which the I still lives in us in the fifth post-Atlantean era is determined by characteristic ways in which the physical body develops. During this fifth post-Atlantean era, the Russian people are not meant to reach the point of directly developing the I as such. The I is not at all intended to impress itself into the physical body with all that lives and weaves in the etheric body. Naturally these words are an approximation only since words have not yet been coined to express spiritual realities. If I say 'dreamlike' a materialist might come along and demonstrate that the people of this nation are not in the least dreamy and so forth. But these are all external objections that actually have nothing at all to do with real inner developments.

We can therefore say that the national traits rooted in the Russian people as yet cannot come to outward manifestation, and that this people has been impressed from without, for the time being, by something that develops and gives expression to qualities and characteristics quite opposed to their real nature. H.P. Blavatsky largely grew out of this Russian culture, and so we can understand that in her, to an enormous degree, the activity of the etheric body—inasmuch as it is cognitive activity—outweighed all physical activity. We therefore have in H.P. Blavatsky very much an individual who can experience a great deal, an infinite amount in her etheric body. This is of course a quite different order of experience from that granted through thinking and perception mediated by the physical brain. By the very fact therefore that Blavatsky emerged from Russian culture, she can experience an infinite amount in her etheric body. But connected with this is the lack of qualities—really she did lack them—that a western European finds indispensable if he seeks revelations from worlds of spirit. Blavatsky lacked all means to think logically, to group her perceptions in a logical way, to say two things one after the other in which the second follows from the first. Thus if we try to translate the inner visions she had in her etheric body into our mode of cognition in western and central Europe, we always get a sense of a millwheel spinning round in our head. Unless we ourselves have a tendency to dismiss serious modes of thinking, inevitably we will experience what Blavatsky wrote as a millwheel revolving in our head. But nevertheless, what suffused her via her etheric body and came to disorderly expression through her etheric power of cognition, still contained significant revelations from the world of spirit. It is important to retain our critical faculty in regard to such things, and see them as they are rather than reading what she wrote in the same way as, say, some scientific or other book which finds its ordinary place in our modern culture.

Thus at a time when humanity was to pass through what one might call its highest charge of materialism, an individual such as Blavatsky appeared. This is simply a fact we must acknowledge: someone is present who emerged from eastern European culture and yet who had in her blood, as heredity, a dash of central European quality. This is very easy to show in her ancestry. This too was present in her, though greatly overlaid by an eastern European element: something that leads towards logical understanding in central Europe, and to will initiative, which the Russian does not intrinsically have at all. What did this result in? If we take the two extreme poles and combine them we can say that ultimately—as we can study in the many English books by Blavatsky available to us—what could emerge from her etheric body due to her roots in Russian culture was encompassed and encapsulated in an English quality, English culture, and appears in her books in a mode informed by this Englishness. But the important thing here is what happened between these two extremes.

To understand what happened we must realize that in western Europe, especially instigated by British culture, the study of occult and esoteric knowledge was always widespread. In terms of English history we can say that extensive occult studies were always pursued. In the whole development of its spiritual culture, central Europe really has no proper idea of the incisive nature of occult study that has always proceeded from the land of Britain and spread across western Europe, across southern Europe too, and so on. If we wish to understand how things really are we will have to take a look at this especially British tinge of occultism. This British hue of occultism certainly exists. The external facts known about all kinds of high-ranking orders of Scottish Freemasonry and so on are in fact only the outer aspects that are revealed to the world. Behind these externalities stand occult schools that work in a really comprehensive way; and to a far greater degree than in central Europe, these schools absorbed and incorporated old occult traditions and occult streams. In central Europe, as you have seen from my various public lectures, people strive more to rise from their own spirituality to spiritual perception, a perception of spiritual worlds. This has been their inevitable striving. Here people have depended less on what has come down to them from elsewhere, especially from older occult schools. If we look back through the centuries, in particular to the beginning of the seventeenth century, we find across England, Scotland and Ireland—less so there but certainly in Scotland—widespread occult communities that have perpetuated, promulgated and in some sense reconstituted the occult knowledge of very ancient times.

If we wish to properly understand the reason for the reconfiguring of this knowledge, we need to know that the fourth post-Atlantean epoch, that of Greek and Roman culture and so forth, which lasted until the beginning of the fifteenth century, had, in a purely human way, to inwardly assimilate the spiritual revelation that existed in former ages. What humankind received as revelations had to be spiritually assimilated during this fourth epoch. Then the fifth post-Atlantean era arrived, coinciding with the beginning of the fifteenth century. At this point the human being needed to start focusing more upon the outer world, living more on the physical plane, and elaborating fewer new concepts. All the ideas and concepts we possess today come from the fourth post-Atlantean era and have all been passed down to us. No new concepts have been formed since the fifteenth century. Not a single really new idea has been formulated, but the old concepts have just been applied to phenomena and processes in new ways. Darwinism did not produce a new concept of evolution but simply applied it to certain processes. Since the beginning of the fifteenth century, no really new concept has arisen; all ideas and concepts emerged in the fourth post-Atlantean epoch. In the fifth post-Atlantean era our focus was to be on the external, physical world, the physical plane, and the British people were especially fitted for this task. And the late stage at which this people's distinctive trait emerged in the British Isles was precisely what fitted them for it.

At the beginning of the fifteenth century a threat developed, the risk that a kind of confusion would emerge. The purely physical endeavours of British culture threatened to be confounded by a much more spiritual striving, one fruitfully informed by a spiritual life originating in very ancient times. This was at the time that parts of the kingdom of France were still under English rule, English dominion enforced from the other side of the Channel. To bring about a real sundering or separation, the world of spirit played its part in the appearance of Joan of Arc, the Maid of Orleans, whose task in a sense was to bring and create order from the world of spirit at the beginning of the fifteenth century, when she appeared. Indeed, it is true to say that the whole outward nature of Europe depends, as I said also on a previous occasion here, on this appearance of the Maid of Orleans. It was precisely then that British and French culture were sundered. Hitherto the Angles and Saxons migrating to Britain under the legendary but in fact occult leadership of Hengist and Horsa[24] had been ruled, really, by a Norman and Roman element, especially a Roman element, and represented a subordinate stratum of society. The British culture predominant today, predominant especially since the seventeenth century, at that time formed an under-stratum so strong that while the French element still dominated and the French spirit in a sense still held dominion over the

British Isles an aristocracy existed which profoundly disdained anything that originated only from the Angles and Saxons. In the tenth, eleventh and twelfth centuries for instance, a curse commonly used by this dominant class, still living at the time over the sea in France, in the French-Norman bloodline, was 'God condemn me for an Englishman.' That was a widely used curse. To be a respectable person one wished to be anything other than an Englishman in the British Isles. This only changed fully after the division I described occurred, and English culture emerged more strongly. Now diverse events occurred—it would take too long to describe them in detail—behind which profound spiritual forces held sway: the Wars of the Roses, the white and the red. The important thing is that at the beginning of the seventeenth century, after Shakespeare had written his plays—especially those concerned with kingship and the Wars of the Roses (and the whole battle between the white and red factions lives in these Shakespeare plays)—a soul incarnated in a physical body in Britain at the end of the sixteenth and the beginning of the seventeenth century. Outwardly this person was not of great importance, but nevertheless exerted great, far-reaching stimulus and influence. This soul in whom there was, really, little British blood but a confluence of French and Scottish ancestry was able to exert an especially stimulating effect. From this individual emanated an impulse both for exoteric and esoteric British culture. And thus this esoteric British culture developed, naturally with many diverse intermediary processes that it would take too long to describe. I said that this spiritual culture was a continuation of the occult streams of the fourth post-Atlantean epoch. This tradition encompassed a huge amount of knowledge, providing in fact the foundation for the predominant importance given to the body, while the etheric body was relegated to a much more subsidiary role. The physical body was here regarded as the instrument for all spiritual life, and for this very reason there was no means in these occult schools themselves to experience very much of the world of spirit. Yet these occult schools preserved ancient traditions, all that had been handed down from ancient clairvoyant seers, and they sought to permeate this with concepts. And so there developed an occult science which really only worked with experiences passed down from seers in the fourth and even the third post-Atlantean epoch. What such seers had achieved was imbued with purely physical concepts, with the conceptual material one has if one thinks only by means of the physical body. Thus a curious kind of occult science arose, but one which nevertheless extended across all domains of life.

Now it is interesting to take a somewhat closer look at certain aspects of this occult science. As I told you, I am relating nothing but facts. It is worth considering what was taught there concerning the destiny of the people of Europe. Let me try to characterize the teachings that were given.[25] Of the fourth post-Atlantean epoch—knowledge of which was passed down by tradition—it was said that this epoch had been bursting with spiritual life, had produced the conceptual world of humankind, its views of society, all kinds of things; that this era had been imbued with spiritual life. It had developed in southern Europe on the Greek peninsula, on the Italian peninsula, and spread far and wide from there. The people of central Europe, western Europe, were still in their cultural infancy at the time the fourth post-Atlantean epoch blossomed, still infants of humanity in a spiritual sense. I am telling you only what was taught in these occult schools. The peoples of central and western Europe were infants in respect of spiritual life and culture and in relation to the achievements spreading from the cultural centres of the fourth post-Atlantean epoch. Gradually these peoples of western and central Europe worked their way out of an infant state, becoming ever more mature as the Renaissance and the Reformation arrived. I do not mean the German Reformation but the English one under James I and so forth. And so these central and western European peoples freed themselves; and now a very particular dogma developed within these esoteric schools, which they adhered to with utter faith, and this was that in the fifth post-Atlantean epoch Anglo-Saxon culture will become ascendant in the place of Graeco-Roman culture. Repeatedly it was emphasized that there had been a fourth post-Atlantean epoch and now a fifth, that Graeco-Roman culture set the tone in the fourth epoch, but that what flows from the nature of Anglo-Saxon culture must set the tone for the fifth. Anglo-Saxon culture, it was said, must hold spiritual sway over the fifth post-Atlantean epoch. And everything conceived in relation to humanity's evolution must help to realize this dogma. In eastern Europe—as taught in these schools—people live in the same conditions in which the peoples of central and western Europe lived when they received Graeco-Roman culture from the Romans. In eastern Europe the Slavic peoples today, it was said, live in their infancy; all who belong to these schools regard this eastern European culture as being in an infant state, and consider that what comes in future will involve these eastern Europeans working their way towards greater maturity in a way similar to that in which central and western Europeans formerly did. But—and here I may use the actual words spoken in these schools—just as the Romans were the spiritual nursemaids to western and central Europe, so now Anglo-Saxon culture must become the nursemaid to eastern European culture, guiding it out of its infancy into a more mature spiritual phase of life. Here they make a distinction similar to the way the Germanic peoples were differentiated into Goths and so forth, according to which the Slavic peoples will also become differentiated. In awareness of the existence of inner powers that point to certain future configurations, they describe how in Russia itself the people very demonstrably live in a kind of infancy since, just as formerly in central and western Europe, a number of local regions and municipalities are only artificially held together within a nation state; yet on the other hand a people held together only by its religion, the Poles, would, despite their endeavours, ultimately be summoned—as stated, I am only speaking of what is actually taught in these schools—to be incorporated into Russian culture. In these schools this is a point of keen persuasion—that the whole Polish nation must be incorporated into Russian culture. For instance they say—and again this is quite literal—that in the neighbourhood of the valley of the lower Danube, various Slavic nations formed isolated kingdoms. However, these independent Slavic nations will, say these schools, only endure until the next great European war that is to come. In other words, there were widespread teachings of a great European war that would create havoc and disorder, and the independence of these Slavic states would only last until that point. And the whole issue is presented as if something not yet existing in the present—and please remember that these are teachings that were given through the centuries already, and so I am speaking as it were from a past present in reference to a future which has already to some extent arrived—will come about in future, and gradually give rise to a quite different form of cohesion between these eastern European peoples as they grow from infancy to greater maturity.

These were the teachings repeatedly disseminated, and always in existence. They were not taken merely theoretically but were inculcated in those who belonged to these schools in a way that led numerous people to try to configure and influence outward life so that facts and realities would also be shaped in accordance with these teachings. And here it would be interesting to cite historical facts showing how such realities can be created in a particular context. People usually have absolutely no idea that things which arise alongside each other have actually been conceived together, organized together. In occult fraternities—such as those in the British Empire of which I am speaking, which encompass broad swathes of the population including ruling groups and figures, and which have their affiliates and adherents throughout western Europe and in Italy—it is known that each person has their own particular task, that each acts in a particular way in life. It is well known what this signifies. Let me give you a specific example. On the one hand English statesmen gradually formed friendships with certain statesmen in a smaller state of the Danube region, a part of Austria. It is well known in these circles what it means to arrange things so that a friendly relationship develops and a certain belief forms in a Danube state in the security of particular institutions in the British Empire, giving rise to the view that these institutions are good ones. But one does not do this alone; at the same time and alongside it one does something else. For example, one ensures that an influential book is published that contains very derogatory things about the people who live in the Danube state. Thus with one hand one nurtures it and with the other does the opposite. Something like this has significance if undertaken methodically—cultivating a friendship which can develop some cultural significance, and on the other hand greatly accentuating the negative qualities of the same people. A devilish undertaking, you may say; and indeed, ahrimanic powers are at work in it. This is how things are done that seemingly are only coincidental. A member of such a fraternity writes a book that becomes influential, sets in motion a dire effect and movement, while another makes efforts to engender and secure the friendship of the same people whom the book disparages. Thus movements are at work behind the scenes of outer life, and people have no idea how such fraternities act with a view to making a particular nation, in this case the British nation, into a ruling and dominant power.

Now imagine an individual like Blavatsky entering this context of occult fraternities. Members of these fraternities, who knew the whole nature of occultism from tradition if not from any fruitful intuition, would learn of the existence of such an individual. To ordinary people who know nothing of occultism, Blavatsky will appear as a rather baroque individual, a little abnormal. But she does not appear so to the occultists, even those of an ahrimanic persuasion like those I have been speaking of. These people know that someone of her kind emerges out of all the developmental powers at work in humanity. This means that an individual emerges in whom the ether body can act in the way described at a time when a very great deal is occurring and unfolding. It is, you see, a time when the greatest conceivable distrust is shown towards those who simply speak of the world of spirit. Little credence will be given in our time, for the many reasons I have given, to those who simply stand up as we should—again for reasons I have given—and with full justification speak of the world of spirit. It was not in the interests of the occult fraternities centred in British culture and spreading outwards from there to cultivate an honest striving for the truth. They were above all interested in spiritual truths being communicated to the world, truths originating therefore in the world of spirit, in a way that was much more tangible and down-to-earth. These truths, in their view, should be adapted in a way favourable to the theories taught as dogma by the ruling Anglo-Saxon classes of the fifth post-Atlantean epoch.

Thus in the 1860s and at the beginning of the 1870s, these occult fraternities sought to use Blavatsky to present to the world spiritual truths of a sort that could be seen to arise not from a perfectly ordinary human brain but from an etheric body and additionally, as a purely future element, from one that had developed within a culture that possesses the foundations for the sixth post-Atlantean epoch. But since this future element does not as yet have full self-possession in the fifth post-Atlantean epoch, people thought they could arrange things in the following way. They thought they could influence Blavatsky—who, being as I described, is not an ordinary medium, but who can nevertheless be influenced by ordinary mediumistic powers—so that these British fraternities could ensure that she would speak in a way they wanted her to rather than as she would when left to her own devices. Instead of these British fraternities themselves appearing before the world and simply announcing that British culture should be dominant, they point to her as an individual who has emerged and who apparently, out of her own etheric body, introduces a new science, entirely new concepts. In fact, through the influence of these occult fraternities, these new concepts were to be formulated and shaped precisely so as to show Anglo-Saxon culture as the decisive and predominant element of the fifth post-Atlantean epoch. That was the aim. And the dogma these fraternities subscribed to made them think their conduct was entirely appropriate. They were taking a Russian woman, a Russian soul, and treating her like an infant, supervising her like a nursemaid and cultivating her by means of western European occultism. The whole thing was embedded in their dogma. Their aim was to present to the world a new occult science, but one at the same time that seemed to the western fraternities a suitable means to achieve their particular ends.

All would have run smoothly if Blavatsky had been only Russian.

They could have moulded her to their ends if she had been. But as I said, there was a certain pinch of central European quality in her. She was far too independent. I cannot trace every detail of the leverage they tried to exert on her to achieve what they sought, but she always, repeatedly, foiled them. Since all the things that lived in her etheric body naturally came to her awareness, she would not have contemplated going to London, for instance, to join an occult fraternity, and letting herself be trained as a higher medium. This is what the occult fraternities wanted, but she would never have agreed to it.

Having initially undergone very fine and proper guidance during which much developed and was continuing to develop very well in her, the whole thing was arranged so that she entered a high-level order in Paris, one however that was subordinate to British occult streams. There she was to be prepared in a way that would allow what people desired to emerge from her soul. But as I said, there was an independent streak in her, and she thwarted the aims they had for her, as she had done previously. She issued conditions for her work in the order that could not possibly be met, that cannot possibly be fulfilled without invoking an absolute storm. And hardly had this process begun, therefore, than she was excluded again. And yet by that time already, retaining her independence and acuity to a certain degree, she had absorbed important aspects of secrets that exist within such occult orders.

And then, if I can put it like this, she developed a taste for the whole role. In a sense she found it agreeable to play a very initial occult role. But she did not wish to become only a higher medium; she also wanted to direct the whole thing herself. And at this point she entered an American order. One cannot describe everything she sought to instigate and to some degree did inaugurate within this American order. Now she was an insider in it, she learned countless secrets which, until then, only high-grade members of the order had been party to. A particular intention was at work, and this was still being pursued. All this led to her receiving a huge quantity of knowledge. Imagine it, a whole new situation was thereby created!

There was now an individual who possessed an endless amount of occult knowledge that occult orders had hitherto kept as secrets. This situation was really an entirely new one. But now she did something in America that made it impossible for her to remain in the order or to work further with it: she showed that she wished to use this occult knowledge that she had gained in a way which the order could not agree to. It was quite impossible for them to agree to this, for it would have led to utter confusion if they had let her continue as she wished.

Instead they resorted to something very dubious that is used really only very, very rarely. They placed her in occult imprisonment, this good, poor Blavatsky, who, as you see, was a plaything of all kinds of powers. This occult imprisonment, achieved through certain means employed in ceremonial magic, allows those imposing it to ensure that everything the soul in question develops reaches only as far as a certain sphere, where it is repulsed. Everything the person in question inwardly develops can be seen only by himself, and he is unable to communicate it in any way to the outer world. It remains something isolated within him, assimilated within him. This is a very curious matter, but the decision was made to impose this on Blavatsky to render her harmless, thus preventing her communicating all sorts of things to the world and ensuring her whole endeavour was repulsed. This is called the repulse of endeavour, or occult imprisonment. The decision was made in 1879 at a gathering of occultists from various countries, and imposed upon Blavatsky. For many years therefore, Blavatsky did really live in this occult imprisonment. It is unnecessary to recount her outward circumstances during this period since to an external view nothing of what I am relating may be discerned.

Now certain Indian occultists were concerned to free her from this occult imprisonment. And this was the beginning of the period during which Blavatsky first embarked on an Indian path. Everything I have so far related is really Blavatsky's early history, and only now did she embark on the developments with which people are familiar. Everything that is hard to comprehend about her is connected with what I have described. Indian occultists who were endeavouring to save her from the grip of British interests employed certain means to dissolve the occult imprisonment. In fact, this was undertaken with the accord of those who had previously imposed this imprisonment on her. And the result of this for Blavatsky was that now, in a sense, everything streamed into her soul that was connected only with Indian occultism. I must continually emphasize the fact that we really are speaking here about revealed secrets of the world of spirit, which manifest however in all kinds of distorted pictures and caricatures. It would be wrong to think that they do not reveal great occult secrets. Naturally, with the huge powers that held sway in Blavatsky through her innate disposition, and then also through all she had experienced and undergone, the Indian occult truths manifested in her to a very distinct degree.

In Blavatsky, therefore, we have a specific instance of British occultism, Anglo-Saxon interests, endeavouring to pursue their predominance by using a soul such as that of Blavatsky, which they regard as embodying an infant culture. All this seeks to completely overlook central Europe, to ride roughshod over it and ignore it. These secret societies really do speak as I have recounted to you, and regard what I have so often described as the central European stream as something that must be discounted and sidelined. Thus through Blavatsky there appeared a form of occult knowledge in many respects dubious and contestable, a kind of kaleidoscope of dazzling colours through which—as you can see from all I have described—political intentions were working. The conditions Blavatsky sought in Paris were pursued with political intentions, and likewise what she was trying to do in America had a political aim. If I were to characterize Blavatsky's intentions in Paris and America, I would say that this involved the inner opposition of her Russian nature to a dependency of Russian culture on western Europe and America. This was why she tried to assert a requirement in Paris that cannot be met, and would have led to a political convulsion in France. In America she herself did not seek to impose the condition, but instead she formed an alliance with someone who had high standing in the political domain, with Olcott, in order to pursue all kinds of political machinations, but with the aid of a pervasive and manifest occultism. All these measures sought to realize endeavours that had been differently pursued under the guidance of Blavatsky's masked, original leader, of whom it is very difficult indeed to speak. This original leader wished to guide Blavatsky into the proper channel; but then he was replaced by another who was anything other than what Blavatsky called a Mahatma—really a completely different figure.

And so, through the most varied forces working together here, a confused text emerged from Blavatsky, the *Secret Doctrine*; and yet it is one that also contains countless great, mighty truths. This book was also capable of having great influence in central Europe. You see—and this is apparent for instance in a very important novel by George Sand[26]—secret societies, fraternities pervaded by occultism, play a great role in political movements in western Europe, albeit often in outwardly imperceptible ways (a subterranean kind of influence). At the end of my public lecture on Friday[27] I hinted that such things are playing their part in current events. Political conspiracies and all sorts of other related things play an important role. As I said at the public lecture, we can point to conspiracies that draw on underground occult streams and foundations, connected for instance with the murder of Jaurès and a whole host of other things that I mentioned last Friday, also the murder of Franz Ferdinand and so on. All these things—usually hidden from the outer world—are involved in a whole loop of plots and conspiracies centred in London and spun across western Europe as far as southern Europe and the Balkan countries, ending in St Petersburg. As I said, these things should not be regarded so much in historical terms like other historical facts but more as things that can shed some light on various events.

What we should remember, above all, is that powers at work in the world of spirit and only manifesting in the physical world play through a soul such as that of Blavatsky. We should discern quite especially how such a soul is gripped by what plays below the surface of the physical plane, how it is carried along on its current, revealing powers at work in historical evolution. I am sure it is clear to you from the many reflections we have engaged in together here that we must gradually become familiar with such realities. Today I was obliged to speak of these matters so that you might see how many of the events of the world and their determining causes remain hidden from view if we do not try to look deeper than people usually do. Under the surface of events run quite different currents; and in a sense we remain blind if we penetrate no further than the surface. The astonishment people invariably feel at events that occur at any particular time would be much diminished if they engaged with the deeper currents and deeper powers at work behind them. But unfortunately the state of affairs today is that many concern themselves only with the apparently linear stream of outward events, unaware that it is repeatedly convulsed and interrupted as if by a vortex surfacing from the depths, while on the other hand there are people who are interested in all kinds of occult matters, but only in their sensational aspects because this grips their interest. Very few people today have any perception that what we can discern in the occult domain can be endlessly enlightening when we seek to understand what is happening in the outer world. Some are extremely interested in the life of Blavatsky while others are not in the least interested in her but instead concern themselves only with outward facts that occur on the physical plane. But if we see how these events are connected with deeper realities, as I was only able to hint at today, we can gain greater insights, and this is important. We are moving towards a time when increasing numbers of people will seek to penetrate and perceive the deeper currents of existence, having the good will to do so.

And within our movement it is particularly necessary to see things such as those I have spoken of in the right light. Immediately after the war broke out, a pupil of Blavatsky, Mrs Annie Besant,[28] railed in very extreme terms in her English journals against what lives in our anthroposophic movement. The way in which she upbraided us showed clearly that the factions she belonged to could not for a moment imagine that our honest esotericism, in its pure search for truth, was not sullied by political interests. But political elements can never play into our quest for truth. It can have a connection with politics only in so far as truth in general can inform politics, but not in the sense I indicated in relation to the western European fraternities. Basically, our movement could only have the mission of sundering those who can be sundered from the influence of these western European fraternities. But in these factions to which Besant belongs, people cannot conceive of anything occurring without impure political motives. Thus it was related, entirely wrongly, that from 1909 onwards I had intended to become the president of the whole Theosophical Society, and to go to India so that I might influence politics from there. On the one hand, therefore, I'd be jumping on the Berlin-Baghdad train,[29] and on the other developing anthroposophy! I am not telling you fairy tales. Assuming a most indignant and angry pose, these circles asserted that I would gradually have won over all the officials of the Theosophical Society, which was very widespread there at the time, so as to exert a political influence to further the aims of Pan-Germanism. In other words, I would have attacked England from my position in India. You can read this in Mrs Besant's essays; and now the whole thing is being repeated in a still more extreme fashion.

You see, therefore, that these people can only think in such ways, and that gradually a sense of truth, of pure, objective, honest striving for truth, inevitably gets lost. The kinds of things said by Mrs Besant can only be called objective untruths. But actually I ought to go a good deal further in the forcefulness of my expressions, for to speak of 'objective untruth' in relation to the nonsensical accusations by the Jesuits,[30] with which you are by now very familiar, falls far short of what is needed. But then something else must be considered too. In 1909 in Budapest I had something very particular to say to Mrs Besant. At the time people were seeking to make a compromise with me, with a view to making this figure of Alcyone[31] into the bearer of Christ. By way of compromise, if I were to agree with this, they would make me into the reincarnated St John the evangelist. This would have been enshrined in their dogmas if I had agreed to engage with all their deceitful ploys. But countering all these developments, an international association of honest people formed. They included Mr Keightley,[32] who in the past had always edited Mrs Besant's books and corrected their factual errors. This international association, based in India, asked me to become its president. And in 1909, in Budapest, I said to Mrs Besant that I would not for a moment work within an occult movement in any other way than in relation to German culture, only in connection with German culture, within central Europe. I said this to Mrs Besant in 1909. Nevertheless, after war broke out she wrote the things I described. Here it is no longer a matter of objective untruth but of an intentional lie, since I had expressly stated my position: an intentional lie rather than an objective untruth.

This is the path one is led down if one does not stand firm on the ground of pure truth, of honest, incontrovertible truth, when entering the domain of spiritual truths. Everything depends on the way in which occult streams must enter the world in accordance with the needs of human evolution. This necessity, and acknowledgement of it, is the all-important thing. When Mrs Besant first arrived in Germany, to give a lecture in Hamburg, she also spoke in a smaller circle. At the time I asked Mrs Besant a question—and the fact that I remember such things is no doubt sometimes very unpleasant for people. I asked her about the great and powerful tradition of German occultism that connected so strongly with German culture at the turn of the eighteenth and nineteenth centuries. Mrs Besant replied—and as I said, this was during her very first visit to Germany—that what emerged in Germany was a failed attempt in occultism, which surfaced in other forms. And because it failed, it had to be undertaken in England instead, so that occultism could now be brought back to Europe from England. You see how politics insinuates itself into these things, and how we must be aware of them.

What I have said to you today is intended as a kind of introduction to reflections that will, however, take us in a somewhat different direction. They will, though, lead us to matters of equal historical importance, such as esoteric perception of the individual human being, of which we will speak more next time.

Lecture 4

4 April 1916

Today I want to pass to more occult aspects of the things we spoke of a week ago. As we saw, certain occult streams, expressed in the form of occult fraternities, can be considered important for human life. As you will have seen from our more outward reflections last week, such occult fraternities of a very distinctive hue are employed—in British lands—in order to achieve certain outward aims. Now it is necessary for anyone who joins a spiritual-scientific movement today with his eyes open to be able to assess such things with a degree of objectivity, to survey the field and current situation. Today therefore I will speak of how we must conceive of the work of such occult fraternities in general, so that we can see from this how they may become an instrument for certain other aims and purposes.

What we refer to here as an 'occult fraternity' is in fact a very complex matter. But this complexity is founded on a substructure in which people are guided in a particular direction by coming together in a kind of rite, and being given certain symbols. They gather together in a kind of ritual manner that comes to expression in symbols. There are a great many people today who think with some scorn of such fraternities, who think, wrongly, that they know enough about them to ridicule them and the symbolism they employ. There is a great deal of short-sightedness in relation to all such things today. To those who lightly dismiss the importance of certain ceremonies and symbols connected with the occult fraternities, we can simply reply that people ultimately no less important than themselves—these enlightened monists and others who scorn and ridicule such things—have placed great value on experiencing ceremonial and symbolic rites. One such person was Goethe, who well knew what he had gained thereby, and repeatedly expressed this in one way or another. Instead of a school education, he was able to undergo a form of education later on that was connected with certain Freemason orders. This may have given less important figures than Goethe less than it gave him; but it gave him a very great deal. People who scorn and ridicule such things might do well to consider this. But to understand the deeper nature of these orders and their rites, we need to be able to study them more closely.

As you know, we have been living in the fifth post-Atlantean epoch since the beginning of the fifteenth century. This was preceded by the fourth post-Atlantean era, beginning around 747 BC and only really ending at the beginning of the fifteenth century. People who today are very, very clever—and almost all of them are, aren't they?—think that what the human soul experiences since the fifteenth century cannot be very different from what it experienced in the two millennia before that, back to 747 BC. But even very external things can show us how fundamentally different the human soul was in the fourth post-Atlantean epoch, the one that preceded ours. From the eighth century BC to the late fourteenth century AD, though of course this waned a great deal as the fifteenth century approached, the human etheric body was much, much more receptive than it has been since then. It was capable of perceiving much more of what surrounded it. And when the ether body perceives things, it perceives the elemental world; it does not only perceive minerals, plants, animals, water, air and so forth as the physical body does, but it perceives, rather, the elemental beings alive in plants, animals and minerals. Today people think that descriptions from those days of gnomes or sprites that were perceived in mountain regions, in mines and caves, were just poetic inventions. But this is not so. The people in those days really did still know of the existence of an elemental world behind the physical world.

Not all present here may know that even external documentation can prove this—that people still knew about the elemental world until relatively recently. I believe I have mentioned here before a picture in Hamburg Museum. The picture depicts the Fall, in other words the event we read about in Genesis. A painter who depicts this theme today is likely to show the tree of paradise and Adam and Eve either side of it, portrayed in a more or less beautiful and in fact often rather ugly fashion. Coiled around the tree, usually, is the snake, a real snake. But is this actually realistic my dear friends? Can we call this realism? Naturally Eve was not yet as clever and intelligent as modern women are, but nevertheless it is a little far-fetched to think that she would be tempted by a real snake that crawls in the grass to commit this act. We therefore cannot consider this kind of depiction realistic.

But we know that the tempter was in fact Lucifer—not a being that can be seen with today's physical eyes. One can only see him with the awoken etheric body, with awoken clairvoyance. We find that he was the being who remained behind at the Moon stage of evolution. From Moon evolution we largely already received our physical body as we know it today, although at that time it was not yet physically visible, existed only etherically. A modern person's head today is a reflection of the head that already existed during Moon evolution. But the rest of the human body attached to it did not yet then exist in its modern form, but only as a snakelike appendage, in what we now have as our spinal column. And thus, if we were to depict Lucifer as he remained behind from Moon evolution, one would have to portray him with a human head and a spinal column attached to it, a snakelike form in other words.

And this is precisely how the painter Master Bertram portrayed Lucifer in the thirteenth, fourteenth century—not as a modern painter does, but in a way that fully accords with spiritual science. You can see the picture in Hamburg Museum, and can discover that a painter of the thirteenth or fourteenth century painted things as they really are. Unfortunately people today are too clever to acknowledge the telling nature of this picture. But it documents the fact that human beings still perceived the etheric world up until the time we have been speaking of.

At this period, the fourth post-Atlantean epoch, arose the symbols upon which occult fraternities are founded. The symbols used were something that people still experienced as vividly alive in the fourth post-Atlantean era, as something living within them. I will try to clarify the ideas embodied in these symbols in the way Goethe communicated them. In his own way, Goethe tried to render symbolism fruitful for outward life, considering that one could make great inner progress, could gain great benefit from engaging deeply with symbolism. As you can see in his *Wilhelm Meister*, he wanted education to be conducted so that human beings grew up within a certain milieu of symbolism. Instead of learning the trivialities people nowadays often learn in grammar schools, he wanted them to be informed by a certain language of symbolism. He wanted them above all to learn, through symbols, what we can call the 'four human venerations': for the world of spirit, for the physical world, for every human soul; and then the veneration founded on these other three: a reverence for oneself. Most enlightened people today would of course probably relate well enough to the last of these, wouldn't they? But in Goethe's view, this reverence, which is in a sense connected with the greatest dangers, would only emerge from the foundation created by the other three.

How does Goethe think that veneration for the spirit should be incorporated into us? He wishes us to learn a certain gesture: arms crossed over the chest and our gaze turned upwards. And in this stance, we should acquire a reverence for the spirit's influence upon us. At a certain still very young age, Goethe thinks, we should connect this gesture with a feeling of reverence for what is above us. Why is this significant? It has a certain importance because, when we really feel reverence for the spirit, we can do no other than give expression to it. And if we placed our physical hands together upon our back, our etheric hands would cross in front; and our gaze, however much we cast it downwards as physical glance, would be turned upwards with our etheric eyes. This is the natural gesture for etheric eyes, turned upwards, and for etheric hands, crossing in front of us. This is something the etheric body actually does when this reverence for the spirit is present. It is inevitable, self-evident that the etheric body assumes this gesture. In the fourth post-Atlantean epoch, people still knew this because they sensed the movements of the etheric body within them. And when they were told to adopt this gesture, they were being told only that they should enliven and perceive the etheric gesture by making the physical correspond to it.

Thus Goethe sought a way to grow into the life of spirit. He knew that there is real meaning in fully experiencing the gestures connected with direct expressions of inner life. In the same way he wanted a person to cross his hands behind his back and cast his gaze downwards when he acquires reverence for the corporeal realm, for everything earthly. That was the second thing he thought people should acquire. And the third thing was this: outspread hands with a gaze turning to right and left should teach them reverence for every other human soul. And this would be the foundation for acquiring a reverence for one's own soul.

This direct knowledge that such gestures, when they are right, are not something arbitrary but are connected with the human being's spiritual organization is something that humankind has largely lost sight of since the fourteenth century. Before the fifteenth century, people were easily awoken to inner experience through such gestures, along with more complex ones. From the fifth post-Atlantean era onwards, it is perfectly possible to teach young people simple gestures such as these if they are taught in the appropriate way. And this is also something that Goethe wishes.

But after the fourteenth or fifteenth centuries the more complex gestural language of 'symbol, handshake and word' as this is current within secret fraternities could no longer be taught to people in a way that enabled them to sense its reality. And so, while these fraternities that existed in the fourth post-Atlantean epoch continued to develop, with three consecutive degrees involving the teaching of symbols, handshakes and words, among other things, the different nature of human souls in recent centuries meant that people no longer really connected with these things. If we stay with the simplest of such things, with symbol, handshake and word, people felt no real connection with them because they could no longer experience the ether body corresponding to these things in a way that accorded with the human soul. It became something outward and external. You see, in the fourth post-Atlantean epoch, the rational and mind soul had chiefly developed in humankind, but now the consciousness soul began to seize hold of them. In other words, people began to be reliant on the powers of reason connected with the physical brain. What we can call the sensitivity of the etheric body receded. And what is surfacing today? Please listen carefully as I describe what must now appear.

Occult fraternities thus continue into this fifth post-Atlantean epoch. Occult brotherhoods continue to be founded or are perpetuated, and they admit people to whom corresponding symbols are introduced. These people learn certain symbols by means of adopting a particular bodily stance and position that expresses them. They learn certain handshakes in which they take hold of another person's hand in other than the usual way. They learn to utter certain words that signify a very specific activity of the etheric body, and other such things. I will only mention these basic aspects. Thus people have been learning such symbols, handshakes and words since the fifteenth or sixteenth centuries, but their nature is now such that the consciousness soul is at work in them. And these symbols, handshakes and words do not influence the consciousness soul but remain something very external to it. Yet you must not think for a moment that such things, symbol, handshake and word, do not still work upon our etheric body. They do indeed. We absorb through symbol, handshake and word what is implicit in and related to them. Thus through teaching a number of people these symbols, handshakes and words, their subconscious learns something that they do not possess in their conscious awareness. Naturally this is something that very definitely should not be done but instead we should proceed in a way that human evolution requires—which is to appeal to the human mind. In other words, we teach people what their mind and understanding can first encompass and learn, which is the content of spiritual science. This content of spiritual science must first be comprehended, and by this means we must first approach people. First people must stand in some way within the spiritual-scientific movement, and only after some time has passed can symbol, handshake and word be introduced to them in a way they can receive because they have been properly prepared. They can find something familiar in it, for they have at least understood it. Normally this is not done in occult brotherhoods. People are admitted to the first degree of an order without previously having learned anything of spiritual science or occultism. Symbols, handshakes and words are conveyed to them before they have learned anything about the world of spirit, and this means that their subconscious is influenced by something unconnected with their conscious awareness.

What is the outcome of this? If one so desires, one can thereby make people into pliant tools for all kinds of plans. You see, if you work upon the etheric body without the human being knowing this, you exclude the powers of reason he otherwise possesses if you do not also give the mind something that spiritual science must be today. You exclude this and then make such fraternities into a tool of those who seek to realize their plans and aims. And then you can use such brotherhoods to pursue certain political aims, or you can cultivate the dogma that 'Alcyone' is the outward, physical bearer of Christ Jesus. Those who have been prepared by these means will become willing instruments to disseminate such things. One need only be dishonest and unrighteous enough, and then one can achieve all kinds of things by such means, by using others as instruments.

These things become apparent to true insight and knowledge. Those who know the difference and the distinction between the fifth and the fourth post-Atlantean epochs, something we keep reiterating, will also know why one must first acquaint oneself with spiritual science and only then be introduced to occult symbols. Wherever spiritual science is being pursued with really honest intent, this course will naturally be followed. No harm of any kind will come to someone who has only become acquainted, say, with what he finds in my *Theosophy* or *Occult Science*, and seeks to understand it. He will not suffer harm through the unexplained communication of symbols.

In British lands, particularly, we see the utter lack of any teaching or explanation as an introduction to such symbols. Explanation does not mean us saying that this symbol means this or that, for here anyone can be told anything. Such teaching should be of a kind that discloses secrets based on a preceding delineation of the course of the evolution of humankind and the world, and only then moves on to show how the symbols arise from this. This does not happen. The symbols are simply given; in fact, they are not even simply given in this way but in another way: instead of basing them on literature such as our spiritual science, they are related to a literature in which, really, everything is given symbolically.

In many respects, the greatest mischief has been done with this occult literature in France by Eliphas Lévi,[33] whose books, *Dogma and Ritual of Higher Magic* and *The Key to Higher Magic* contain great truths, certainly, but all mixed up with very dangerous errors. Their nature is such that they cannot easily be rationally comprehended, as our spiritual science can, but must be assimilated symbolically. Read Eliphas Lévi! *You* can read him without danger, of course, because you have been sufficiently prepared. If you read his book *Dogma and Ritual of Higher Magic* then you will see how the whole symbolic method differs from what we do. Yes, my dear friends, if one instructs others in purely symbolic ways as Eliphas Lévi does, then one can basically use them for whatever purposes one desires.

Things became still worse after Eliphas Lévi with the appearance of Dr Encausse,[34] otherwise known as Papus, who gained such devastating and dangerous influence at the Court of St Petersburg. He repeatedly stayed there and played a disastrous political role in events. Papus, as he calls himself, communicated certain occult secrets to humanity but in a dire, dangerous way; and those who allow him to influence them hold fast to his teaching, once they have got beyond the basics, with a rigid fanaticism. It is not a matter of refuting Papus, for as paradoxical as this may sound, the worst thing about him is that he writes a great many things that are correct. It is the way in which he gives them that is so dangerous. To trickle into weak souls the things contained in Papus's books means to prepare them to utterly lull their reason to sleep, so they can be used for whatever purpose is desired. People like Papus exert an influence today. Anyone who has some experience of these things will know that Papus exerts a major influence. I traced this influence through Bohemia and Austria. His influence is far less great in Germany, though here too it was present until a certain point in time. But he is particularly influential in Russia, and this was also achieved through a certain dishonesty that is connected with all these matters.

In the eighteenth century the teachings of Jakob Boehme,[35] of whom we have often spoken, were transplanted to France by Saint-Martin,[36] the so-called 'philosophe inconnu'. He reproduced them in a really very charming style, and so, when they were translated back into German again, the works of Saint-Martin were of course much more readable for people than had been the works of Boehme himself, whose difficulty is widely acknowledged.

I myself have a fond memory of translations of Saint-Martin, this 'unknown philosopher'. The book by him, *Des erreurs et de la vérité* ('Of Truth and Error') was beautifully translated into German by a fine, well-known German poet. I have a particular interest in this since a small pamphlet by me,[37] entitled *The Mission of Spiritual Science and its Building in Dornach*, will shortly appear. There I try to refute some common errors about spiritual science in a brief, popular form. This essay, soon to be published, arose from a lecture I gave in Switzerland because there, in Dornach itself, a very clever Protestant priest had suggested a great many things. But in the end I did not wish to confine myself to what this priest had said, although it was rather typical. People raise all sorts of things; and, without specifically mentioning the priest, I was able to refute some of these common errors people entertain about our spiritual science, especially also about our building in Dornach. In a lecture the priest gave he quoted a poem—I spoke of this once here—by Matthias Claudius. He recited a verse of this poem, seemingly one of great pathos, to show that people really ought not to speak of something like a secret science or doctrine since even the moon was beyond ordinary comprehension. But if you read further in this poem by Matthias Claudius, the next verse reveals that the poet's meaning was precisely the opposite of what the priest wished to convey. The interesting thing here is that Matthias Claudius was the translator of Saint-Martin's *Of Truth and Error*, that it was he who translated Saint-Martin. Such things can show you, my dear friends, what kind of people oppose us today on what they call 'good grounds', and what the nature of these motives are. I could expand at great length on the kinds of people we are dealing with here, but it is a shame to waste time refuting people who oppose us in this way.

But sometimes one experiences much more curious things, and one of these I would like to relate now because of its great interest. It happened to me since we last met here. You all know—for I mentioned it again last time—that, for reasons to do solely with truth, I could not and might not go along with what Mrs Besant, president of the Theosophical Society, was doing with her group, a large number of whom she had prepared in the way I just described to you. I could not go along with this. In the name of truth I had to take a stand against this frivolous view of Christ associated with the Alcyone boy, all the more so since I saw that even scholarly individuals were very taken with the little pamphlet said to be written by Alcyone—called, I believe *At the Feet of the Masters*—and heralded it as one of the greatest phenomena of modern times. In those circles around Mrs Besant, though, some did have a sense that I was serving the truth. They sensed this. But at the same time those who felt this were in doubt as to whether truth was really something that should cause them to take a stand against Mrs Besant for being less than truthful. And then I find in a pamphlet by a member of our society, E. von Gumppenberg,[38] also due to be published shortly, a statement, a judgement about me. It is quoted word-for-word, this judgement about me. Frau von Gumppenberg quotes a comment about me by someone else, and then says: This is reminiscent of another verdict on Dr Steiner, made on one occasion by an English lady, who said: 'The good Dr Steiner is a philosopher; and this may be why he is so careful with the truth. What does it matter if Mrs Besant is less truthful? Don't we all tell fibs? Surely it is inevitable. How would we get through life if we were always strictly truthful? We cannot all be philosophers. Let us therefore allow people to fib, for it will only cause trouble if we oppose them.'

My dear friends, I cannot help thinking that a bandit is a more decent person than someone who holds such a view! That is really what I think and feel, however finely dressed the person who holds this opinion. I am sure the lady in question was indeed dressed in the finest fashion. But from such things we can see how dangerous it is to be sparing with the truth today, in particular where matters not accessible to direct, sensory perception are concerned.

Hypocrisy holds sway in the dissemination of spiritual views by Encausse, by Papus, for these people call themselves 'Martinistes'. Here we really have to defend the honest 'unknown philosopher' and his upright quest for truth, along with his endeavours to serve the eighteenth century. We must guard his name from wrongful use by modern Papusians.

Now it is very important to know that every occult brotherhood is founded on three degrees. In the first degree, when symbolism is used in the right way—by which I mean of course what I have just intimated as the right path for our fifth post-Atlantean epoch—souls advance to a point where they have a precise inner experience of a knowledge independent of ordinary physical-sensory knowledge. What is contained in my *Occult Science* is, broadly, what every member of the first degree should know in our fifth post-Atlantean epoch. In the second degree or grade, each person should know—and that means having a living, inward knowledge—what is contained in the book *Knowledge of the Higher Worlds*. And at the third degree, having received the significant symbols of sign, handshake and word, one should know what it means to live outside the body. These would be the rules if schooling were properly handled.

And that is in fact what was achieved within these grades or degrees in certain regions of Europe up until the eighth or ninth centuries. In Ireland,[39] for instance, what I have described was to a great degree achieved fully by individuals, by a great number of them, before the eighth or ninth centuries—and also in other regions of Europe though not in such great numbers as in Ireland. Certain things were avoided, simply through lack of ability—that is, the capacity to work towards a real science of the spirit. For many reasons this real science of the spirit is only now approaching us. But as I said, occult brotherhoods have always existed, and they work out of nothing but symbolism. This is especially significant when people work out of nothing but symbolism within a nation, a national community that has not yet reached full maturity. This was the cause of the mischief and confusion that arose immediately under Catherine the Great, and her successor Emperor Paul, when an attempt was made to transplant certain secret societies from the West to Russia after Voltairianism had suffered something of a setback. This attempt was comprehensive in its scope, and what occurred at this time under the influence of occult brotherhoods transplanted from the West to Russia has had a great influence since then on the whole of Russia's spiritual and cultural development—a much greater influence than people can credit. Naturally, such an influence affects different fields in different ways: novelists assimilate it through their novels, political authors in politics. But on certain, always present paths, such an influence always has an impact on subsequent developments. And in fact everything of significance in Russian culture up to Tolstoy points us back more or less to the time I have referred to when certain occult brotherhoods were transplanted from western Europe to Russia.

Now I said that a certain substructure exists, the three degrees through which members of the occult brotherhoods advance. Then there are those who attain so-called high degrees, higher grades. Naturally this is a realm where vanity has a great deal of scope, for there are fraternities in which one can progress through 90 levels or even more. Let us consider for a moment what it means to attain such a high status in an order of this kind. The so-called Scottish degree system, founded on the three grades that develop as I described, has 33 degrees, and this is simply because of an error arising from grotesque ignorance. First come the three levels which, as you see, have a deep significance, but then there follow 30 more. You can imagine that if one has already acquired the capacity in the third degree to have body-free experiences, one must indeed be a very advanced adept if one can progress through a further 30 grades after this. But this is based on a grotesque misunderstanding and misperception. You see, in occult sciences numbers are read in a different way from the decimal system, based instead on a system appropriate to the numbers under consideration. So the thirty-third degree in fact, in the system of numbers under consideration here, signifies 3 times 3, or 9. This played an important role for Blavatsky. In her *Secret Doctrine*, you can find a long debate about the number 777. People came up with all sorts of fantasies about the meaning of this number. In reality it is 343, or in other words 7 times 7 times 7. In occultism one multiplies written numbers with one another, and so to find the real number involved here one multiplies 7 by 7 to get 49, and then that number with 7 again to obtain 343. Accordingly, 33 is 9, the product of 3 times 3. It is only because people are unaware of this that they read it as 33 instead of 9.

Leaving such foolishness and vanity aside, there are, then, six further legitimate grades after the first three. And when a person is properly schooled in them, they endow him with very significant advances. But no one in our present era can, really, fully undergo these stages of schooling. It is simply impossible. No one can undergo these stages in their entirety since in the fifth post-Atlantean epoch humanity has not developed to the point where this would be possible. So far, you see, not enough knowledge—well, not knowledge but activation of knowledge—of worlds of spirit has emerged. This still has to emerge, and will do so gradually. Since around 1413 we have been in the fifth post-Atlantean epoch, which will last a long time, roughly 2160 years, and will not end therefore until 3573. Thus we are still only at the beginning of this period. During this fifth post-Atlantean epoch a very great deal will happen, and the development of spiritual science is integral to this. But this can only slowly manifest, although we can certainly already discern the broad outlines and can also convey many details too. But a very great deal will only emerge through meeting resistance and developing strength by this encounter. And this resistance will keep growing ever greater.

As you can see from the things I have related during these lectures, and will see too from diverse other things I can relate, we now live in relatively idealistic, spiritual times compared with what is to come. We live at the end of the second Christian millennium, but shortly after this millennium ends humanity will experience strange and curious things—which today are only slowly being prepared. We can say that two poles are rapidly developing, are in preparation respectively in East and West. Towards more eastern regions—but emerging from national traits, and quite obviously not from those circles that now misgovern the peoples of eastern Europe—a quite different kind of thinking about the human being will increasingly develop. In the not too distant future people will come to see the developing child in a quite different way from current tendencies. When a child is born people will try to ask what might manifest in this child. They will discern a hidden spiritual being slowly developing within this child and will seek to decipher the riddle of this being. A kind of ritual will be connected with the growth and development of the child. This is in preparation in eastern regions and will naturally play over into Europe too. The consequence will be a huge respect that develops for the genius of each child, a search for this genius. It is self-evident, isn't it, that when an age develops towards this outlook, the educational traditions that are currently so prevalent must die away. This era is approaching from the East, but will encompass a smaller portion of humanity.

The greater portion of humanity will be affected by influences from America, from the West, and this will pursue a different form of development, one that is so far showing only its first idealistic traces and sympathetic beginnings compared with what will come. We can say that our current times are in pretty good shape compared with what will come when western development increasingly puts forth its blossoms. Not very long after the year 2000, a kind of prohibition on all thinking—though not a direct one—will issue from America: a law that will have the aim of suppressing all individual thinking. The beginnings of this can be seen already in what materialistic medicine is doing, where no account can be taken of the soul any more, but where, based on empirical experiments, the human being is treated like a machine.

But please don't misunderstand me, since even in the so-called 'spiritual' domain much here is done in a hugely misguided way. People can sometimes come along and say: I had all kinds of orthodox treatment and was not cured. Then I went to a person who treated me spiritually, who told me there are evil spirits in my body and I must get rid of them, initially by praying. This was what someone told me recently, and so I asked him whether it helped. No, he said, I got much, much worse. And so I asked him to reflect on what situation he had been placed in. Do not think, I said, that what the man told you was wrong. It is quite true that there were certain spiritual beings in you that caused your disorder. But it is precisely because the man told you something correct, something you had to acknowledge as true, that he had to harm you in this way. Think of it like this. A good-for-nothing nuisance comes along and breaks a machine. He is the real reason why it no longer works. So how do I get the machine to work again? Following the method of your spiritual physicians I would have to get hold of the fellow, give him a beating and then, when he runs off, imagine this means that everything will work properly again. He told you that once the evil spirits have gone all will be well again. But just as little as the good-for-nothing running off will mend the machine, which still needs to be fixed, the same is true for you. Whether you get rid of the spirits or not is ultimately of as little importance for your healing as if I were to give that fellow a beating so that he runs away. Actually I could let him stand there and watch as I mend the machine.

So with a spiritual outlook too a great deal can be misperceived, since people are not very good at thinking nowadays. Rather than swinging back and forth between one extreme and the other, between either/or, we should try to gain real insight into the fact that spirit indwells all matter, and that the body can only be cured through knowledge of the spirit. But as things are set to develop, the spirit will be excluded from the whole picture. That is one of the beginnings we are witnessing.

And here is another. Today we already have machines for adding and subtracting, don't we. All very useful and easy—we no longer need to calculate for ourselves. And this will become the norm for everything. It will take only a couple of centuries to arrive; and then people will no longer need to think or reflect, but only push things around. For instance, today if we need to send 330 balls of wool to Liverpool we have to think how to do it, don't we. But soon you will need only to push or press and the thing will be done. And to ensure that the firm coherence of social structures is not disrupted in future, laws will be issued that do not directly prohibit individual thinking but whose effect will be to exclude it, render it void. That is the other pole towards which we are tending. By comparison, life today is really not so bad. Today we are still allowed to think, aren't we, as long we don't overstep a certain boundary. But what I have described is implicit in the development of the West, and will emerge as the West develops.

Spiritual-scientific development must also place itself into this overall course of development. It will have to perceive it clearly and objectively. We must be clear that what seems paradoxical today will come about. In the year 2200, roughly, and a little more, thinking will start to be suppressed in the world to the greatest possible extent. And spiritual science must engage with this tendency, must—and will—find enough to offer as a counterbalance in cosmic evolution to these tendencies.

We have seen only the beginnings of these trends so far, and they will become increasingly apparent. It is certainly true that the six higher grades of initiation can only partially be achieved, only partly worked through. But instead of this one can engage in something quite different, can just let people pass symbolically through the three first grades. And indeed there are brotherhoods today in which only symbols are given and nothing more. The people concerned are often even proud of this fact—that nothing more than symbols are offered. They are admitted to the first grade, advance into the second, and then the third, and actually they acquaint themselves there only with symbolism without actually absorbing anything of spiritual science. And if you ask them whether this really satisfies them, whether it is enough for them to learn certain ceremonies, handshakes and symbols, to witness certain symbolic actions and rites performed around them in a temple room, many say that they are perfectly satisfied with this since they do not need to think anything during these rites, and because each person can interpret them as he likes.

But the astral body thereby conveys real knowledge into the etheric body, and in this way the etheric bodies of those involved receive comprehensive knowledge. And if you take a look at the most narrow-minded of Freemasons today, you will see that actually they possess vast knowledge in their etheric body—not in their physical body, in their conscious awareness, but in their etheric bodies, especially when they have reached the third grade. They possess a huge, subconscious knowledge. This knowledge, that can be conveyed and passed on through symbolism, can be used in the manner suggested both for honest and dishonest purposes. There are, you see, the most diverse occult connections, and again these appear at two extremes. The character of the one is worldly and Christian, while that of the other is Christian in an ecclesiastical sense. The Freemasons must be counted amongst the worldly Christian symbolic brotherhoods, while the Jesuits have ecclesiastical symbolic connections. The Jesuit is led through the three grades in the same way, likewise in association with symbols, and through this symbolism he learns to acquire a language of huge efficacy. This is why Jesuit orators are so immensely influential; they know how one builds up a speech in order to influence the uneducated masses, how to keep intensifying their message. An educated listener will sometimes find what they say very trivial, and yet it is hugely influential. On one occasion I wished to see the effect that emanates from an influential Jesuit sermon—see it clairvoyantly I mean. I listened to a sermon—

this is many years ago now—given by Father Klinkowstroem, one of the most effective Jesuit preachers. Before a crowd who had gathered to hear him—naturally all uneducated people—he sought to impress on them the need for Easter Confession. He was trying to show these uneducated people in irrefutable terms—so that they would accept it as something self-evident, without any need for real understanding—that the Easter Confession was not arbitrarily ordained by the Pope, but was established by higher, divine powers. He said the following.

My dear Christians, imagine that you see a cannon and a gunner beside it holding the fuse. Someone gives him the order to fire. Imagine, dear Christians that the cannon is about to be fired. What happens if a cannon is to be fired? The gunner stands expectantly beside his cannon. What is he waiting for? For the word of command—Fire! He waits for this word of command, Fire! This lives in his soul. He knows very clearly that this will come. And then it comes: Fire! He shoots. The cannon thunders. Dear Christians, please picture these things very clearly. Now consider the cannon as the assembly of customs relating to the Easter Confession. Previously the laws and commands about this Easter Confession had not yet been given. But the cannon stood there. These commands were to be given. The Pope stood there as the gunner with the lit fuse. And from heaven, dear Christians, came the command: Fire! The Pope heard it—fuse! The cannon fired! The Easter Confession now existed! Can we not exactly equate this cannon and the ordaining of Easter Confession? But the unfaithful, dear Christians, claim that the Pope himself invented the Easter Confession! You need only remember the cannon. At the command, Fire! it shoots. Would it ever occur to you to say that this gunner, who shoots the cannon on the command 'Fire', had invented the gunpowder that fires it? And equally, dear Christians, you cannot say that the Pope invented the Easter Confession. The Pope did not invent it just as the gunner did not invent the gunpowder!

All were convinced. The whole church was won over. This was very cleverly done indeed, very skilfully done in pictures. Such people also pass through their three grades, in their own way. And naturally the most diverse nuances exist between such orders, just as not all occult brotherhoods are Freemasons. In Germany we even have the Illuminati and suchlike.

But in both kinds, the worldly and ecclesiastical, three higher grades follow the three lower ones. Those who are admitted to the higher grades, and those who progress to the highest grades of all in certain fraternities—in some but not all of these societies of course—form a kind of community with each other, and so for example it is certainly possible for a high-ranking member of a Jesuit order to belong to such a community or association. Of course the Jesuits are very fierce in their opposition to Freemason societies and the latter equally fierce in their opposition to the Jesuits; and yet high-ranking Freemasons and Jesuits also belong to the higher grades of a special brotherhood, forming a state within a state that encompasses the others. Just picture what you can achieve in the world if you are on the one hand a high-ranking member of a Freemason order, who employs this community to exert influence, but at the same time you can agree a joint action with a high-ranking Jesuit that can only be undertaken by using the means at the latter's disposal. On the one hand you can mobilize the forces available to you through your brother Freemasons, to vigorously pursue some aim through all channels. But if you only instigate something from one direction, it comes to nothing. At the same time you have to unleash forces of opposition to combat it from the other direction, and do so with the same fire, the same enthusiasm. Imagine what you can achieve if you have such a mechanism available to you. Something like this happened in a certain country in north-western Europe, between Holland and France, where Jesuits and Freemasons together set something very effective in motion without the rest of the Jesuits or Freemasons knowing of it. This had very powerful effects—not in very recent times but for a long period—which had many repercussions and served the interests of both streams.

We have run out of time now. In a week's time, my dear friends, I will pursue these reflections in a more tangible way. Today I had to consider their more abstract aspects. We needed the whole foundation first, since only then can we understand how influences act in this way, in this domain, in the outer world.

Lecture 5

11 April 1916

In the grave times in which we live, whose difficulties impact on us each day with increasing force, it seems fitting to engage here in our circle in reflections which can acquaint us with the great goals of human history and the deep impulses of humanity. In our day it is profoundly necessary to turn to great, significant revelations we can receive from the world of spirit; and this is because what we are experiencing today will most definitely lead towards times when people experience a huge need for all that can bring the human soul strength, solace, hope and assurance from worlds of spirit. It is all the more important to cultivate such thoughts since we are also living in a time when true spiritual deepening—that is, profound contemplation of the reality of the spiritual life that we need—is becoming endlessly difficult for humanity, and encounters immeasurable obstacles. These are hindrances which, in a certain higher sense, modern people can do nothing about, encountering them simply due to the circumstances and developmental impulses of modern times that hold them back from a true engagement with the life of spirit. The latter is essential, though, and becomes more so with every passing week, and will be especially necessary in the period swiftly following ours which in many respects will be by no means easier than the times we are living through right now.

In preceding lectures I have attempted to reflect on the connection between insights and practices cultivated in various spiritual communities and humanity's overall course of evolution. Today I would like to deepen these observations in a certain regard, although what I have to say will stand alone and quite separately from what has so far been said, and can be understood without reference to it. I will preface these thoughts, however, by reminding you that across the whole educated world, and also in less scholarly quarters—perhaps even more so there—exist certain human communities which cultivate occult knowledge. They use it, too, to inform their actions in certain ways, in their efforts to influence the course of humanity's evolution as they wish, for purposes either benevolent or not. But it is noticeable in a large majority of such communities, especially as these have been developing into modern times, that so far there is no understanding of the distinctive new need that inevitably must enter such communities. In other words, they retain the old traditions as these were passed down to them, but as yet have failed to understand what must complement and renew them, the new element that is now being revealed from the world of spirit. In a great many of these spiritual societies, therefore, that cannot as yet call themselves fully contemporary, a certain common formula predominates, a formulaic phrase which they use to refer to the creative potency pervading and pulsing through the world. When they wish to refer to these creative powers imbuing the world, to divine, spiritual powers pulsing through and pervading the world, these societies speak of the 'sublime master builder of the world'. This is a much-used phrase: the sublime master builder of the world.

Those who can draw on spiritual science to understand the course of human evolution will know that such a phrase, used, say, in certain Freemason societies as well as in other occult brotherhoods, tells us that they have existed since very ancient times and are founded on very ancient institutions. It tells us that although it is not entirely wrong to see these communities originating at a later historical period, in fact they have roots that go a very long way back to earlier and different forms, that these roots go back in an unbroken line to ancient communities that existed in the fourth post-Atlantean epoch amongst the Greeks, the Romans and also the ancient Egyptians. In fact we can trace them still further back. The modern fraternities thus originate in these very ancient communities, and are as I described them except that in their modern form they do not have such direct communication with the world of spirit as did their forebears in the more ancient communities. Instead they preserve the knowledge that has been passed down to them as tradition.

If we wish to understand the meaning of this formulaic phrase about the sublime master builder of the world, the great architect of the universe, or why it is used, we will have to recall various matters that certainly could be known today but have as yet not entered the common awareness of humanity, or even the more specialized knowledge of scholars. In certain modern texts by more enlightened theologians or specialists in ancient history, you can find the term 'primordial revelation'. What does this mean?

This term figures today in books that have some academic standing and are not regarded as crazy nonsense, as our books are. The term 'primordial revelation' does appear in books, therefore, that are accorded some degree of academic respect. It is a term that we can understand particularly well if we try to familiarize ourselves with ancient religious texts. We need only look back to the writings that originate with Gautama Buddha. In such texts, in ancient religious documents—if we are open-minded enough, and not as foolish as, for instance, the person who wrote an article on conditions in ancient Egypt in the last issue of *Zeitgeist*—then we can discern that those who helped write them in long-gone millennia had a knowledge that humanity has now lost, that has gradually dried up under the weight of increasing materialism. As I said, you need only read available documents recording the utterances of Gautama Buddha and you will see that what is written there is founded on a great knowledge, although one that even in his day had been passed down by tradition and points back to much, much more ancient times: to a primordial knowledge therefore. This knowledge of course cannot be attained in the way that knowledge is disseminated today in the academic world. I believe that an open-minded observer of modern Academe will not dispute this. Nor, indeed, one whose mind is closed, since such a person rejects all such knowledge and regards it as foolish and misguided. He regards it in historical terms, and will acknowledge historians who discourse upon it, as long as they cite chapter and verse in the approved academic manner, but not the knowledge itself that is studied there. He cannot admit, therefore, that such knowledge might be achieved today, since he does not accept its validity, does he?

So here we are led back to a primordial knowledge, and accordingly we must assume—as every open-minded person will on reading these ancient religious texts—that we can look back from our current time, from our glorious modern progress that includes, doesn't it, the terrible slaughter, to older periods of human evolution: to earlier centuries when people knew things that today, with their wonderful advances, they regard as a confused garble, things such as those we find in the writings of Jakob Boehme, Paracelsus and such figures. And then we come back to the time when people did alchemical things in their retorts, then further and further back when, even if they were scholars, they lived according to modern views in 'superstitious beliefs'. Back and back we go; but as we look back, with an open mind, through the Roman, Greek and Egyptian eras, we arrive at a stage where humanity once possessed a knowledge spread across the globe in a way that is impossible today. Naturally it is difficult for people today to grasp this, since in the time we are speaking of now they think the human being was still only an ape, *Pithecanthropus erectus*, or apeman. But despite all these theories about the apeman, an open-minded person will, as I have said, see from ancient documents that originally a knowledge existed that is beyond the scope or reach of modern human beings with all their cleverness: an endlessly profound knowledge encompassing worlds of spirit to an outstanding degree. He will see that this knowledge contains not only an awareness of the human capacity to rise into worlds of spirit but of the possibility, too, of finding there other beings not incarnated in the flesh. These are the beings we refer to today as the ranks of the Angeloi, Archangeloi and so on. In these primordial religious texts, we even discover that people speak of these higher spirit beings as ones with whom they communicated. This can be demonstrated in these texts themselves.

What is the underlying basis of this? Well, from a certain perspective made possible by a particular stage of initiation we can grasp the reasons for this secret. But even at a lesser degree of initiation, one very commonplace and easily attained, we can understand what underlies it simply by means of an analogy. We know of course that besides what sensory evidence tells us of the world around us there is another underlying aspect, that of the so-called elemental world. We can only speak of this, describe it, by resorting to ancient mythology and using its terms to identify various types of elemental beings: the gnomes that underlie the mineral realm, the undines in the watery and plant realm, the sylphs in the enlivened atmosphere and the salamander beings at work in the whole earthly domain.

To speak seriously of such things in any other than this present, enlightened circle can engender a sense of reticence, even shame. But today, amongst ourselves, we can do so. Thus the natural world surrounding us is founded on elemental beings; but we should not imagine that these beings are simply there so that people who become clairvoyant can perceive them, and that they serve no purpose otherwise and the rest of the time simply rest lazily on their laurels. That is certainly not true. These beings have their good mission in the world and have a great deal to do. They take care of things that external, materialistic science thinks take care of themselves. But they don't take care of themselves. Anyone whose eyes are open for the beings of this elemental world will see that really they have to pass through an annual cycle, and that the influence upon these beings that descends from worlds of spirit varies from spring through summer, autumn and winter. The elemental realm of these beings therefore surrounds us and underpins the kingdom of nature, and powers stream down to them, almost a kind of instruction, so that in spring they acquire the capacity to draw forth the earth's plant cover. Certain spirit beings bear downwards the powers of the Spirits of Form, conveying them to these elemental beings so that a new world of forms sprout and burgeon in spring. As summer approaches, they receive a subsequent influx, and can thus accomplish what occurs towards summer. During the course of the year, therefore, changes occur in the nature of the mutual interplay between the spirits of the higher hierarchies and the elemental beings that live and weave in the natural world surrounding us. There is a continual upwards and downward streaming of spirit beings of the higher hierarchies, whose 'pupils' are the elemental beings who must deliver the enlivening powers for all that shoots, sprouts, arises and fades again. Things do not merely grow forth from the earth but are also in direct interplay with the heavenly, spiritual realm. And those who think that the plants and creatures that reawaken each spring do so only by emerging from earthly forces can be compared, say, to worms who, living below ground and never rising to the surface, might think as they crawl from plant root to plant root that roots are all that exist, that the world of leaves and flowers above is a fantasy. Then, when one day such a worm does poke its head out and sees that from the roots emerge leaves and blossoms above, reaching up towards sunlight, and comes back to tell the other worms below about this, they will say, no doubt, that he is a crazy worm with distorted ideas, and that what he is describing cannot possibly exist. Well, this is probably not true of worms, for they are likely to be brighter than that. But something similar is true of human beings.

Thus as I said, what sprouts during the year is in direct interplay with the beings whose powers stream upwards and downwards, and pour these into the elemental world. Yet in the same way, my friends, that sylphs, gnomes, undines and salamanders receive influences from these beings of the higher hierarchies that rise and descend depending on the time of year, so the human being, when he was not as yet so closely bound up with his physical body, received instruction from the rising and sinking spirits of the higher hierarchies. And all the myths and legends that have come down to us and tell us that in ancient times the human being enjoyed instruction from such beings descending from worlds of spirit are based on truth. The human being himself was one amongst the spirits accounted for today only by gnomes, sylphs, undines and so forth. These elemental spirits receive the powers by means of which they develop forms that sprout from the earth and fade again through the seasons, and similarly, in ancient times, the human being received instruction from the rising and sinking spirits of the higher hierarchies. The last vestiges of what he thus received in primordial days has been preserved for us in the extant texts that have come down to us, in which an open-minded person can discern the nature of this primordial revelation.

This primordial revelation existed. And in the eras preceding the eighth century BC, the last vestiges of this primordial revelation flowed down to humanity. We can be fairly precise here: around the year 747 BC, the further evolution of human physical nature excluded us from immediate participation in such instruction, though naturally these things phase in gradually. All the ancient knowledge flowed into human beings through the direct instruction of spiritual beings. And these primordial disciplines, though no longer understood, reached humankind by this means and are recorded in extant texts. The last field of knowledge that reached humankind in this way is one we will now consider. What did human beings learn as time passed, from the original period of ancient Atlantis onwards, when such primordial revelation flowed down to them? They learned of the connection they themselves had as human beings with the worlds of spirit. You see, the human being is a microcosm in whom unfold, in miniature, all the powers and processes at work in the greater world. The last thing humankind learned in this way, by influx from without, was geometry and arithmetic. And anyone today who still allows geometry and arithmetic, in the true sense, to work upon him, will have a sense that something approaches him in this domain that is different from other knowledge. We gather other knowledge from experience, compile it, but in geometry and arithmetic we can feel a sense of its truth quite apart from all outward experience, sensory experience. No one can prove that a triangle's angles add up to 180 degrees simply by drawing one or reproducing it from sensory experience. This can only be proven through an inner thought experience. And likewise no one can prove that three times three are nine merely by outward counting, but only through inner picturing and thinking. You don't need to have beans or peas to count with, nor your fingers; you need only inwardly conceive this, and thereby arrive at the truth that three times three are nine.

But in its further scope, the thinking that underlies geometry and arithmetic comes to expression in architectural forms. In Egyptian times people referred back to an older, primordial knowledge in which geometry and arithmetic were revealed. In Graeco-Roman times, ancient knowledge was conveyed to people in the mysteries in the following way. By entering into profound contemplation, they were told, you can bring forth from you what was revealed by the spirits of the higher hierarchies when you lived on earth in earlier times. This was not necessary in the Egyptian mysteries, since these high beings still themselves descended. In Graeco-Roman times a master would gather his pupils round him and tell them that in former incarnations they had passed through a phase of human evolution in which the spirits of the higher hierarchies participated. This reality became embedded in their souls and they could, they were told, draw upon it and bring it into awareness. Such a master in the Greek and Roman mysteries had his pupils draw up what lay in the human soul. You see, everything can be found in the human soul since it all streamed down from spirits to human beings through the primordial revelation. What we draw forth from us today, really draw forth from within us, is something that we once underwent in the form of instruction from the higher hierarchies.

Then came the year 1413/14. And, since the materialistic age properly began at that point, human beings could no longer be aware of what is actually within them as legacy from their former spiritual instruction. From then on, the soul's close union with the physical body covered and concealed what there is in our souls. But in the whole period from 747 BC to AD 1413, it was possible to draw forth from the soul, raise from it, what had once streamed into it in earlier times as I described. Just think how someone must have felt in the olden times, especially in ancient Greece. He would have said that the geometry coming to expression in the forms of a building once flowed down in divine, spiritual instruction from without. This geometry was embodied in forms, and the human being was surrounded and encompassed by such forms. But when a person wishes to draw a triangle today, he takes a piece of chalk and draws it. The ancient Greek had no need of this as yet; he needed only to reflect on the form and could then see it before him as if clairvoyantly, in etheric clairvoyance. He could draw the geometry in his inner, clairvoyant perception. This is how it was in still older times, primordial times, with written script. One did not need to merely write on a papyrus but could also write things before one's inner vision, clairvoyantly. But as I said, people placed around them what flowed into architectural forms. At a certain period of the Greek mysteries, people were taught the following: 'Reflect clearly upon yourself, and if you reflect upon the divine human being living within you, and therefore do not only consider your transient, earthly human being, there will arise around you an edifice created from the forms of geometry, with you at its centre.'

As the spider spins its web around itself, so a pupil of the Greek mysteries span etherically around himself a whole geometrical configuration, in which the rest of human knowledge then found its place for him. He then needed only create this around himself outwardly, in the form of the Greek temple. The Greek temple is nothing other than the geometrical forms arising clairvoyantly around the human being and then filled with physical material. The Greek temple adds only the stones to these configurations, and this is why the ancient Greek always also tended to place a statue of the god inside the temple, representing in a sense his own divine human nature within it. Thus in the times when this was done, he did not only erect a temple but within it also a divine image, Pallas Athene or some other god, since these things belonged together: the surrounding macrocosm together with what emerges from and manifests out of the cosmos, but must now of course reveal itself from within for the reasons described. Thus we see here a connection between the building of the temple and an original clairvoyance.

Those who erected buildings in these times therefore saw something divine in the art of building, something that was most intimately connected with all inner human revelations. They did not build as we do today, having learned the profession at university or college, mastered all the required skills, and then practising the craft, but they had a quite different feeling about how to go about building. That is why people today look so askance today on our efforts to found what we are building here in Dornach on our own spiritual science. They would think it right if an ordinary building company built it, an architect who, in their view, would not need to know the least thing about our spiritual science. People no longer know that the purpose served by the building must come to expression in the whole outer surroundings and edifice. In times when people experienced a building as the revelation of the Spirits of Form, they did know this. This is why Vitruvius,[40] a great architect at the time of Augustus, speaks in such a remarkable way of the builder and his art. He speaks of the moral qualities a builder must possess, his sense of the divine meaning of the universe. I would like to read you a striking passage from Vitruvius where he says the following about an architect or builder:

> He must therefore not only possess natural talents but also an eagerness to learn; for neither genius without academic education nor academic education without genius can make a perfect artist. He must have skill in writing, be experienced in draughtsmanship, knowledgeable of geometry, not unknowledgeable in optics, and well instructed in arithmetic. He must know many stories, have attended conscientiously to philosophy, understand music, have knowledge of medicine, be familiar with law and acquainted with star lore together with the course of the planetary bodies.

Why, in Vitruvius's view, should the architect and builder know all these things? It is because the forms of a building are the revelations of higher hierarchies. People in those times were aware that the real architects were the beings of the higher hierarchies. This is of huge importance. And what feeling did such a builder have? A modern architect would make a long face, wouldn't he, if he were required not only to know what is taught about his profession at college or university but in addition to this medicine, philosophy and even astronomy and the movements of stars and planets. In a sense, therefore, he would have to be someone initiated into the spiritual sciences. Why was this so? Vitruvius himself still felt that when he created a building this must not arise from himself as a finite human being but this finite being must become the instrument of a being of the higher hierarchies working through him.

It was however only in the occult mysteries that people acquired the means to enter into connection with the higher hierarchies in such a way that when stone was laid on stone to create a building the spirits of the higher hierarchies worked through a finite human being. One had to be initiated into the connection between the divine and human worlds. It was necessary to know about medicine because the forms of a building should be configured so as to make them a real expression or reflection of the human being, comparable in a sense to the way a snail shell reflects the nature of the snail, constructed out of the macrocosm in correspondence with the inner nature informing it. Thus a human being felt that this divine, spiritual nature was at work in him, that it guided his hands and governed his mind to work into the forms that architecture created.

It is because the forms of architecture were the last revelation given that everything living in the occult societies I spoke of last time emerged from this true architecture and the mood of the builder in the practice of his craft and profession. Albeit in distorted, caricature form, these occult societies preserve a sense, above all, that someone admitted to them enters upon a path into worlds of spirit. At the second grade or degree he establishes with the other members of his occult community relationships that are not governed solely by outer social circumstances, are not determined by these, but arise purely from soul to soul. At this second level he becomes a friend, companion or confrère. And he learns to feel, finally, what it means to stand here as a human being and feel himself to contain or encompass what lives in him as spirit being with whom the beings of the higher hierarchies speak, to whom they incline themselves—someone who may speak no word that is not inspired by these spirits of the higher hierarchies. It is true, however, that there is little awareness of this today in those who reach the third degree of such occult societies and then call themselves 'master', masters of the third degree. And yet this reality underpins such societies. And because revelations are no longer forthcoming, because no such intensive influence is experienced since there is no longer any direct connection with the world of spirit, people rely instead on tradition, on what is passed down. They spread a veil of secrecy over this, forbid others to partake of it, keep this knowledge hidden. Yet an original knowledge is preserved in such communities, passed down through the centuries from generation to generation, although frequently distorted and misused, wrongfully influencing humanity as I described last time.

The fourth post-Atlantean period ending in the fifteenth century, around 1413, existed so as to gradually allow our direct connection with the world of spirit to dry up and disappear. But the remarkable thing is that finer, more sensitive minds continued to feel their former connection with the spiritual world even at a time when this had faded and vanished. During the whole period from 747 BC to AD 1413 a certain connection with the world of spirit still existed, as I have suggested. At least it was possible for people to enliven this connection inwardly during this period, enliven it through memory at least. But in the fourteenth century this came to an end. But beyond the fourteenth century sensitive minds still felt that the spirit plays into human life. Students of history today, as I have often said, are taught that human nature has always been more or less what it now is in our age of 'glorious advancement'. But this is not so. If you wish to understand the fifteenth, sixteenth and seventeenth centuries, you first have to develop some sense that these were times when a last breath of spiritual life still encompassed the earth. And in older eras a person felt his surroundings to be composed not only of plants, clouds, winds, storms and lightning but also of elemental beings that were no less real to him than plants, creatures and so forth. But this awareness faded and disappeared—naturally not all at once—so that from the fourteenth century and on into the seventeenth more sensitive people knew that the spirit lived and was active around them.

In those times people did not yet regard an influx from the world of spirit as they do today. Today it is called hysteria, yes, hysteria! And yet this tells us nothing. It may manifest in an hysterical form, certainly, but the world of spirit may still be playing into behaviour described as hysterical. These two things have nothing to do with each other. Today people accept merely materialistic interpretations, but in the times I have spoken of they still knew a thing or two, and did not regard an influx from the world of spirit into human life as merely pathological—although it can also be so, in our materialistic sense. If we do not grasp this we cannot comprehend certain things at all.

A modern historian may speak, say, of the period of Savonarola[41] in the fifteenth century, and in doing so will often speak of Florence at that time as if he were talking about a modern city—will speak of it as if he were describing the way people nowadays congregate outside grocery shops and chat to each other. No thought is given to the fact that one must first transpose oneself back, imagine oneself back into the mood of that time, a mood in which people still felt something of spiritual reality. Let us ask what it was, in a certain week in Florence, that made people on the street walk about as if deeply troubled and burdened. It was because Savonarola had told them, the previous Sunday, that if their moral conduct continued as it was, another Flood would inundate them all. He concluded his sermon with these words: *Ecce ego adducam aquas super terram*—I tell you that the waters will flood the earth! And spirit enlivened these words, streaming forth from them. And the inhabitants of Florence felt the spiritual influence of these words for a week, and walked about the streets as I have described. One of Savonarola's contemporaries was Pico della Mirandola,[42] Count Mirandola. He lived at the end of the fifteenth century and was wholly immersed in this mood that spread over Florence at the time. This was the time of transition between the fourth and fifth post-Atlantean epochs. Pico della Mirandola was one of those sensitive minds I spoke of. They felt the spirit was fading from the world around and at the same time they experienced an inmost longing to feel it still, to seek its entry into them. Yes, there were a whole number of people in Florence at that time who lived in this mood. They felt that the spirit was vanishing from ordinary human life but that they must bring it back into them. These Renaissance people called themselves neoplatonists, and no one could enter their academy unless he had had some experience testifying to his soul's connection with and direct vision of the spirit living and active around us. This was in the fifteenth century still. One could not enter the Florence Academy, which cultivated neoplatonism, the revival of Plato, if one did not first endeavour to have an experience that gave one direct knowledge that the spirit works into sensory life. Pico had several such moments, and therefore he understood the words of Savonarola which, albeit in an idiosyncratic way, were imbued with such spiritual insights. In his own way Pico understood Savonarola but was too vain to engage with what Savonarola wished for him: to become his close ally and comrade. Pico della Mirandola could not reconcile such a thing with his vanity; and when he drew near to death, still as a relatively young man, he had another such experience. As he saw his end approaching—and he was still very young—he was able to look into the world of spirit. In such an experience, the forms in which the beings of the world of spirit are configured are oriented to a person's subjective perception. The spiritual world revealed itself to Pico clothed in the image of the Madonna. In brief, the Madonna appeared to him, we can say, and spoke thus to him: 'I will not deliver you wholly up to death.' Mirandola did not immediately understand what this meant. He thought it meant he could go on living as a physical person. But he died, and Savonarola himself held the funeral oration. And it is important that we can transpose ourselves into the whole mood at this transition between the fourth and fifth post-Atlantean epoch. It may be helpful for us to remind ourselves of the words spoken by Savonarola at the grave of Pico della Mirandola, for we find in these words a recognition of the importance of such a person's relationship with the world of spirit, revealed to him in this way in an image before he died. Standing at the grave of Pico della Mirandola, Savonarola spoke the following words—and we can see them at the same time as evidence of the fact that funeral orations in those days were not mere flattery but truthful occasions.

> None amongst you did not know Giovanni Pico. God magnanimously endowed him with great deeds of benevolence and lofty favours. His knowledge was manifold and his spirit towered over mortals. For the Church too his death signifies a great loss. If he had not lived so briefly, it is my firm conviction that he would have outshone all scholars of the last eight centuries. A divine voice in his heart called him to take holy orders and he was at first willing to follow this call. But he continually postponed his entry to the cloisters, whether through ingratitude towards God or because a sensual nature held him back from this, or because he was anxious at the thought of the hardships of a monastic life due to the frailty of his body, or, finally, because he felt himself already to be serving religion through his scholarly works. For this reason I have been threatening him for the past two years with the divine scourge, and I here acknowledge that I called upon the Highest to discipline him a little for his omissions. But God nevertheless showed him lenience. While the soul of the deceased has not yet entered upon the bliss of heaven in the lap of the Father, yet it is not condemned eternally, either, to the martyrdom of hell. For a certain period it will make its atonement in the fires of purgatory. What I tell you of Pico's death is not refuted by the promise made to him by the sacred Madonna. At first I thought this promise to be the machinations of a demon

—here Savonarola is speaking of Pico della Mirandola's last vision—

> but then it became clear to me that the dying man, in the sensory confusions of his last hour, thought that this promise was of the first death, but that the Madonna was speaking in fact of eternal death.

In other words, according to Savonarola, the Madonna was saying he would not suffer eternal punishment but would be chastised only for a short period after death.

I merely wished to characterize the kind of mood voiced on such occasions in relation to spiritual matters. This is a good example, for Savonarola is not someone who would have invoked spiritual matters hypocritically, simply in his role as a priest. He was a man of whom we can be assured that he followed the voice only of his personal conviction in every situation and circumstance. He did not speak only to please the Church, which in fact did not regard him kindly, and treated him accordingly, but he spoke of the world of spirit from his own experience. What Savonarola received as direct revelations from the world of spirit naturally far surpassed the knowledge of it that Pico possessed.

I wished only to describe this to you because it is important to consider the mood people had towards the world of spirit if we are to understand this sudden, swift transition from the fourteenth to the fifteenth century. What we have heard can strike us as a longing to return to the time when people still more easily received impressions of the world of spirit. But now these people were isolated and more lonely. They had to undertake special ascetic exercises to acquire what they desired, at least at certain moments in life, perhaps even in a distorted form. It really is not true to say, as modern scholars do, that everything developed so slowly and gradually. Nature takes no sudden leaps, it is said. But that is the stupidest idea. It takes no leaps as such, but continually one finds metamorphoses or transitions, incisive ones. The green sepal does not slowly transform into something a little less sepal-like and then a little less sepal-like again into a coloured petal, but the plant passes from one to the other without any intermediate stage. It is nonsense to say nature makes no leaps! But such phrases are bandied around without thinking.

The next mission in humanity's development was to invoke the powers that must replace an old capacity to absorb the spirit. Ordinarily there were two means to do this. One was simply to perpetuate tradition. People were content with what the ancients had perceived and revealed, and perpetuated it by means of tradition; and this gave rise to many secret societies. But there were also people who endeavoured to draw upon the new power of soul that had emerged. They sought to translate what had previously existed in a quite different form, as picture and direct vision, into the form of rational thought bound up with the body—this capacity to reason that we now have as ordinary people in the fifth post-Atlantean epoch. The great Amos Comenius was one of those who now sought to raise into a proper, contemporary context the former building principle, although of course conceived of in a quite different way, in pictures and symbols. I do not think many people know anything much about Amos Comenius any more. He was really the founder of our whole modern schooling system, and he established reading primers. Living in the sixteenth century, our whole approach to teaching children originated with him. It may be of interest to read you a few excerpts relating to this because there is so little awareness today of Amos Comenius. Amongst the various books and anthologies that have been published, not all of which are good, is one entitled *Comenius and the Bohemian Brotherhood* by Friedrich Eckstein.[43] Eckstein was a colleague of mine in Vienna at the end of the 1880s, and together we were part of a theosophical group. Later he went his own way and I heard nothing from him for a long time. And now this little book by him about Amos Comenius has been published, a very useful compilation. Eckstein says of the so-called *Orbis pictus* that

> its primitive illustrations, albeit in modern, mutilated and truncated editions, gave all of us pleasure in our youth. In the 150 woodcuts of the original edition, with their brief text in German and Latin, entirely in keeping with the principle of teaching simultaneously through tangible and verbal means, the chief concepts and principles of life were conveyed to the child's mind, beginning with God, the world, the heavens and the elements, plants, fruits, animals, the human body and its limbs, through to the various forms of work and craft, and this with a moving, heart-warming simplicity and clarity of words

> and pictures. Looking at it we can immediately understand why this book made such a deep impression on the children of many generations. Herder and Goethe loved it more than anything in their childhood, and no doubt drew from it impulses that accompanied them through their lives. 'At the time there were as yet no libraries for children,' writes Goethe in the first book of *Poetry and Truth*. And he continues: 'The ancients themselves still had a childlike outlook, and found it easy to convey their own culture to future generations. Apart from the *Orbis pictus* by Amos Comenius, no book of this kind fell into our hands.'

The whole way of creating children's books, that is school books for children, was based on Amos Comenius. But Comenius was a man, born in Moravia, who formed connections in the course of his life with numerous secret fraternities throughout Europe, similar to the ones I have described. They existed everywhere you see. And he formed real connections with all of them, and tried to influence them all. What he writes in his *Pansophia* especially, shows how he did so effectively.

Here therefore, in Amos Comenius in the sixteenth and seventeenth centuries, at the beginning of our era, we find a person who knew that change was afoot, that a new, different age was dawning and that what formerly existed must now be recreated in the form of outer reason rather than being preserved and perpetuated as tradition. Tradition was founded on the last revelations to be received, on temple building, irrespective of whether this concerned the Greek temple or that of Solomon. The nature of temple building, symbolic, imaginative pictures concerned with temple building, were the foundation of everything else.

In his *Pansophia*, Amos Comenius set about transforming everything into a mode corresponding to the soul nature of the fifth post-Atlantean epoch. He writes:

> We chose the name 'Pansophia' because we wished to give a stimulus to all people to perceive everything and in general to be wise, to fill the mind with the truth of things rather than

> with the smoke of opinions. One might also call this the Science of the Best, of the Select, or even the Science of Unknowledge if we wish to recall Socrates or the Apostle. But why should the temple of Pansophia be erected according to the ideas, standards and laws of the greatest master builder himself?

Here Amos Comenius is addressing the 'sublime master builder of worlds', invoked in a true knowledge of the art of building in ancient times. We should take this quite literally, although in a spiritual sense. But Amos Comenius now seeks to translate this into the language of the fifth post-Atlantean epoch. Listen to how he does so:

> But why should the temple of Pansophia be erected according to the ideas, standards and laws of the greatest master builder himself? Because we follow the archetype of the whole according to measure, number, position and purpose of its parts in the way that God's wisdom itself ordains; and as we first see in Exodus when the tabernacle was erected, then in the Book of Solomon when the temple was constructed, and finally in Ezekiel when the temple was rebuilt.

He could equally well have referred to the Greek temple.

> If we wish to erect the temple of wisdom, we must always remember that the temple to be built was great, glorious and praiseworthy throughout all lands because our God is higher than all other gods. Worthy and industrious builders must therefore be called upon wherever they can be found so that they may discover and create what is needed. The temple of Solomon was built upon Mount Moriah at God's command; Moriah means 'the countenance of God'.

And in the same way the human being was built out of the lap of the Godhead! So as we have seen, Vitruvius required a builder to possess in his mind all wisdom about the human being—'The foundation of the temple of wisdom will thus be a countenance of God'—and in the same way the countenance of God, which means the revelation of God, should be revealed through the new form of knowledge:

> That is, the invisible Grand Master of the world, in his omnipotence, wisdom and goodness should be perceived by the human spirit as working through all that is visible. The building materials of the temple of Solomon were stones, marble and precious stones, and sappy and aromatic woods, firs and cedars, and the purest metal and gold. Three forests supply the wood for building the temple of wisdom . . .

And now he translates this:

> . . . in other words, the senses, reason and divine revelation; the first supplies what can be grasped, the second what lives, and the third what is intransient and eternal.

Formerly this was embodied in the images of stone, wood and the gold inlay; but now he translates this into the language of the fifth post-Atlantean epoch: the first supplies what can be held and grasped, the senses; reason supplies the living element; and revelation supplies the intransient and eternal. Here you have the translation. And then he goes on:

> Of the stones walls were built, of wood the carved reliefs; and of gold were made the sheets to adorn the reliefs and the marble tiling, and then also the sacred vessels and tools. And thus the walls of the temple of wisdom are raised from sensory certainty . . .

. . . in other words, what the senses give us forms the walls of our temple of wisdom . . .

> . . . while the reliefs [the wood] give us our reasoned conclusions, what we add to the senses; and the gold inlaid upon it arises from the harmony of perception with revelation. The temple of Solomon arose from perfectly dressed stones, and during the construction no sound was heard of hammer, axe or iron tool. In the same way, when building the temple of wisdom, there should be no altercation or dispute, but all must be undertaken in perfect proportion so that it need only be placed

> together; wisdom must have already been discussed and concluded in advance, and have been elaborated in all things.

No altercation and dispute in the search for wisdom! That is why, my dear friends, we should seek in our society for a spiritual wisdom dependent on absence of quarrel and dispute between members. If our aim is to be achieved, quarrel and dispute must be excluded from our ranks. Especially recent times have shown, as you know, the degree to which this golden rule is adhered to. Then Amos Comenius continues:

> The parts of the temple of Solomon were in the finest and most perfect relationship of number and measure, and an angel with a measuring cord etc. made the ground plan . . .

. . . here you have again a reference to the angelos . . .

> In the same way in the temple of wisdom, too, all should be well measured so that the spirit is preserved from all error and deviation. In the temple of Solomon there were adornments, carvings, embossed work, cherubim, palms and flowers. In the temple of wisdom beauty, fine representation, should be the adornment. Everything encompassed within the temple of Solomon was sacred. So too must it be with the temple of wisdom: its contents should be pure and sacred, dedicated to the highest goals. But what God once promised to the builders of the temple of Jerusalem—his presence, his help, his blessing—can also be expected by those who build the temple of wisdom. For he says: I love those who love me etc. and load them with treasures. Finally, when the foundation for the walls was laid in that temple of Solomon, the Levites and the priests in their adornments stood there and praised God with cymbals and flutes, together with the people.

As you know, things are done similarly in our day! Here spiritual wisdom is sought, as worlds of spirit reveal it, and the priests of all confessions, as you know, stand outside with the people and praise what is found with cymbals and flutes. I am sure you have seen this being done by the priests and scholars of our day!

> Thus when the temple of wisdom is erected, all devout people should gather together and praise the name of the Lord from now to eternity, from the rising of the sun to its setting. We desire a school of wisdom, universal wisdom, a pansophian or all-wisdom school, that is, a workshop where all are admitted to be schooled, receiving practice in all that is necessary for life, both as it is today and in the future, in a fully comprehensive fashion. And this should happen by such certain means that there would be no one there who knew nothing of these things and was unable to make the necessary use of this understanding.

We can say that what Goethe portrays in *Wilhelm Meister*, especially in *The Journeyman Years*, and what he seeks to make of the human being there, is a continuation of what Amos Comenius wished. And then in turn, without being immodest but looking objectively at the goal of our endeavours, we can see how a beginning was made in the sixteenth and seventeenth centuries of what we can now take up and further in our own efforts for humanity's evolution. Then what we seek will be very much the right thing: not what arises from subjective capriciousness, but what the evolution of humanity requires and necessitates.

We can see things like this (and I have often expressed it): modern science is working from one direction and spiritual science from the other, and they must meet in the middle to produce the whole truth. Science and spiritual science do not contradict each other. Like tunnel builders working from two directions towards each other, who meet in the middle if everything—the levels and angles and so on—has been calculated correctly, so modern science and spiritual science, if it proceeds in an authentic and honest way, will meet each other. And they can and will do so. There is already evidence of this today, and I would like to speak of this now. I could offer a great deal of evidence for it, but I will only mention the following by way of conclusion.

Just the other day a book by Carl Ludwig Schleich[44] was published, one based on modern scientific enquiry, entitled *The Mechanism of Thoughts*. It is an extremely interesting book, by an honest researcher and physician who endeavours to draw on everything afforded him by the whole scope of sense-based knowledge. The book also contains a very remarkable chapter that is bound to mark a new departure in our time, for we can see how, working from one direction, it must meet what spiritual science is bringing towards it from the other. This chapter is entitled, 'Hysteria—a Metaphysical Problem'. Here the author describes a series of curious cases of hysteria. Let me just read a couple to you:

> A hysterical young lady sits on her sofa. An electrically powered fan stands in a corner of the room on a small table. To the physician who visits her she says, in terrible anxiety, in a really hysterical manner: 'My God, that's humming so loudly! It sounds like a huge bee.' Remember this is a fan. 'Well, Miss,' I said, 'if it were a bee we would chase it out of the window.' 'No, no, it might sting me. O God, what if it stung me in the eye!' While I tried to calm her by saying that even that would not be fatal and could be cured, the poor lady's lower eyelid started swelling up as she continued to lament her plight, forming a clearly inflamed and very painful oedema the size of a hen's egg, of doughy consistency.

In other words, the thought that a huge bee is present in the room was enough to give rise to a real lump on her lower eyelid as large as a hen's egg! Other anecdotes recorded here may be less suitable to read out. But I would like to read another interesting case that is in fact very significant, and originates, as the author says, from 'very recent clinical experience at a military hospital':

> A corporal, dark as an Italian, with burning, dark eyes and a wild and not easily controlled temperament came to us with both elbow joints shot through, and suffering severe ulceration to the wounds. We succeeded in assuaging the condition: in

> other words, the fever abated and he regained enough movement in the upper arm stumps to enable him to play the mouth harmonica again, the favourite instrument of our soldiers. But then another soldier was admitted and placed in the bed opposite him, suffering from a head wound, feverish and half-unconscious, with intermittent convulsions. As a possible operation was being discussed, someone unwisely said out loud, 'It might be tetanus.' It was not tetanus in fact. A piece of the skull was removed and the patient recovered but in the meantime, on the third day after the man with the head wound had been admitted, our corporal with the now almost healed upper arm wounds, did suddenly contract tetanus, four months after he had been admitted.

In other words, this happened simply because he heard the word 'tetanus'. He had been in the ward for four months and so any infection must be excluded, especially since the other man did not even have tetanus!

> All symptoms of the condition were present except that he had no fever. We injected antitoxin into the spine without success. I was very perplexed by the state of the patient. We undertook the normal, absolutely reliable test for tetanus by injecting a rabbit with the blood serum from the patient's vertebral canal, and the results were negative. No tetanus bacilli were discovered. After a few days a cure was effected by stating categorically to the patient, 'This is not tetanus!' In other words, the case was a hysterical attack of 'tetanus'.

In other words, he did not have tetanus at all in physical terms. Then Professor Schleich continues:

> And now let me present a few experiences that demonstrate how hysteria can lead very near to a final curtailment of life. There are cases of 'apparent death' due to hysteria which Arndt also refers to . . . Other authors have reliably recorded such cases although I myself have not witnessed them.

I expressly emphasize here that such cases are very well known to spiritual science, and are by no means to be considered anything out of the ordinary, although they do surprise modern physicians. But here now is a very remarkable case:

> A very wealthy businessman, who ran his office in person, came to me one day and begged me to amputate his arm as he had stabbed his fingers with his pen and now knew that he would otherwise die of blood poisoning. I would have laughed, except that fear was written all over the man's face and stifled all mockery. He had already consulted several excellent surgeons, even Bergmann, who had all refused to amputate his arm. He said I should take pity on him and take off his upper arm which was already tingling and itching. Naturally I too had to send him away after all attempts to reassure him. I went to see him the same evening: no raised temperature, no sign of swelling or inflammation around the wound which I had cleaned, bandaged and even sucked out. But he was still very agitated. 'Why will no one amputate it? I could be saved!' The next day the man was dead. My friend Langerhans carried out the post-mortem examination: no infection, no toxins in the blood, no cause of death whatsoever. My diagnosis was: death by hysteria.

And so we see that, as Schleich fully acknowledges, thoughts can not only cause a swollen eyelid and so on but even death. That is the power of thought. And this induces a modern physician, who is honest in his research as in this case, to say that in the first case, that of swollen tissue caused by a hysterical impulse, we see the metaphysical problem of incarnation: a thought incarnates itself, becomes flesh as the soul embodies itself when it descends from worlds of spirit and kindles the whole organism. In other words, the modern physician here comes a very great way towards us, speaks of incarnation. And in the second case he refers to mediumistic perception: a kind of clairvoyant vision of possible illnesses. The honest modern scientist must indeed speak of clairvoyance and incarnation if he wishes to reflect on his actual clinical experiences.

You see, it is not capricious and vacuous to say that science and spiritual science must work towards each other from two directions. They will meet each other in the word. I say this not arbitrarily or with some kind of fanatical impulse but out of an awareness of the needs of our time. Naturally, though, further enquiry is needed here, for it is easily seen that an ordinary thought cannot of course engender a swelling. Try it yourself—however hard you try you cannot think a lump into appearing. Thank God you can't, thank God an ordinary thought cannot do this, and will not kill you either. You can be reassured on that score. There are mysteries underlying all such cases. But above all, one thing in particular underlies them which we can never discern as long as we remain with the ordinary I and the ordinary content of our thoughts. What occurred in the case of the hysterical lady whose lower eyelid swelled up? Her thought in response to the electric fan became a vivid image for her, an imagination, and furled down to the astral body, from there incarnating through the etheric body into the physical body. We must be clear about this. The case cannot be explained without going beyond our ordinary ideas of the ego and seeing how this works down into the astral, etheric and physical body. The I-formed thought alone did not kill the businessman either, but what lived in this I-thought penetrated down into the astral body which is in direct connection with the powers of life and death. In other words, to explain such cases we must first discover what spiritual science can offer science from the other direction. Sadly, we often speak in words that do not engage with each other. We meet in facts and realities but our words are often ships that pass in the night, and it would be good if this were no longer so. To say that we do not meet in words is certainly not meant as a criticism of this excellent book, which might really mark a new departure in research, also from the perspective I suggested. It is probably more worthwhile to highlight this failure to connect in words in relation to a thoroughly honest researcher than in instances where there may be some doubt about this. You see, Schleich speaks in the preceding section of this book about the 'myth of brain metabolism'. For him metabolism in the brain is just a myth. That is very finely put, and innovative. But now he goes on to say that Goethe already knew that the skull, the bones of the skull are transformed vertebrae. Of course this is widely known. But he states that we can explore this further. Again, Schleich is to be greatly commended for realizing that we can pursue this idea further, and see the whole skull in fact as transformed ganglion, transformed parts of the spinal column. And then Schleich says that Goethe was really a visionary in his own way, and that he might also have been able to come up with this idea that not only the skull bones are transformed vertebrae but that the whole brain itself is a metamorphosis. Schleich concludes his chapter on the myth of brain metabolism very beautifully by saying:

> If Goethe, this visionary and prophet, was able to discern so many connections in the divinity of nature and could show that the skull with all its plates is nothing other than an unfurled cervical vertebra and that all constituents of the latter can be detected in the brain's bony capsule, I would be most surprised if he had not also conceived in the labyrinth of his thoughts the idea we have just expressed of the 'configuring of the brain from the elements of the spine'. I would not be surprised if some page of Goethe's notes about this should surface. For to what purpose would the vertebrae have sought to arch upwards as if on swan's wings if not to receive, cover and protect the rising dome of that central organ?

In 1916, therefore, Schleich says he would not be at all surprised if some note by Goethe should be found suggesting this. Actually I discovered such a note in 1892, in the Goethe and Schiller Archive, and have repeatedly publicized this whole idea, which Schleich now reproduces, along with this finding from the archive. So you see, what Schleich suggests already happened back in 1892, and is in the public domain; and you can also see therefore that we are passing each other by like ships in the night, talking past each other. We can see this quite objectively, and it is because, unfortunately, there is no self-evident meeting place in these different areas of research and publication, no clearly recognized need for such encounter. Here we have a very striking example of this, in which someone with the best will in the world, and with the necessary brilliance, arrives at the idea that such a thing might exist, and yet it has already been available for over 20 years! This is very interesting, isn't it, in relation to the whole way in which science and spiritual science interact. We can learn a great deal from it, especially when we are sure that no spark of bad will underlies it but that the research in question is being undertaken with absolute authenticity and integrity. But at the same time you can also see that what spiritual science undertakes is truly not capricious but is founded on a perception of the inner necessity at work in humanity's spiritual evolution. And this spiritual course of humanity's evolution really does tell us that a certain sum of spiritual insights must stream into humankind and be shaped in a way that succours humanity.

In this respect our time is ready for many things; and we must not overlook the fact—now that the spilling of blood heralds the dawn of a new age, when so many souls are speaking to us after they have passed, as our time's sacrifices, through the gate of death—that the world of spirit is knocking at the gates that lead from it to our world. The call for spirit today must not go unheard, for the spirit is coming and announces itself in all kinds of ways. This spirit need only be directed in the proper channels. But here it has to be said that those who seek to walk on such paths will not always meet with their proper due. When we endeavour to introduce the spiritual world in a way really borne upon a scientific approach, this certainly is not met by the cymbals and flutes of the modern equivalents of priests and Levites, but instead encounters all sorts of opposition, sometimes of an objectionable kind. One need only consider the whole significance underlying this fact. On the one hand we have efforts founded on scientific rigour to convey to humanity the revelations of the world of spirit. These efforts are met, as they invariably are, by those whose opposition is already familiar to us, through to very clever-seeming characters such as Thassilo von Scheffer[45]—people who respond to our efforts with vacuous phrases. But on the other hand we see certain truths of the spiritual world flooding in through the channels possible today. I am thinking not just of Strindberg's important *Dream Play*,[46] which we can regard certainly as an influx of the spiritual world, in which much can be recognized and acknowledged, but also of lesser, and less important types of influx of the spiritual world into our physical world. For instance, there is a modern writer who is very popular today, partly because he can really be of interest to people since he gains extraordinary access to the world of spirit. Much streams into him that is greatly distorted, caricatured—but therefore becomes all the more interesting perhaps to modern readers. And by this means he can exert a popular influence, for he describes futuristic scenarios, not as painter but as writer. If you read *Golem* by Gustav Meyrink[47] you can say that a hugely powerful current of spiritual life is breaking in here, but in distorted, caricatured forms in which it can do more harm than good for those who are not solid in themselves. But this is a phenomenon of our times, too. A living current is breaking in from the world of spirit, apparent for instance in the excellent short story 'Cardinal Napellus'. Especially here you can discern the author's insights and perceptions of the distinctive workings of the Akashic Records and suchlike, wonderfully conveyed. This is described in fact without any of the wild, runaway futurism that we see in *Golem*. Here you do really find that the world of spirit is seeking entry—and a great many such phenomena can be discerned today. The seriousness to which we are now so strongly prompted includes gaining an understanding of the importance of opening our heart, soul and head to the currents entering from the world of spirit.

And then, as I have often said, we can meet the grave circumstances of our times through spiritual-scientific endeavours, accomplishing what it is essential to accomplish.

From the courage of fighters
From the blood of slaughter
From the suffering of the bereaved
From the people's deeds of sacrifice
Spirit fruit will grow—
So that souls with spirit awareness
May guide their mind into the spirit realm.

Lecture 6

18 April 1916

It seems a difficult thing to engage in Easter reflections in the way one might in other less grave times and circumstances. Nevertheless, today I will share some thoughts with you about the approaching festival. In recent lectures we have spoken of various things that have a strong connection with the Easter festival or also with the Easter service, even though no mention was made of their relationship with it. We spoke of how human culture and cultural evolution, in so far as it is spiritual in nature, is informed by a wide range of associations and brotherhoods that express their solidarity in the form of symbolic rites and actions, and that these in turn are drawn from certain imaginative conceptions. The most important symbol of such societies is connected with the idea of death and resurrection. It repeatedly becomes apparent that these fraternities connect the idea of human death and that of resurrection in a way that together gives rise to that of immortality. The things to be considered here are often regarded as these societies' secret rites, and yet there is now such a wealth of literature with extensive details about the rites of these fraternities, conveyed in images at least, that we can say a great deal about their symbolic content without in any way violating their secrecy. The things I wish to discuss have been published in countless books.

All this is centred, one can say, on a symbolic representation of circumstances in which a person is led towards death, dies and is buried. In most of these fraternities, the human individual to whom this symbolic context relates is regarded as Hiram, and this context is therefore called the Hiram Legend. Hiram, the master builder of the temple of Solomon, whom the legend states built it in association with King Solomon and was then killed by certain enemies who were subordinates of his, is seen in the symbolic context of this death. First his burial is depicted, and subsequently this leads to a certain form of resurrection from the grave—Hiram's emergence from the grave. By means of this symbolic context, efforts are made to impress upon the soul the idea of immortality in a more comprehensive or incisive way than is possible through merely theoretical considerations. In symbols or imaginative pictures that elicit a person's unconscious powers they seek to show the nature of the passage through death and resurrection.

If we consider that Hiram's death and resurrection is represented in the temples of these societies, their lodges, then we already find here a connection with the Easter thought. As you know, Catholic rites also contain a symbolic representation in which, after the Maunday Thursday festival, Good Friday follows and symbolically Christ is then laid in the grave. Contemplation of Christ Jesus in the grave continues through Easter Saturday until, according to more recent customs, the Resurrection is celebrated on the evening of Easter Saturday; that is, the Christ arises from the grave and his Resurrection is celebrated. If we consider these Catholic rituals with their symbolic content, we find that they are really fully equivalent to the burial and resurrection of Hiram in occult brotherhoods. You can see therefore that the Easter thought is in a sense at the very centre of these occult brotherhoods. The meaning connected with this ceremony is that a person can enter more deeply into his inner self, in a sense invoking the deeper powers that lie there and are not present in ordinary awareness. A symbolic rite of this kind would have no meaning if it were not assumed that powers exist in the depths of the human soul where consciousness does not delve. Anyone who gives credence to human accomplishments that cannot originate in ordinary consciousness must assume that such powers exist—and this includes for instance anyone who is serious about art. What empowers the artist to create works of art cannot, it is generally said, originate in the soul's ordinary, conscious powers; it must bubble up from the subconscious and enter conscious awareness. This is why an artist will often have little patience with rules and guidelines for his work. He cannot be governed by such things, but must open himself to the elemental powers that give wing to his sensibility. It may be that he can only afterwards embark on some kind of explanation of what underlies his soul's creative activity.

Thus we must assume that many other, hidden powers hold sway in the soul and do not surface in our conscious mind. We can say, as we often have, that the human being's astral life is far, far more extensive in scope and breadth than our conscious ego life, and that these powers surface out of astrality into conscious experience—that, in other words, they exist below in a subterranean realm. In our time a very great number of people have gradually adapted to a purely outward, material life and there seek their whole *raison d'être*. Even in their inner life of soul, basically, there is nothing but habituation to this outward, material existence, which is the conscious realm. Our present, conscious life on earth does need to develop under a material influence, and is bound up with material life. This is why I have often said that what seeks to live in our awareness under the influence of our outward surroundings does not pass through the gate of death but, after a soul has passed through death, can live on only in the memory of another I, and gleams out when this person in turn passes through the gate of death. There below in subconscious depths, therefore, a different kind of life holds sway if a person has not accustomed himself to merely outward, material life, as a great many people have today. And we can certainly notice the difference. If one shows people who are orientated only to outward, material life a symbolic representation of, say, the death and rebirth of Hiram, they may even laugh at it, find it funny—something superfluous and pointless. But those who feel and sense something by drawing on the subconscious powers of soul that hold sway in the astral realm will be deeply moved by such a symbol, invoking in their soul the capacities that can understand immortality. Ordinary powers bound up with physical life cannot, by contrast, understand this idea.

Now the Easter festival preserves something of what was connected with the whole idea of a festival in humanity's primordial awareness. We have often spoken of this. When do we celebrate Easter? People with a materialistic outlook have often sought to change the way the time of the Easter festival is determined, thinking it is a nuisance if the date keeps altering every year—it can come at the end of March, or the beginning of April, or even at the end of April. Modern people think it should always be celebrated on a fixed date, say the first Sunday in April, so that account books are not disrupted by Easter falling at different times every year. Let us not forget of course that a materialistic outlook is indeed connected with keeping accounts. I have nothing against account books but I do naturally object a good deal to the materialistic outlook. Something can be perfectly good in itself but this does not mean that other related things always have to be governed by it.

For the time being at least—though this will change—there is still a sense that the Easter festival ought not to fall on the first Sunday in April but should be established in accordance with certain cosmic circumstances, the reciprocal positions of sun and moon. If you go out in the evening at the moment, and there's a clear sky, you can feel what the shining full moon means for human sensibility. Easter is celebrated on the Sunday after the first spring full moon, or in other words after the full moon following the beginning of spring on 21 March. Thus the date of Easter is determined by relationships between the sun and moon, so that a festival celebrated here on earth is made dependent on conditions in the cosmos.

In setting the date of the Easter festival in this way, the human soul declares implicitly that not everything here on earth should be governed by earthly circumstances but that what most deeply affects the soul should orientate itself to super-terrestrial conditions. The human being is directed towards the symbols of immortality, burial and resurrection. In images—whether in ritual pictures as in Catholic worship or in more conceptual form as in other confessions—

humankind is presented with the idea of life's immortality, the passage of the soul through the gate of death. But this picture of burial and resurrection is to hold sway in our soul at the time when sun and moon stand in the corresponding position, as we can always see from the calendar. This is a protest by the human soul that such an important symbolic context ought not to unfold under merely earthly circumstances. It is a recognition that contemplation of these symbols must be related to cosmic, super-terrestrial conditions.

Let us ask ourselves whether this idea is founded on a reality. Because of the temptations and misguidance of our materialistic age, we tend not to engage enough with the thought of true reality. The more materialistic people are today the more they give themselves up to the hallucination that they are contemplating reality. Why are people such materialists? It is because they do not recognize the reality of anything that is not material. People have a materialistic outlook because they delude themselves that they know reality. Yet basically it is true to say that nothing diverts us so much from reality as materialism. A simple thought can bring this home to us. You are all sitting here and listening to what I am saying. Now what I have just said is not as dire as other things I have said elsewhere—dire for a materialistic thinker, I mean. Let us assume that instead of you, this audience, the room is full of materialistic thinkers, for instance a band of monists. If this were so, surely something quite different would be passing through human souls as I speak if this were a gathering of monists listening instead of you. Why is this? If you consider realities, what lives in souls, you will have to acknowledge that if a crowd of monists were sitting here something quite different would occur. Why? You will admit that in purely abstract, hypothetical terms, though not in reality, one could also say that your karma might have led you to join a band of monists rather than to be here. This is not so, of course; the whole thing is hypothetical and an unreal assumption, though one we can make in the abstract. But given this assumption, it would not be too far-fetched to say that within your bodies something quite different would be listening than is presently listening in you since you have absorbed various aspects of spiritual science. Truly, what we develop over the course of our lives always also listens in us, always also resonates. And one can say that with many or most of you something is also listening that has lived its way into your soul over the course of the time that you have spent within the stream of spiritual science. We continually become a little different through the life we lead and the experiences we have. But to speak in this way of people in the abstract is unreal. Speaking of the human being in general has no reality at all. The moment we engage with realities, we discover how unreal we are if, as so commonly today, we speak only in anthropological rather than anthroposophical terms.

Now it is easy for you to overlook this, to fail to see the effect upon your soul of spiritual science. But your soul is also formed by a very great many other things. A great deal informs the nature of human souls, and here you need only consider how a subconscious, astral nature is connected with the human soul; and then you will see that what plays into your soul from the outer world without your awareness, which remains in the subconscious, may be the most significant and powerful factor. Sometimes people allow a quiet awareness to resonate in them, something also of an infinitely sweet and loving awareness of the fact that much that is not even earthly in nature plays into their under-psyche. Who of us does not know delightful, beautiful poems, love poems, that relate to the shining light of the moon, which testify to a quiet, sweet sense that this under-psyche, the unconscious soul, is connected with non-earthly realities that shimmer and gleam from and in the moonlight? Try to call before your soul the lyric poetry that speaks of lovers walking in the moonlight, and how in so much of this there quietly and sweetly resonates the fine weaving of the silver moonlight. And no one will try to claim, surely, that the human soul with, in this respect, its coarser upper consciousness can say what exactly it is in the moonshine that wafts and weaves through this soul. A hardened materialist will of course say that the moon has nothing at all to do with these loving feelings. But today we will not engage further with objections of such a nature but instead let us trust more in the quiet, sweet surfacing into awareness of what the lyric poets have spoken and sung. Here we can say that something like a ray of cosmic, superterrestrial reality shines into our awareness, and is related to the subconscious weaving and working of the human soul. If you recall what was said on Thursday, and again at the public lecture on Saturday,[48] about the working and weaving of the folk soul element into human soul life, then you will have to acknowledge that this folk soul element also holds sway much more in the subconscious than in conscious awareness. You see, the working of the folk soul element that often rises up from the subconscious into consciousness and is formulated in ideas and concepts is also of this nature. That is simply so!

Truly, an important part of what holds sway in the depths of our soul and rises to resonate quietly in our conscious awareness, what holds sway there in the astral body, is not earthly. Someone whose soul is open to impressions of the world of spirit knows that our earth is different in spring and autumn not solely because vegetation burgeons in spring and is harvested in autumn, but because the region of the earth upon which the moonlight shines is different from the region when it is not moon-illumined. Instead of thinking that it is just a silver ball or silver sickle floating in the heavens we must picture a tissue of light surrounding us, a spiritual fabric, in which we ourselves live, weave and swim with our souls in the same way that our bodies can swim in water. And what weaves and lives in or around the earth keeps changing depending on the changing relationship between the moon and the sun.

After 21 March, the sun stands in a quite different relationship to the earth than before this date. And the sunlight that shines back to us from the moon to the earth is therefore also quite different in quality after 21 March than it is before then. The first full moon after the beginning of spring, which gives us back the first strength of the resurrected sun, is something different from every other full moon. Our astral nature would therefore not be the same if, let us say, it looked upon the symbol of burial and resurrection in December rather than during the week after the spring full moon. Our soul is something quite different at this time. If our soul becomes different to a small degree by our absorption of spiritual science, as opposed to monist outlooks, so it becomes substantially different in the moonlight after the spring equinox from what it is after the winter solstice. Thus our soul can experience something different at this time than at another. Oh my dear friends, if only people would consider what the human being actually is and what he is connected with! They would then speak of the divine nature within them with enormous piety. And doing so would not make them arrogant but very humble, for it would become clear to them how very much is necessary in the world so that this being they find themselves to be can stand here in the world.

When spiritual science appears today, one of the many reasons for it doing so is to widen the human being's scope of vision—a vision that has become so constricted through materialistic developments. The soul's thinking, feeling and will, its whole sensibility, really is widened when one absorbs spiritual science authentically. People today fail to realize that materialistic developments in humanity have not only brought what is called materialism but above all also a curtailment of our thought life. Our thoughts have all become small and they must grow great again. Amongst humankind it must again become possible to see things in much broader contexts. In everything connected with the arts, for instance, in which a person also includes himself in the material on which he works—and that is ultimately true of almost all the arts—I wish that people would feel this: that an idea drawn from spiritual science such as the one we highlighted last Saturday really can lead us to deeper understanding. Just consider what it means if we can realize that we consist of two parts, a head standing at a much later evolutionary stage, already more hardened than the rest of the organism, and the latter standing at a less advanced evolutionary stage. Consider all that can emerge from this for the interplay between this human organism apart from the head, and the head itself. Whenever we move our hand we perform a movement, and underlying this is the etheric body that accomplishes it. What happens when I move my hands? I have previously described this here: the physical hands and the etheric hands accomplish the same movements. Whenever I think, the left and right cerebral lobes, as etheric head, also perform movements, and these are very similar to my hand movements; but the physical part is chained, enclosed in the fixed skull—a Prometheus Bound. And this is the basis for thinking. If not through external constraint but through organic enchainment the human being were as he will be when earth has passed away and the Jupiter stage of evolution arrives, when his arms will be as bound as his cerebral lobes are now, what would remain of the movements of the hands would be thinking.

But I wish to use a much more tangible example to show something that can clarify a few things, specifically in relation to modern times. The thoughts of the best figures of our age have been curtailed so that they survey only a small span of space and time, as opposed to the broad scope that we need, a larger scale of thinking that can survey much more. Let me give you an example.

By his own view, Eduard von Hartmann,[49] the philosopher of the unconscious, was certainly not a materialist. Yet this self-appraisal is of less importance than discerning whether our actual habits of thought are materialistic. One can establish an entirely idealistic philosophy and yet still have material habits of thinking, and these habits of thought will then determine whether our ideas are limited or of much broader scope. Now alongside some useful philosophical works, Eduard von Hartmann has also written on politics. I will cite him in this context since in his day he was really greatly esteemed as a political writer. In the most eminent sense we must call him one of the greatest German, or Prussian patriots. No one can doubt that Eduard von Hartmann held these patriotic views if they read certain published letters he wrote about what happened in 1866: 'And although the Danish war, and what followed from it, inevitably took an unfortunate course, I believe that Prussia must become dominant within Germany simply because the evolution of ideas necessitates this.'

We can therefore regard Eduard von Hartmann as one of the most dedicated patriots. In the 1880s, in 1889, he wrote some very fine essays about the general situation in Europe. They were widely read at the time and of course suffered the same fate to which all writing succumbs today, whether it is good or bad: things are read and forgotten. I don't believe that what he wrote 30 years ago is still read very much. As a political commentator he did not start from abstract and idealistic ideas—this is something he was also esteemed for—but he was, as you can see from numerous reviews of his work, a person who espoused *realpolitik*, in other words someone who reckoned with actual circumstances. Naturally Eduard von Hartmann's ideas were sufficiently broad in scope to encompass the constellation of the various great powers of Europe: Germany, Austria, Italy, France, England, Russia—and then all the small neutral states between them; and he was painstaking in his research when writing an essay on the diverse political interests of these various states. In a noteworthy essay he wrote in 1888, which appeared in book form in 1889, he reflected on the best possible potential political constellation for Europe. As I said, he was a real patriot, not just for Germany but for a wider Prussia, and was therefore of course speaking from this standpoint. He conceived of alliances he thought should be formed, considering that Germany, and a Europe encompassing as powerful a Germany as possible, would best be served by an alliance under English leadership between Switzerland, Belgium, Holland as an alliance of shared neutrality. He thought this would be the surest means to create conditions that a German and Prussian patriot would most ardently wish for. And this was back in 1889!

Switzerland, Belgium and Holland united under English leadership! I beg you to consider this most seriously, and compare it with what people are now obliged to say after this only half came about prior to the war: Belgium under England's leadership! Eduard von Hartmann wanted to see Belgium, Switzerland and Holland under England's leadership. It is interesting to see such a tangible example—and if we considered all areas of life we could find countless examples of these and similar circumstances—of how people were thinking 30 years ago, and to ask what intelligent people are thinking today. Everyone is intelligent of course these days! But how far-reaching is the scope of their ideas? How long will they remain true? And surely the important thing about an idea is that it exists within and relates to reality—that our thinking can realize our actions in the world. I am sure you can see where this is leading: the whole materialistic evolution of our age curtails human thoughts, renders them of use, in temporal terms, for no more than two or three decades. There is no point in employing such short-term thinking when we need to consider longer periods of time. Political views such as those of Eduard von Hartmann appear outdated after 30 years, and, if one writes a book on Hartmann, one may no longer even need to consider them. You see a fair number of books are written today without considering all the factors that should be considered.

But in another domain we really do need to consider a longer duration, for example in the realm of medicines. Views about medicines are not as easy to evaluate as political judgements. And yet the philosopher Lotze,[50] who is thoroughly conversant with medicine, was quite right to say that the enthusiasm accompanying the development of a new medicine today usually lasts only five years or so. Not only does this enthusiasm fade after this period but along with it also the huge popularity that first greeted it. People do notice this a little more than they notice it with political views. Gustav Theodor Fechner,[51] a witty and intelligent man, wrote a very interesting treatise in the 1820s, at a time when a new medicine, iodine, had just arrived on the scene. People started to list all the countless conditions and disorders that iodine could be used to treat. Fechner wrote a neat little essay in which he applied all the rules of science to prove that the moon is made of iodine, and that one therefore need only devise a method for capturing moonlight and would then be able to use this wonderful universal panacea. Later, as you know, Gustav Theodor Fechner established a scientific conception of aesthetics, founded psychophysics, and was also an outstanding physicist. So we do not need to see him as one of those dubious theosophists, do we? Even people who have more than half a foot in the monist camp take Fechner seriously. Those with both feet in it, on the other hand, do not. Everywhere we come upon a certain curtailment of vision, a certain adherence to short-term views and ideas.

This is true particularly wherever we find modern science raised from its proper domain into the realm of humanities, or what are called the humanities, and there employing the same methods. Yes, this is very dismal indeed, and the only way in which people can overlook this desolation is to stick with just one or two authors who write in the same vein, rather than perceiving the chaos and confusion that arises, for instance, if one considers a couple of differently minded authors—or researchers as they like to call themselves. Try comparing two authors with different perspectives on what is called the 'psychology of nations'. I'm sorry to say this but you will be flabbergasted. Using the modern mode of thinking to study the various peoples of Europe, in, of course, a purely 'scientific' and 'objective' manner, you will see that an author describes the people of central Europe as 'Germanic' or 'Norse' in origin. Such an author then goes on to characterize the qualities of these people. But if we turn from him to a French author who describes the French nation, whose people are, as he has been informed, descended from the Celts, we will find that he ascribes to these ancient Celts the same characteristics that the other author ascribed to the Teutonic peoples. The only thing people are unaware of is that there is much more of a Celtic quality living in central Europe than in French-speaking western Europe. People do not know this.

Indeed, we can encounter still more breathtaking assumptions. I could tell you about a well-known author, a commentator on national psychology who, as other authors do, focuses on examples of individuals descended from a particular people or nation and illustrative of its qualities. This commentator refers to Byron. One can see he loves Byron, but this is only because, in considering him, he comes to the view that Byron was not really English at all but really a German at heart! This is seriously stated in a book on national psychology. Byron is really a German! Another author, who probably likes Byron less, also writes about him but finds him repellent because of his entirely Celtic characteristics!

I could cite countless examples of this sort of thing: conflicting ideas that show how little substance they have. Certainly, when modern, so-called 'sure' scientific methods are transposed into the domain of culture, the humanities, we quickly see how unreliable are the ideas that emerge from this. Just consider how necessary it is for the spirit to inform this realm. But how long will it be before we possess a soul science as I tried to describe this in ideal terms last Thursday?[52] And yet only a soul science of this kind can bring us an understanding of what really holds sway in Europe, and can also introduce the mutual understanding between peoples that is necessary if European culture is to continue.

Much has been written in recent war months. Well, I'm not sure whether reading is the right use for all that has been written. But books by the Swede Kjellén[53] are amongst relatively good things that have been written. There you will find a very positive assessment connected with current events, a judgement more general in character which we can summarize as follows: in humanity's evolution we have gradually developed an enormously material culture which comes to expression everywhere. The spiritual scientist, as I have often stated, has no need to disparage the greatness of this external, material culture. But if we compare these material values with spiritual ones, we have to acknowledge that the latter are simply incapable of mastering and governing such an intensely materialistic culture. And this is the greatest plague of our time: our incapacity to master and govern the products of material culture through spiritual values. It is here that spiritual science really must engender the necessary feelings, giving rise to the insight that we must not sin against the great spiritual laws of the cosmos. The prevailing truth demands its rights. Just conceive of any domain of life without spiritual values, however marvellously equipped in material terms. This materiality, whether of a state organization or other structure, will not thrive because the world is such that a soul is essential for every body. I can give you a tangible example of this, one that may be close to home for us. I am not speaking here of what anyone *ought* to do or think, but just offering an illustrative instance.

Within the Anthroposophical Society we cultivate the science of the spirit. A whole range of characteristics make this Anthroposophical Society different from all other associations, and it cannot be like them, at least under current circumstances. Why is this? What do other associations do when they are founded? They draw up programmes, agreeing on certain planned courses of action. When one leaves such an association one thereby states that one no longer agrees with its programme. If the whole association is dissolved, no one is injured by the items on the plan or programme, are they? One can form an association and dissolve it again, and this is true of every mechanism in the world. Weismann[54] once tried to characterize the organism in scientific terms. Naturally he only drew attention to a negative characteristic, yet it was true: What is the nature of life? asked Weismann. It is what leaves a corpse behind when it departs. Naturally this is not a description of life as such but we have to acknowledge there is some truth in it, an accurate negative characterization of life as leaving a corpse behind when it has gone. Our Anthroposophical Society is really already a living entity by virtue of the fact that our members have in their hands now a certain number of lecture cycles which, given the nature of the Society at present, non-members usually do not get to see. But this means in turn that it is not so easy to leave either, for otherwise the person in question will take these lecture cycles away with him. But I did not wish to speak of this, for actually you can already buy these cycles in second-hand bookshops! Such things have occurred. And we must recognize that the Anthroposophical Society is an organism. You see, if the Anthroposophical Society were to be dissolved it would leave a corpse behind: the lecture cycles exist! A different society, structured on mechanical principles, can dissolve itself without leaving any corpse: its members go their different ways, and its programmes and agendas are really not a residual corpse. As I said, we cannot contemplate reforms or suchlike in these present, grave times, but what I mean is something else. Please do not think, my dear friends, that we can simply say that the Society can go on existing, for why shouldn't it? In this case it does not truly exist, does not truly live! If it lives in the assumption that lecture cycles cannot be found in second-hand bookshops, then, if they can after all be found and bought there, it is not living in truth, in reality, but in a lie. That is quite self-evident. And to further spiritual science, truth, absolute truth is needed. We can overlook this with our abstract thinking, but someone who knows that truth is a reality that works in the world cannot overlook it.

When spiritual science becomes something we really feel inwardly, then we begin to sense how every thought stands within reality, whereas abstract thinking, which accords with materialism, does not care how a thought relates to reality and stands within it. But it can be a curious experience if one tries to record in writing thoughts that live in reality. What is the nature of this experience? One finds that people regard these thoughts, at best, simply like anything else that can, say, be found printed in the newspaper, though perhaps not as long-winded an article as I read in the *Piccolo della Sera* about some matter or other—bristling with indignation over three columns. But reading on, the whole thing was in turn repudiated. One did not have to wait for the next issue the following evening to find a repudiation of the article; it was there in the same edition! Things may not usually be so extreme, but as I said the best you can hope for today when you try to present true, truthful thoughts—in other words ones you not only believe but know to be in the domain of truth—is that they will merely be regarded like anything else. People read them as they read the things in newspapers, which are mostly only relevant for 24 hours. Yes, this awareness of our responsibility to live with our thoughts in reality is something that must come with spiritual science. And if the serious nature of our times is calling on us to develop one quality, it is this: to feel responsible for one's thoughts.

My dear friends, all this shows how restricted thinking becomes if it limits itself only to the conscious realm, which initially is bound up with material reality.

We should not be surprised, therefore, if the cultural streams in humanity's evolution, which must take a deeper hold than daily life does, also seek to take account of things that go deeper than ordinary consciousness. This has always been true of deeper religious impulses. Why did something like the Easter rites and services enter humanity's evolution? And why were these Easter rites connected with cosmology, with what occurs between sun and moon in the broad expanses of the heavens? It is because we would lapse into the most extreme short-sightedness, in our feeling, thinking and will, if we were limited to our earthly experiences alone. We can only gain a broader view of life, can only make our thoughts more wide-ranging, if we not only integrate our physical I consciousness into earthly experiences but also our astral subconscious into the great cosmic events in the heavens.

When the most important thought, that of immortality, is integrated with the cosmos, that truly has a good underlying reason in respect of religion. You see, if we only originated in earthly conditions we could never even grasp the idea of immortality. If we were merely more developed apes, as scientific materialism would have it, there would be nothing in us that could conceive of this idea of immortality.

I can actually give you a nice little example of the short-sightedness of scientists in this realm when they wax philosophical. A few days ago I opened a book whose author—who may not be a monist as such, but might be—was writing in a materialistic vein about the connection between human beings and apes, though not in the justified sense that we have often discussed it. In one of his essays at the very beginning of the book, this author states that he can give examples of travellers who, arriving in a certain region, have witnessed people whose culture had degenerated to such a degree that they displayed the same instincts and drives as apes. He goes on to say that if human beings can sink to the level of apes, can develop downwards to apelike behaviour, then it is logical than the human being can likewise evolve from the ape. Self-evident isn't it, logical! We might just as well say that a person develops in his lifetime from a child to an old man—something we can see without travelling abroad. We can draw a parallel between a child becoming an old man and a person becoming apelike through cultural degeneration. And it would be just as logical as this author's claim to say that an old man could turn back into a child. It is the very same logic. What is worrying is not so much the development of such shaky logic but that all this is read by people, absorbed by them, without them noticing that it is based on utter drivel.

We could never arrive at the idea of immortality if we were really connected only with earthly conditions, if our intrinsic being were only earthly. But—whether through spiritual science or by some other means—we can connect the human being with the cosmos, with super-terrestrial realities, and then the idea of immortality can blossom in us. People can also come along and say that talking of super-terrestrial conditions is mere fantasy. That's possible: the human intellect can discount the spiritual element from its view of the human being, as monist materialism is seeking to do in all domains today. But the spiritual element cannot be sundered from the human soul, since we do not belong only to the earth and are not composed only of earthly conditions. In a science and cultural orientation that limits human thoughts and feelings to earthly things, supersensible powers are nevertheless still present in the depths of the human soul, though people have to suppress this. And this will gradually give rise to the cultural illness of suppressed spirituality in the human soul.

The times are serious, and we must seek to conceive this seriousness to the very greatest degree. But we will only rightly conceive what must hold sway in these grave times if we do not think only of the outward aspect, of what should come about through the hard trials of our times, but at the same time also recognize that these events must speak to us of a spiritual elevation of the *whole* human race.

Only if a small number of people, at least, emerge from these grave times with the profound sense that humanity needs to be spiritualized can these grave and challenging times of trial develop into something that accords with the spirit of the universe. Good will only follow from these events, whatever their outcome, if this is so.

We only comprehend spiritual science if we see it not just as a

Christmas annunciation but an Easter one as well, in the sense of understanding the wider implications of the idea of immortality for the human being's whole nature. We can only grasp immortality if we comprehend the immortal aspect within us. Fichte, Hegel and many others knew that the human soul does not become immortal only when it has passed through death but is already immortal, and that this immortality is found within us. Therefore we must seek a science that takes full spiritual, soul account not only of the mortal body but also the immortal human soul.

It is quite natural that over the past four hundred years as science made such brilliant advances human vision of the spiritual life has receded, along with an increasing disinclination to perceive the spirit in the outer world. But a time must come once more when Hiram or, as we say, that portion of Christ that is always with us and speaks to us of the supersensible, resurrects after being buried in the grave of cultural evolution's Holy Week. We can really see it like this: when the great Copernicus, the great Kepler, Galileo and the rest appeared, and directed human thoughts, as they had to, to the external world, this was the cosmic Maunday Thursday, which was followed by a Good Friday. Vision of immortality was buried. But now the time has come for the universal Easter Sunday, when we must celebrate the sacred resurrection of human soul and spirit knowledge. It is very fitting for us to have a Good Friday mood in our present times. But only if we find the strength to fit ourselves for the universal Easter Sunday will we be able to accomplish an inward Easter service in ourselves to accompany the outward rites and services. In Holy Week we bear a black and grievous mood. The priests embody this mood in black mourning robes because the corpse of the dead Christ rests in the grave. Then comes the Resurrection: cordial, bright, spring garments replace the black clothes of mourning at the moment the thought of resurrection replaces that of the grave. It is fitting that we bear mourning and grief within us today. But let us fit ourselves to wear the spiritual garments of Easter when the times have once more changed.

LECTURE 7

25 APRIL 1916

TODAY I want to start once more from matters we have discussed in other recent reflections. I have spoken of the customs of certain brotherhoods and described some of what happens there, in particular illustrating how, in various ways, the deeper impulses of occult brotherhoods have become an arid shell in modern Freemasonry. Last time I referred especially to the custom that represents burial and resurrection, which basically is nothing other than an Easter ritual. Today my starting point will be something else relating to these matters.

Endeavours within these circles are formulated and expressed in terms of a search for 'the lost Word'. It is beyond the scope of my lecture today to go into the details of this, but if, with the means available, one enquires into what is meant by this phrase, one need only consider the beginning of the Gospel of St John, 'In the beginning was the Word.' In Greek, the Word was always the Logos. 'And the Word was with God, and a God was the Word.' This Word, as we have often discussed, is of course not at all the same as what we mean nowadays by 'word'. We can only approach its real meaning if we recall—as we have done in recent lectures—that humanity possessed a primordial revelation in ancient times, a primordial wisdom. If you picture this primordial wisdom given to humankind in its infancy in ways we have here discussed, conceive of it in its whole scope, and call it the Logos, the primal Word, then you will have a rough idea of what is meant by the Word or Logos. And we can say that the wisdom given to humankind in its infancy through the mediation of higher spirits, far exceeding everything we can as yet know today even in our science of the spirit, has been lost. And it is a fine custom if a feeling at least is kindled in these brotherhoods that such a thing has been lost and must be sought again. Of course it is not found there, for otherwise all those who attain a certain degree within such brotherhoods would be wise as were those primordial people whom the gods once instructed. If this were so we would see it not only in those who had achieved certain grades in their brotherhoods, but the whole world would inevitably look different too. But in their ceremonies and rites something does become apparent that offers a picture of this loss of primordial wisdom and rediscovery of it. Something of this nature must embed itself in human souls so that they become able, at least, when they pass through the portal of death, pass in turn through the world of spirit and return again to the earth, to develop an understanding of an earthly wisdom that would be necessary for them—and in fact already is so today.

So the lost Word is sought. And basically all our spiritual science is a search for the lost Word. But when this lost Word is expressed today, that is, if anything drawn from the science of the spirit is spoken, along come all those who have grown wise in our time—and in so many fields we have made such glorious progress—and say: fantasy, nonsense, dream, or worse things. But in the first part of our reflections today, since we are alone together here, let us enter into a realm of spiritual science that is capable of deciphering many riddles of human existence. One cannot even say that the knowledge that should be furthered through spiritual science was always so absolutely unknown. I myself have spoken in public[55] about a forgotten tone in modern culture, a forgotten stream, in which lived much from which spiritual science germinates. If we consider the human being today, we know that what our eyes perceive is only the outward aspect, the physical body. The etheric body is alive within this physical body, and acts within it. But we won't get very far if we know no more than this, that the human being has an etheric body. If we know this word and, at most—and many think this sufficient—that the etheric body is just somewhat finer than the physical body, more nebulous and luminous, this is not yet much. This etheric body in fact is a highly complex configuration. If we consider people as they are today, we find differences between different peoples, don't we. Europeans are different from Africans, who are different in turn from Asians. We have to acknowledge these differences. But if we survey all humanity, we have to admit that despite all the differences, these people of the globe all resemble each other much more than animals do. Even though Europeans and Africans are markedly different if we consider subtler distinctions, we cannot say, can we, that the difference between them could ever be as great as between a stork and a mouse. Thus animals are much more different from each other than human beings. Animals belong to different species, whereas the human race is a single species. The most diverse animals exist across the globe. Let us keep this in mind as we return now to consider our etheric body. During life, between birth and death, the etheric body coheres through the elastic power of the physical body. Try imagining the following, something that can't be done of course, but if it were possible even a research scientist would be persuaded: imagine that we could, in an experiment, sunder a person's physical body from his etheric body, drawing out the etheric body and then also separating out the astral body and I from the etheric body. No longer governed by the physical body's elasticity, this etheric body would fracture into many small pieces. This etheric body is, in fact, a multiplicity formed of many, many parts, and only coheres because of the elasticity of the physical body.

And if we could separate the physical body from them, what would these small parts look like? However strange this may sound to modern, clever people, it is true that these parts of the etheric body would assume forms that approximate to an outspread animal kingdom; in other words all possible animal forms would appear. A certain part of your etheric body—that of the head—would really shape itself in a birdlike fashion while the part originating in the area of the larynx would become a very beautiful, almost angel-like animal form, and so forth. Basically we bear the whole animal kingdom in our etheric body. This is the truth. Our etheric body is the outspread animal kingdom compressed and cohering through the elasticity of the physical body. In ancient, primordial times when evolution was at a different stage, the whole human form was indeed distributed across all the many animals. Only if we reflect on this can we grasp the reality underlying Darwinism's much coarser and heavier-handed ideas. Humanity prepared itself by developing, as if in the different species of today's animal kingdom, separate aspects of what was later to become the etheric body, though the animals at that time were somewhat different from today. Our animal kingdom nowadays is no longer something from which humanity could be derived, but quite different in nature. But the powers that were at that time spread out across this animal kingdom were in a sense extracted and are still present today in our etheric body. So now let us consider for a moment all that is basically within us. With this animal kingdom we possess all the instincts, all the diverse animal drives, though now harmonized and placed in an overall context of mutual relationship through being united by the elasticity of our physical body. We are human beings because we are physical human beings, and we received our physical form from the Spirits of Form during earthly existence. As physical human beings we keep everything that is in us in check. Sometimes one or other drive comes to the fore when some part of the etheric body gains the upper hand.

Just think therefore of the complex multiplicity that constitutes us human beings, and how it is impossible really to present such things to people although it is only by means of them that we can properly understand the world. We can see this on occasion when someone, in a moment of sudden insight, has an inkling of the truth. There have been such people in modern times: for instance Oken,[56] a pupil of Schelling, had a flash of genius in the idea that the human being is composed of the whole animal kingdom. He did not see this in Darwinian terms—I said last time how illogical modern people are when they develop and discuss Darwinian concepts. No, Oken had an inkling of the truth. It was not yet possible for him to draw on spiritual science to express such things as we are discussing this evening, but he glimpsed something of the fact that the whole animal kingdom is contained in the human being, and he ably articulated this. But he was ridiculed, especially by following generations. After all, what other response can a very clever, endlessly clever person give to Oken's suggestion that the tongue is an octopus? But what I have just been describing from spiritual-scientific research is something that Oken found through brilliant intuition and wished to present to people. He wished to show that the separate parts as elaborated from the etheric body have a connection with the form configurations of animals. For instance, he traced the ear's genesis to a sort of mouse-stork combination, and the tongue to an octopus. Naturally people ridiculed him. But something that appeared so ridiculous was in fact a premonition of profound knowledge, which must develop amongst humanity in coming times. It will not be possible to comprehend the world's phenomena without such knowledge. People will only be able to judge reality by knowing such things.

You see, the Spirits of Form act primarily upon our physical body, and during Earth evolution they give form only to the human being. The animals possess their inherited form from ancient Moon evolution, and this animal form is therefore luciferic in nature—is a form that remained over from ancient Moon evolution. What was only etheric back then has hardened. From the Spirits of Form we have our outward physical form, whereas our inner nature is less subject to them. In other words, the Spirits of Form work less upon our etheric body than do the Spirits of Personality, the spiritual beings we refer to as Archangeloi or Angeloi. They act upon the etheric body, and have something to do with governing this multiplicity in the etheric body which I spoke of. And if we enter into precise spiritual-scientific facts, then we must for example be very clear that all the powers that originate in the folk soul also act upon and influence our etheric body. What we grasp with our physical body, what we see with our eyes, hear through our ears, is first and foremost international.

Qualities of nationality sit much deeper in the unconscious nature of the etheric body for instance. I presented this here on one occasion, about 18 months ago.[57] Briefly, we can see how complex our being is, and that we must seek to understand ourselves in terms of the primordial wisdom that once held sway.

And this will offer us deep pictures, insights and wisdom that are conveyed to humankind and that can be understood if one has the will. Think of the activity of speaking or singing. It is simply a preconception to think that only the physical body is somehow involved and in motion in this activity. The movement primarily occurs in the etheric body, with the multiplicity of which I just spoke. And this is why what comes to our awareness in singing or music surfaces from subconscious depths and is so hard to express in words—because it is connected with the whole complexity of the etheric body. And we can gain a real sense, in turn, of our affinity with the rest of the world when we know that the animal kingdom spread wide around us lives in our etheric body in the way I described. Naturally, if a drive surfaces in us it must rise into the astral body. These things are not contradictory if we consider them carefully in reality. Thus in speaking of the presence of drives and instincts in the human being, we must of course ascribe them to the astral body; and yet they are founded upon the resemblance of form with the animal kingdom as I have now outlined it.

And if, similarly, we could separate out our astral body in the way suggested for the etheric body, it would disintegrate, since it too only coheres through the elasticity of the physical and etheric body. It would disintegrate and would appear as something similar to the whole realm of plants. By virtue of the fact that we possess an astral body, we really do contain all the forms of the plant kingdom we see spread around us in the outer world in such diversity. If you study the whole plant world and the way one plant form relates to another, you have an outward picture, a subdivided picture of what has been drawn together and united in the human astral body. This too belongs to the 'lost Word'. Primordial wisdom had a sense of these things, and for this reason it was said that there is something in the human being that expresses his deep and most inward affinity with the nature of trees and plants. If you read Norse mythology—for mythologies are in fact only a later expression of this primordial human wisdom—you will discover that the human race is said to originate in ash and elm, and here you find an awareness of the human being's affinity with plant nature, which is due in turn to the fact that the human being was at the level of the plant kingdom during the evolutionary stage of Old Sun, whereas during Old Moon he was at the level of the animal kingdom.

And within the astral body, in turn, we bear the actual I. In outward, physical life, after all, we know little enough of this intrinsic I. Philosophers of course know a great deal about it! For instance, they know that this I, as a person perceives it in the physical body, remains constant from birth to death through all the inner soul changes he undergoes. Philosophers know this, and you can read it in countless works of philosophy. It is as if they had forgotten that we always fall asleep in each 24-hour period. Every time we sleep this constancy of the I is interrupted. But philosophers are not troubled by such thoughts for they are, after all, extremely clever!

When we speak of the I, we must speak of something that for instance not only has awareness in our waking life but is also present when we sleep, but then unfolds its powers out into the whole universe, there to be irradiated, woven and pulsed through by the spiritual powers of the cosmos. We bear this unconsciously within us. And if we could extract it from within us as we imagined in the case of both the etheric and astral body, we would gain from it the whole picture of the mineral universe with all its diverse cosmic secrets. In this I exists, in compressed form, everything that is spread out through the whole cosmos. Thus we bear the mineral cosmos within us.

In this way we acquire a picture of what we really are and of our affinity with the cosmos. And if we speak of the fact that the human being is composed of physical body, etheric body, astral body and the I, then this should be more for us than mere words; we should recognize that we will only understand what underlies these words if, through spiritual science, we can really consider the whole connection between the human being and the cosmos.

Yes, that is an important realm of spiritual science, one people ought at least to engage with a little in our time. Today people speak about the human being in a very ill-informed way because everyone is so clever in the modern world. But what they say is very ill-informed. And the times present us with challenges that are too great to be resolved by an ill-informed science and its narrow wisdoms. And yet people are up in arms when you offer them an idea such as the one I have just presented. In fact it is not a matter of knowing these precise things but of learning to think in a mobile, flexible way that enables us to discover them. Someone who understands what is happening today knows humanity will face very, very grave tasks and trials in the coming period—tasks of which very few may perhaps have an inkling as yet. But people do not possess sufficient mobility and elasticity of thinking to meet these challenges. If we consider this in direct connection with the severe trials of our time, we can gain a quite different sense of the need for spiritual science to inform human sensibilities in future. The earth is soaked in blood. But in future there must develop on this blood-fertilized earth something that can only be encompassed by a kind of thinking different from what has arisen from the more or less materialistic developments of the nineteenth century. As you know, the spiritual scientist does not repudiate these developments at all, their importance and their great achievements. But the karma of these materialistic advances in the nineteenth century has led to the rivers of blood we now witness, and the tragic occurrences of our day.

People will not, I repeat, find the courage to develop what is needed, even if they gain a fleeting acquaintance with spiritual science or even work on its behalf as far as possible. You see, this spiritual science is strangely ridiculed and mocked—in words—as fantasy and dream. But do these words equate with the reality?

Here I would like to raise something that can show us the depth of lies in which we are immersed today. Let me offer you an example, close at hand, to show how untruthful are the conditions that currently hold sway between people. In one lecture cycle[58] I discussed Christian initiation, speaking of the first initiation stage called the washing of the feet—a symbolic expression, simply, of something a person should practise inwardly. There a description was given of how a person should develop certain feelings that support his sense of a connection with all the kingdoms of nature. If we gaze down upon the animal kingdom with deep, inward feeling, we must recognize it as the foundation of the human kingdom. What would we more developed creatures be if that lower kingdom did not exist? To really enliven this feeling within us is the first step in the first stage of Christian initiation. And then to recognize that the animal, in turn, in a sense looks down from its higher level to the plants and likewise says: 'To you, plant I owe my existence, though you stand lower than I in the hierarchy of creatures.' And then the plant too would feel its way down to the mineral realm from which it grows, to the mineral soil, and say: 'To you I owe my existence.' Likewise the Angeloi look down to the human kingdom in recognition that they owe their existence to us at our lower stage of evolution. And so on upwards through the hierarchies. As we reflect in this way, what we can thus conceive and discover transforms into a fundamental tenor and feeling of the human soul.

Our dear friend Christian Morgenstern, who supported our concerns so courageously and faithfully, created a beautiful poem that encapsulates this washing of the feet. In his last collection of poems entitled *We Found a Path*, and published after his death, we find these thoughts about Christian initiation in the fine poem 'Washing the Feet':

> I thank you, dear, dumb stone,
> to you incline:
> I owe my plant existence to your being.
>
> I thank you, herb and flower,
> to you bend down:
> from you I raise my creature power.

I thank you stone and herb and beast,
to you bow down:
the three of you have raised me to myself.

We thank you child of humankind
and reverently to you descend:
for it is due to you that we exist.

In oneness and in the manifold
nature of all God's being, thanks arise:
in gratitude all life itself enfolds.

And Christian Morgenstern, whose sensibility lived for many years in our midst, bravely acknowledged in his last book of poems all that flows through our world-view. Naturally he has not the slightest responsibility for what I now need to express. You see, if Morgenstern still lived amongst us today in physical form—he died two years ago of course—he would assuredly serve our cause today still more powerfully and courageously. But now someone has published a critique of Morgenstern's poems, naturally also containing good things about him—and why not? Back then, before he died, he was already recognized as an important poet and there is no reason now to forget this. Naturally the author of the review does not mention that the whole current of this book of poems is deeply connected with our movement. But he does say something else. He cites this poem I have just read to you and says that it shows how one can have a metaphorical view of spiritual things that is, nevertheless, devoid of metaphor. The author writes as follows:

> There is no picture contained in these wonderful verses; but amidst these free-floating, very spiritual poems, this poem in particular has a special potency because it makes earthly things visible: they are still visible in it. It seems to address reality itself, rather than to be metaphorically conveyed, rendering past earthly aspects of the human journey. Now the human being continues onwards, and these verses proclaim it. This admirable poem partakes of this earthly reality, and for my

> feeling, therefore, is the greatest poem in this book, the greatest that Morgenstern ever wrote, and one of the greatest poems ever written in the German lyric tradition.

Christian Morgenstern would of course be the first to say that this poem of his could never have been written without the whole context of spiritual science, though the critic Ernst Lissauer fails to mention it. Morgenstern would of course bravely assert that this poem drew on a very particular spiritual context; and here you have an instance of the lies in which we live today, and the way in which people praise the fruits without acknowledging the ground from which they spring. More than this: they praise such work as the finest flowering of cultural life yet regard the soil it grows in as nothing but fantasy, illusion and deception!

This is what we have to deal with, my dear friends. Truly, I wish I could offer you more uplifting Easter reflections. But our times, our times of bloodshed, make it necessary for us to inscribe deeply in our soul a sense of the karmic conditions in which we now live. These are grave times, and we have to recognize this fully. That is the most uplifting feeling we can cultivate today. We must look reality squarely in the face. Let us look at things in close detail—for instance examining the capacity for judgement, or rather, misjudgement, which we experience every day and every hour arising from what developed in the nineteenth century and has found its way into the twentieth. Every day we can gather experiences in this domain. I will offer only a few examples of such things.

Soon after the outbreak of war, people repeatedly sent me or gave me a poem said to be from Robert Hamerling's literary estate,[59] and regarded as a prophecy of contemporary events. But even a passing acquaintance with Robert Hamerling's poetry could show that not a single line of this poem could in fact have been written by him. Hamerling died in 1889. A whole range of newspapers expressed admiration for his prophetic words. Some individuals were singing the poem's praises even when they could long since have realized that it was a fraud. I was astonished, for instance, that Maximilian

Harden[60] in the *Zukunft* journal started praising this poem so late in the day. Harden resorts to 'fine' words—note the inverted commas—to express his admiration for Robert Hamerling's exalted muse. A few days ago still, in an evening paper, a leading article discussed the bitter pill, the 'Easter pill' if you like that we have had to swallow recently; and the degree of seriousness with which this was expressed can be gauged by the fact that this poem by 'Robert Hamerling' was again cited in the context of such a grave and bitter concern. Here is an example of how much credence we should give to all articles that betray such a capacity for judgement—or rather misjudgement.

And this evening countless people will believe what they read in their evening newspaper about circumstances in Switzerland, about the political, military and economic plight of the Swiss. This will all be explained to them. But what I wonder is whether people will look at the author's name and draw some apt conclusions: he is Max Hochdorf, the same man who wrote that stupid article[61] about our movement. I referred to him in a public lecture at the Architects' House. Naturally one will be able to search his article tonight for signs of the same love of truth he displayed when he wrote about us. If we drew the proper conclusions we would discover how heads are knocked together to drum idiocy into them, how dull-witted and thoughtless views prevail in people who allow such views and verdicts about our age to be hammered home in relation to all contemporary phenomena. To counter this one has to keep stepping back and seeing things in context—and then we can see how worthless are all the contemporary views of our age that are hammered into people's skulls.

Quite a lot is hammered home in this way. It is not too much to expect, really, that people today should have an elementary understanding, at least, of the progress achieved in Europe when we passed from a culture rooted in Norse and Teutonic mythology—though of course this drew on primordial wisdom and profound worship of the figures of the Norse gods—to Christianity. An elementary grasp of this would not be too much to expect, you might think. And yet if you read a journal that has just been published you find an expression of regret that Norse myth gave way to Christianity:

> The split in our thinking into which we Germans fell through the introduction of Christianity was something unknown to our forefathers. Their views of the world embraced the conflict in nature as the eternal law of life. It appeared quite natural to them. Like the battle between light and darkness, an eternal war was waged between the sons of light and the children of darkness, of good against bad. They knew that their gods were only images . . .

Goodness, what nonsense this is!

> . . . through which they grasped the world of phenomena. The world of their beliefs and concerns was at the same time that of their poetry . . .

Such self-congratulatory cleverness—

> . . . but have we really advanced beyond them today? I fear we have not; and the difficulty of those who cling to old orthodoxies in solving the terrible problems that currently beset us show us only that the roots of our strength lie in the heroic world-view of our ancestors.

In other words, we should reintroduce Wotan and Thor worship as quickly as possible. This journal, by the way, is one that has also published the most insulting attacks on our movement. People today are already having blinkers put on their vision, so that they cannot dwell in shades and subtleties that exist between one extreme view and another. The most extreme world-views and principles are acclaimed and subscribed to. The world-view so trivially called the 'theosophical' is not free of this general befuddlement, which has assumed very great proportions. This happens when one or another drive gains the upper hand because a part of the etheric body becomes rampant—and now, after my characterizations today you can picture this. Pride and arrogance, for example, is something that pervades all written discourse. Each author lets it be known how very important he is. Without this outlook it is becoming almost impossible to write anything today. As I have often said, esoteric development involves not only recognizing nonsense as nonsense but the capacity to experience bodily pain in consequence. This physical pain, which could lead one to despair, is something one can very, very frequently feel today when reading various—otherwise perhaps very clever—articles.

Here is a small instance. Here I have a little book—I don't wish to say more about its contents. The author is Thomas Mann,[62] whom many regard as one of the most enlightened minds of our day. Here he speaks about how we should regard the causes of the present war. Well, I don't want to go into this much. But he quotes the views of others, and says: 'Gentlemen, a little courage for mental clarity is required!' He thinks others do not have this courage to perceive and judge clearly. The man is therefore not modest! And now comes the passage that can really make one cry out in pain. He wants to prove where the causes of the war lie, and he says:

> War requires conflict between two sides or more, and if Germany had been willing to pursue the highest rationality, even if the other sides had not been 'intent on war' as the phrase goes, preferring it to an embrace of German diplomacy—well, the war would not have happened!

Naturally, this is the kind of logic at work in people's minds today—war takes two sides, and without this war does not happen. This means that if one side attacks, without there being two sides that seek conflict, there will be no war. That's the kind of logic at work today, my dear friends, one accentuated apparently by saying, 'Gentlemen, a little courage for mental clarity is required!' The 'modesty' implicit in such statements reminds me of a poem by Matthias Claudius, a fine poem about supposed humility. I will let the poem speak for itself. It is called—forgive me—'The Donkey'.

> Nought can I delight in,
> misshapen and dumb I am,
> devoid of power and courage.
> All people pass me by
> without regard, or mock me.
> I'm neither cold nor warm.
> There's nothing I can delight in:
> misshapen and dumb I am;

He's truly humble you see!

> I chew on straw and thistles,
> grow old beneath rough sacks—
> Ah, nature when you made me you were careless:
> your only gift to me a lovely voice!

That is about the extent of modesty you find in people who assert their world-view today. They are universally modest, even in regard to what they feel obliged to learn before they propound their world-view. But they know, of course, that nature did at least endow them with the 'courage for mental clarity'—in the same way, forgive me, that the donkey praises his own beautiful voice.

However much such things seem concerned with mundane matters, we do need to consider them seriously. You see, it is far more important for us to acquire the capacity for flexible, mobile thinking than to possess specific spiritual-scientific truths. Practising a strength of clarity in thinking, and making this thinking broader and more flexible, as we must do if we are to acknowledge spiritual-scientific truths, we will inevitably sense the prevalence today of lies, pride and all possible things of this nature. They dominate life today. This is not the fault of the broad masses of the population. People who know a thing or two of human life also know that if it was merely up to human nature alone, two-thirds of the population of Berlin would be drawn to spiritual science. It is not the fault of the general population but is due instead to current conditions and leading individuals. This is something we must be fully aware of. It is not even the leading individuals themselves so much as the currents in which our age has constrained them, which has led to the belief that any and everyone today can form a view about world events without any foundations of insight. It is said that many clever things are written today, but in fact there is much more heat than light. You might even say there's much more coal than flame, if you think of Professor Kohler at Berlin University,[63] who is a jurist and neo-Hegelian. Try giving thorough scrutiny to the charcoal created by such neo-Hegelians! As I said, one has to have an open mind and clear eye for what lives in modern culture and thinking.

Truly, as heroically as people are spilling their blood, so they would incline to the spirit if this spirit could approach them in the right way. It is not due to the general population, and we can see the signs of this in all the great sacrifices and deeds of ordinary people today.

My dear friends, aspects of spiritual science such as those we have spoken of again today should give us the will to have an open mind and clear eye for what lives in our surroundings. Recently I spoke of how people so often speak past each other. I cited a particular example, a ground-breaking book by Professor Schleich, of how people can speak past each other. Do read a few chapters of this book. It really is a good example of how truth is something quite different from human opinion. The really honest enquirers are already working towards each other, tunnelling through to each other as it were, and will meet somewhere in the middle. For instance, read the section which ends with the remark about a possible note by Goethe that might one day be found—but which has been extant already since 1892. The chapter is called 'The Myth of Brain Metabolism'. Read it, and you get a sense of how an honest, serious researcher such as Schleich, and at the same time a thinker, makes an important discovery based on his anatomical and surgical research, and his duties and work as a surgeon. If you read this chapter you will see another angle on what Schleich describes: he is actually describing the reality of the head's etheric body! The real facts impel him to describe this etheric body.

It will be a blessing to discover that spiritual science is tunnelling through from the other side! You see, what mainstream science brings from one direction will get nowhere on its own. Oh, it is painful to see how researchers are digging away from one direction, making as much headway as they can; and yet one has the sense, based on the broad, comprehensive outlook of spiritual science, that although they hold key things in their hands they do not see them correctly. It is like someone who holds a horseshoe in his hand, magnetic iron, but recognizes only the iron itself and not its magnetic properties. He takes a horseshoe and shoes a horse, well and good, but completely overlooks the other properties of iron. This is how modern scientists approach things. You see, a horseshoe does not actually have to be magnetic iron; it might be better if it weren't. Just think of everything that the discoveries of mainstream science could give rise to if people would really come towards each other with an open, unprejudiced mind. And then think of what actually happens in all domains of life. Research in the field of modern economics is helpless, endlessly helpless, however clever the people who pursue it. They have no inkling of what modern economics might become if they engaged with what spiritual science can offer. It is the same in absolutely every field. People hold iron in their hand, metaphorically, and have no idea it is magnetic, that it contains an invisible power. We must feel this fully. The imperatives of evolution are pushing people everywhere towards the spirit, but opinions are so narrow that they do not recognize or acknowledge it.

What we are currently experiencing in the context of modern history and related events is, truly, a sign of the need to acquire this feeling. And, as I recently said, our time is distinguished especially by the complexity of circumstances and events, and by the fact also that people's thinking cannot begin to encompass them. Everything is fragmenting. Each person finds his own method in his own specialized field, and is unaware that there is an historical imperative at work for all these things to be illumined by spiritual science.

Now I have often said that every physical event has its spiritual aspect. The extent of our affinity with the world becomes apparent when we are given back to the world, when we pass through the portal of death. What I have said about the etheric body relates to the time between birth and death. Things change when, held together still by the I and the astral body, the etheric body maintains its coherence for several days after death and then returns into the cosmos. Then it exerts an effect I have often described. Many such ether bodies of young people who have recently passed through the gate of death are currently in the spiritual sphere and remain there with all the spiritual content that accrues from a sacrificial death. They can offer help for the spiritualization of humanity in future. But there must also be human souls on earth who understand what hovers etherically around the human being as precious remains of the souls who give their lives in sacrifice. This will be a very real, not merely abstract process of memory. It will be up to those who remain here on earth to place these powers, available from young ether bodies, at the service of humanity in the way these powers seek. If human souls here do not have the maturity to do this, these powers will inevitably flow instead into ahrimanic-luciferic currents. My dear friends, spiritual science shows us not only insights and feelings, but also responsibilities, and they are ones we must faithfully enliven within us.

And fundamentally, the right outcome of reflections such as those we have engaged in today in various directions will be that we learn to feel the responsibility that the human soul also has towards developments in our time, and the events played out upon blood-fertilized soil. Only when, with genuine, serious feeling rather than in superficial sentiment, we find edification in considering the connection between the human being and the world, as spiritual science can teach it, will we rightly understand the words that have often been spoken here, and which should remind us of the feelings so necessary to modern people in view of the great events of our time:

From the courage of combatants
From the blood of slaughter
From the suffering of the bereaved

From the sacrificial deeds of the people
Spirit fruit will grow—
Will guide souls to awareness of the spirit,
To find their purpose in the spirit realm.

Lecture 8

2 May 1916

We have been reflecting on matters connected with occult brotherhoods, as we have called them, and last time we attempted to shed some light on one of the most significant symbols that reappears time and again in such fraternities: the rediscovery of the lost Word. This is a theme I could go on speaking about for years on end without ever exhausting it. Today I wish to add something to it that, in the world that knows little or nothing of spiritual science, could not be seen to have any connection with these occult brotherhoods, even though it informs them, flows through them as teaching, as rite, as world-view. In other words, we will speak of something that has a kind of connection with other subjects we have discussed, but in a way we can only understand if, at the end of our deliberations, we enter into the whole spiritual-scientific aspect of the question we will be dealing with today.

Here we must speak of a gloomy chapter in history which, specifically from the perspective we will explore today in connection with spiritual science, could also be entitled 'How religions sometimes arise'. You may remember from your schooldays that Henry VIII sat on the throne of England from 1509 to 1547. I imagine that you will remember him as someone of less than exemplary qualities. You will probably recall first and foremost that Henry VIII had six wives, two of whom he had executed, one because she no longer pleased him and the other really for the same reason. He wanted to execute his last wife too, the sixth, but this did not happen because she was a little more cunning than he was and got round him in a very coquettish speech that took place between them. Now as you may remember, he did not find it particularly easy to divorce his first wife as their marriage had been performed in accordance with all ecclesiastical rules, and, if all the outward customs and views of the world had been retained, Henry VIII's divorce would have had to be approved by Pope Clement VII. But the Pope found there was no reason to approve it, and continually refused the latter's petitions. These negotiations went to and fro for many years. The Pope refused to issue the divorce. A desperate situation! What does one do in such a case? Well it cannot always be done, but if one is Henry VIII one does it anyway: one establishes a new religion, founds a new Church. Thus Henry VIII established the new Church which, after some modifications, now lives on as the Anglican Church in England, which today has 20 million adherents. Henry VIII founded a new Church. When others do this, they develop a new teaching. But Henry VIII was not a clever man, as we can see from his conversation with his last wife, and he could not conceive of any new teaching as the basis for his Church. So he retained the old doctrines and founded a new Church; that is, he gradually persuaded the illustrious men of parliament, of the state, to agree no longer to regard the Pope as the head of the English Church but instead himself, Henry VIII. Through the famous Act of Supremacy that was passed at the time in England, Henry VIII—and thus also of course all of his successors—were declared to be the head of the Church. And so now he could get his divorce. He had achieved his goal, had he not? But perhaps it is legitimate to consider such a thing in its connection with the ongoing events of human evolution.

One of the men whose life was closely connected with the establishment of the new Church by Henry VIII was the renowned figure Thomas More.[64] As you no doubt know, he was the author of a book entitled *Utopia*, from which later utopian treatises took their name. You may remember a work in this vein by Bellamy.[65] People believe that a great many such utopian works have been written. As we will see in a moment, though, this is simply hearsay. Whenever someone writes about an ideal state of some kind which 'clever' people do not believe can be realized in practice—which is often also true—they are regarded as utopian after the country 'Utopia' which More describes in his work. In his Utopia More described various institutions of his—let us first say imaginary—state, and one of them was that religious tolerance for different confessions should prevail. This would therefore be a state that declares religion to be a private matter. There is a Redemptorist—a kind of Jesuit—who not so long ago wrote about Thomas More, and questioned whether Thomas More can really have believed that religious tolerance should hold sway in an ideal state. He was not wrong to ask this, but we should not forget either that it would be difficult for a Redemptorist to accept such a thing, for after all the Catholic Church beatified Thomas More, and this beatification was so greatly emphasized in the 1890s that one can see that the Catholic Church probably intends to make him a saint in the not too distant future.

Yes, my dear friends, in such an instance the Catholic Church is usually fully conversant with its historical records, for sanctification is a very laborious procedure, and one that draws fully on the files and records. Above all, the *Advocatus Regius* must accentuate everything that supports the belief that the person in question really was a holy man and that miracles were accomplished by him. You can't be made a Catholic saint without performing miracles. This whole procedure takes a long time. Then the so-called *Advocatus Diaboli* must speak too, proposing everything that could be held against the person in question. Now let us imagine, where sanctification of More is being considered, that the Church exposes itself to the danger of the *Advocatus Diaboli* objecting to his acknowledgement of religious tolerance! This would rule him out as a saint, wouldn't it! But there is really much else too that speaks against such a thing. And if we perused the biography of Thomas More in detail, in so far as it is known, we would find that there is a great deal that runs counter to the idea that More merely sought to preach religious tolerance through the vehicle of his work *Utopia*. And yet a prime trait of his may, after all, favour this view. Although a very pious man, Thomas More was, we can say, greatly favoured by fortune. He rose through various state appointments, became a member of parliament, and eventually Henry VIII's Lord Chancellor. For a saintly person, therefore, he achieved very high rank and status! Thomas More was, though, a pious man, as I said, and true to his conscience. And because of the special relationship he had with Henry VIII, he was required to give his verdict on the establishment of the new Church. And lo and behold, he did not endorse it, despite being not only a pious man but also pliant by nature. Thomas More refused to give his verdict, as Lord Chancellor, that Henry VIII's actions were right.

What does one do in such a situation if one is Henry VIII? Does one try to refute More's cogent arguments? No! One locks him up! After some to-ing and fro-ing, Henry had More thrown in the Tower. And it now fell to the very illustrious Court of Lords to decide what verdict to issue in his case, one of the first great sins under the new Church. My dear friends, it is not without interest to consider this verdict. More was led from the Tower to the illustrious court, and, with the aid of the Sheriff or state prosecutor William Pinkston, was condemned to be taken back to the Tower, and from there to be led forth again and paraded through the city of London in a tumbril to Tyburn, and to be hanged there—but only until he was half dead; then he was to be cut down and drawn and quartered. This meant that his body would be cut open while he was still alive, his innards taken out and burned and his body, apart from the head, divided into four parts and taken to the four ends of the city of London to be set up on spikes. As a terrible warning to the populace, his head was to be planted on a high spike on London Bridge. The illustrious Lords issued this verdict. In fact it was not carried out. The sentence was mercifully transmuted to mere beheading in the Tower, and the rest of it was not done, except for his head on a spike on London Bridge.

These are the historical facts concerning the end of Thomas More, and all this took place in the first half of the sixteenth century, really not such a very long time ago. And so we find it unlikely that Thomas More really propounded religious tolerance, doing so only in faithfulness to the Catholic Church and by way of resistance to Henry VIII, and in consequence being beatified as a martyr. It is clear therefore that Thomas More was not a rationalist of the Enlightenment type in the eighteenth century, not a free spirit who preached religious tolerance. But now let us look a little more closely at his work *Utopia*. This is however an elaborate and lengthy book, and I can only consider a couple of aspects relating to it.

Utopia contains ideas about an imaginary state which, we are told, was established on the far-away island of this name. The chief characteristics of this state would doubtless appear very instinctively desirable to a great many people. And yet there is much to show that merely dry, sober reason holds sway in this state. More describes, for instance, that all the houses are built on square foundations and are all identical, and that the streets, too, run in symmetrical arrangements. We are told that there are strict, one could say police-enforced injunctions stating how many youths and men, and maidens and women, may live in each house. If there are more than the prescribed number, some must leave and go to houses where there are fewer. Thus it is regarded as important that 'human material' is distributed evenly between the various houses. No one may acquire private property, but the economy is run on roughly communist lines. To avoid undue value being placed on private ownership in the form of gold, strict jurisdiction assures that each person can only earn a certain level of income, and everything over and above this is ceded to the state. In particular, no individual can acquire gold, all of which belongs to the state. But to avoid the idea that gold is especially desirable, any potential superfluity of it must be made into chains used to bind criminals; or otherwise it is distributed in the form of vessels used for menial purposes and suchlike. Thus gold must always be used in a way that counters any possible idea that it is of special value. Police powers are not completely unbounded in the state of Utopia. Thus it is expressly stated that there is no prescription regarding the number of children who may live in a house. House comrades take meals together and there are strict regulations about where the elders or youths should sit, who should serve and so forth.

This state is a fantasy rather than a future ideal. Its rational measures have, it is said, liberated the inhabitants to so great an extent from passions and desires that eating is not regarded as something done to please the palate—which would run counter to higher human development. Instead people are grateful for the blessing of enjoyment that accompanies the necessary consumption of food. You discern the subtle distinction, I am sure! And in particular the inhabitants of Utopia say that one should be grateful that hunger, which can be called an illness—since starving is as bad as falling ill—does not need to be cured by poisons and bitter remedies like other diseases, for otherwise one would have to consume them every day, and this would be unpleasant. It is also expressly ordained that at table, before eating, one should always read out or listen to a moral sermon given by one of the illustrious minds in Utopia, who in every other way also lead and guide the populace, and are at the same time priests.

There is also a discourse on the principles of worship in Utopia: how one can rightly serve God, even if it might please Him to be worshipped in different ways by different kinds of human being. And this was one of the reasons, perhaps the chief one, for Utopus, the founder of Utopia's state institutions, allowing full religious freedom. This religious freedom is really very reasonable, for it allows each person to express what he regards as his personal religious persuasion. However, the basic assumption here is that there is and can be no one in Utopia who would deny the existence of God, the immortality of the soul and judgement of the soul after death. These, writes More, are common principles of all religions, and everyone will acknowledge this. As the rational counterpart of this religious freedom, no one can insult, let alone, harm another person because of his religious views. To sum up, if one engages with the content of this book *Utopia* by Thomas More one finds it is founded on some curious outlooks that one can only regard as in every way rational. And wherever More inserts such things as I have mentioned, such as praise of the blessing of food being tasty, or similar, this is based on very specific assumptions that refute any suggestion that this was all ironic, that

More was saying the whole state was nonsense. What he sought to say, in fact, was that human beings are by no means always disposed to interpret rational teachings in a rational way, but instead distort them and make a caricature of them. There are in fact other societies, not in Utopia but elsewhere, in which for instance equal entitlement, equal acknowledgement of different religious communities holds sway, and in which people make efforts to realize rational doctrines, but where, nevertheless, not every individual always behaves rationally when he recounts the views and outlooks he has drawn from a rational realm. I will refrain from naming the 'far-off' places where such a thing occurs!

From a certain point of view, therefore, we should take Thomas More and his island of Utopia very seriously. We ought not to forget, either, that Thomas More was not only very pious from childhood on, but also someone who tirelessly practised his meditations and spiritual exercises. In the profoundest sense he took this practice seriously, spending hours every day conducting his soul into worlds of spirit by means of meditation. On the last day of his life, before being executed, More sent to his daughter from the Tower the secret matters of his spiritual practice, so that those who came for him would not find them in his cell. He continued his meditations until the very moment he was executed. This man, who took the development of his soul so seriously, repeatedly expressed the fact that, in accordance with the conditions of his day—this is a time of course when Protestantism was starting to spread—he sought nothing other than to be a true son of his Church, the Roman Catholic Church, that is. And for the sake of this Church he allowed himself to be executed.

There are various other aspects of the book *Utopia* that we should also consider. Primarily this: upon this distant island, said to be far removed from any geographical connection with Europe, ancient wise men landed only on a single occasion—wise Romans and Egyptians, who instructed Utopus to found the state in the way he did. Then we hear further curious things, contained at least in older editions of Thomas More's work. We are introduced to a certain alphabet consisting of right-angles and their combination, which is supposedly used in the Utopian script. If you look at the customary books today that reproduce the script of some Masonic orders, you cannot help seeing a strong resemblance between this, as used in some Masonic contexts, and the script More says is that of Utopia. More also gives certain phrases and sayings that supposedly govern modes of conduct in Utopia; and these combine Latin, Greek and Hebrew texts in a rather remarkable, albeit very veiled way, which is reminiscent of certain formulae used in occult brotherhoods. Then another curious thing is said: it is expressly stated that Roman and Egyptian wise men landed on the island, but nothing of Christianity arrived there. Everything becomes more and more mysterious. Remember, Thomas More was a pious Catholic, someone devoted to his spiritual practices, but he wrote a book, *Utopia*, describing an island with institutions which he undoubtedly meant seriously, not ironically at all, but in which Christianity does not figure.

What is one to make of this man? How can we understand him? Well, we need only recall the fact that he undertook a spiritual practice. If we give proper consideration to various things he said, which are connected with his spiritual exercises, we will find that Thomas More really did get somewhere with them. But now remember also the era in which More lived. Recall the fact that this period in England was dominated by the king, Henry VIII, in the sixteenth century, and thus shortly after the transition from the fourth to the fifth post-Atlantean age. Not long ago I described this period of transition to you when I spoke of Pico della Mirandola, Savonarola and so forth, trying to show how this era comes to expression in certain individuals. But in Thomas More, too, we have someone at the beginning of the fifth post-Atlantean era, a time whose most intrinsic aspect was the fading of ancient occult capacities. These faded in the general populace but were still available for those who engaged in spiritual exercises such as those practised by Thomas More.

Now a certain thing can happen: through spiritual exercises, as is really always the endeavour of a proper practice, we can at the same time come to see the connection between our ordinary human conception of daily life and what rises from the depths of the soul as vision of a higher, spiritual world. But something else can happen as well, and this is what occurred in the case of Thomas More. Through the practice of his spiritual exercises, More was transposed in sleep into the astral world, and was there able to have quite different experiences from an ordinary person who does not undertake such spiritual exercises in the astral world. And yet he could not bring these experiences back with him in a directly conscious way. He was able to experience a great many things in the world of spirit, and though he could not bring them back into consciousness, he did bring them back with him, and what he brought back in this way he described in his book *Utopia*. This book is only mere fantasy—forgive me—for very clever people. For someone conversant with reality, it embodies a spiritual experience in which the connection between the latter and ordinary thinking has not come to full consciousness. But such spiritual experiences are all the more compelling in consequence. One can be a good, pious Catholic, and even be so pious that one is later beatified and made a saint, is martyred in the Catholic cause, and yet can still write down the spiritual experiences one has had on the astral plane—for one has experienced them, and such experience exerts an elemental power.

It has struck me that translators of the book have often also tried to translate the name of the island of Utopia. In German, the name 'Nirgendheim' has been imposed on it, or in other words 'the island that does not exist'. Clearly those who do such a thing have understood nothing of the whole business. You have to grasp what is at work here to properly translate the name Utopia. You see, if you actually enter the astral world, the laws of ordinary, three-dimensional space as these obtain here no longer apply to astral experience. These laws, of which we learn in geometry, really only hold good for the outer, sensory world, and we cannot speak of what we experience in the astral world in the same way. We can use spatial designations metaphorically in this case, but must at the same time know that such pictures have a different meaning. It is impossible to speak of experiences in the astral world in the same way as we speak of things and beings in the world of the senses. It would be completely meaningless to speak of the astral world as one does of things and entities in the sensory world—that a lady sits here and another over there, say. Such thinking cannot be applied directly to the astral realm, but there instead we become aware of being in a non-localized world where we are compelled to negate the spatial localization of the sensory, physical world. And therefore we should translate the name Utopia as Non-Locality. It is this that conveys the quality of the world into which Thomas More gazed.

What especially did he encounter in this world? It is scarcely surprising that he met here something that resembles the principles and customs that hold sway in occult societies. As we said, these customs of occult brotherhoods originate in ancient wisdom, deriving also from ancient observations of this astral world. This vision faded, and then lived on in various fraternities as tradition, preserved by people who knew of such things as history related them, and as they were passed on pictorially and, if you like, by dictation, but who themselves had no direct insight into them any more. But when people such as Thomas More undertook spiritual exercises, they were able to pass into the world of spirit, and something similar came towards them there, which they then described. It is scarcely surprising therefore that what lived in many occult brotherhoods as a doctrine as yet untouched by Christianity was also described by Thomas More. He conveys this as something that informs the state institutions on the island of Utopia, originating in ancient Egyptian and Roman but not yet Christian sources. We are here in the domain of occult societies that see their lofty importance precisely in the fact that they originated as Egyptian orders, and still further back.

And now let us connect what has been said here with our knowledge of the deepest nerve of the Christian world-view. I have often spoken of this. Christianity is of course founded on the fact that a spiritual potency we call by the name of Christ descended to indwell the body of Jesus, spiritualizing it entirely in the thirtieth year of his life. Jesus had gradually acquired the capacity for this to happen by passing through the souls of the two Jesus boys. What actually occurred? A spiritual power that was not interwoven with earthly evolution until the Mystery of Golgotha from then on united with this evolution, first dwelling in the body of Jesus of Nazareth and then passing into Earth evolution through the Mystery of Golgotha, uniting ever more profoundly and completely with it as our evolution continues. We have often spoken of this. From spiritual heights where it once resided, this power descended to the physical, earthly plane. Thus whenever a wise and truly clairvoyant initiate of ancient times—this too I have mentioned in the past—raised himself into spiritual heights in the era before the Mystery of Golgotha, he naturally encountered the Christ there. At this time, those able to speak of the Christ therefore became prophets who foretold his coming, for they found him there in worlds of spirit, and saw him in a sense on his way towards the earth, descending as sun spirit so as gradually to become the spirit of the earth. Thus they could look ahead to a future moment in earth's evolution when what they saw only in lofty spiritual heights would unite with the earth. No sign of the Christ was to be found on earth before the Mystery of Golgotha, however far one searched, however deeply one plumbed all that might be known of it. For this reason, of course, ancient earth knowledge amongst peoples and cultures before the time of the Mystery of Golgotha did not possess Christ. But when the initiates of these mysteries had attained to a certain level, Christ's coming to earth was made known to them.

Think how different everything is now since the Mystery of Golgotha, the very opposite of circumstances before it. Since the Mystery of Golgotha, if we enquire into earthly evolution, we find Christ interwoven with the whole history of the peoples imbued with Christianity. To give an account of history without reference to this is really nonsensical. Even the historian Ranke felt this,[66] asking himself at a great old age whether history has any meaning at all if one does not trace the Christ impulse through all its diverse phenomena. But in the worlds into which one can ascend, from which Christ descended to unite with earthly evolution, Christ is no longer so directly present. From those heights one must then look down again upon the earth to see how he united with it.

You see, what I have said is a reality that underlies the terrible fear that some religious confessions have of occultism. Naturally they understand nothing of true occultism, nor of how the Christ can be found through true spiritual science. However, they do sometimes make the acquaintance of that shallow form of occultism that states Christ is *only* on earth and that one must strip away this Christ when one rises into elevated spiritual heights, since he is not to be found there. This is the fear that certain orders of priests have—that through an occultism they know only in this shallow form people could gain access to this secret; it has deeper Christian aspects than they are aware of if one knows the facts, but can endanger Christianity if one knows only of a shallower occultism. This is why the Church is so much in conflict with occultism, a reality on which its antagonism is founded.

Thus we really must hold on to what can be learned of Christ within our earthly existence. I have so often spoken of this. When we cross the threshold and rise into worlds of spirit, we must not forget what can be learned about Christ by occult means when we are still on earth. That is a deeper spiritual science compared to a shallow form that tells people either that Christ is only present to earthly vision, or embodies himself in Alcyone and suchlike.

Now let us put ourselves in the shoes of Thomas More, who undertook exercises that enabled him to gain full clarity about Christ. When subsequently the world was in danger of suffering confusion in relation to Christ, then the Jesuits—albeit through still greater, colossal confusion and error—tried to prevent this with their Jesuit exercises. Thomas More did not practise these kinds of Jesuit exercises, but ones instead that really did enable him to experience the whole reality of Christ Jesus. If he had entered the world of spirit in full consciousness, naturally he would have perceived Christ there and have seen how he had descended to the earth. But he was unable to establish a complete, conscious context of understanding, and this resulted in him writing down half unconsciously what he had experienced in the spiritual world where Christ, however, was not present. He expressed this by saying that Christianity had not yet arrived on the island of Utopia. And now we can also understand why *Utopia* contains something that would contradict all Thomas More's honesty, authenticity and love of truth if he had composed it in full consciousness, I mean from the perspective of ordinary consciousness. He could never have written about the institutions of religious tolerance. But he did write down something whose whole foundation did not fully enter his conscious awareness. Religious tolerance was implicit in all that he perceived in Utopia, in the sense that the particular form of worship and ritual is of no account. To a very great degree Thomas More was compelled to recognize two souls living in his breast, one here in the physical world and the other, living during sleep, which experiences a quite different world into which it cannot carry the Christ impulse. If we seek the basic tenor of feeling at work in a man such as Thomas More, inspiring him to write a work such as *Utopia*, we find the following. Occult perceptions and insights that are not fully experienced, laborious inroads into the world of spirit as Thomas More doubtless engaged in, are accompanied by anxieties which the soul does not experience as such; instead what is really a sense of fear remains more or less hidden in the subconscious. Then one seeks other reasons for one's experiences and actions: a masked anxiety that in conscious awareness is transformed into something quite different. The fear that Thomas More had was transformed into something quite different. As occult experiences churned in his sensibility this gave rise to fear in him. And what would this fear have become if it had risen consciously into his soul? What would Thomas More have told himself? Let us assume for a moment as hypothesis something that cannot have happened: that into Thomas More's full consciousness had entered the thought that he saw something—which he later described in Utopia—in the astral, elemental world and wished to describe it. He wishes to describe it. Why? If he had fully understood the fear in him and, through writing, had perhaps succeeded in dispelling it, the following thoughts would have occurred to him. In the present world era one must, with every fibre of one's soul, do everything to fully perceive the Christ impulse and sustain it for and within humanity's evolution. But if people could somehow return to an ancient clairvoyance, they would see something that appears as his Utopia and contains nothing of the Christ impulse. Oh guard yourself, this fear would have told him, from anything that can divert you from the path of the Christ impulse! This is what he would have told himself, and what he would have written if he had truly been able to feel his fear. But he did not fully experience it; it remained in his subconscious. And therefore he wrote down what he did as he saw it inwardly, and simply left the world with the riddle of this apparent irreconcilable contradiction between what he saw and his whole nature as a conscientious, candid person devoted to the truth.

But having considered this, let us put ourselves in the position of the members of certain occult brotherhoods. Thomas More wrote *Utopia*. He is already held in suspicion but this in itself would not have induced the illustrious lords to reach the verdict they did in his case. But remember that he is already regarded with suspicion for having acted against Henry VIII's intentions, and that the lords were also under some compulsion. Now let us assume that the majority of those sitting in the Court of Lords belonged to occult brotherhoods. What could and must they tell themselves? And what, from their perspective, was even fully required by their conscience? This man Thomas More had written the book *Utopia*—and this they saw as a betrayal of the secrets they were obliged to preserve! A complete betrayal. In his book stand many hints of all kinds about these secrets. Not only is the book a betrayal of them, but it shows how these things work on in the outward culture of mankind. It would have been clear to these people that if he had been initiated into an occult fraternity and had attained a particular degree within it he would have had to swear that he would not betray its secrets; but this is what Thomas More had done. The wording of one of the oaths customarily sworn at the time in these societies is almost identical in its formulation to the verdict passed on Thomas More in London. Anyone who attained a certain degree within an occult fraternity in those times would have had to swear an oath that was very close indeed to the words of the court in London when the lords sentenced More. He was thus regarded as having betrayed, in his *Utopia*, the secrets of an occult brotherhood.

You see, my dear friends, that to understand history it really is not sufficient to draw only on the 'accepted fable' that people nowadays think of as history. Instead we need to delve deeper into humanity's development and try to see what plays into human souls. Something like the death of Thomas More stands before us as a great emblem, a cipher we must decode in order to understand what is at work in history. It can only be deciphered if we come to see how supersensible impulses play into historical realities, and this can only be done through spiritual science. There are many, many moments in history that require this insight. A great deal presented to us as the 'fable convenue' of history can only be fathomed when we know a little of what was playing in to the souls of those involved in the events in question.

And the great demands that our current age is making of us include this: that we shed a customary thoughtlessness about certain things. You see, ultimately no one can objectively assess the value of something like the Anglican Church without knowing what 'saint' has founded it, without knowing that there lived in the mind of the man who established it the capacity to execute two of his wives and to attempt this with a third. Clearly such actions are a prelude to saintliness! When we reflect on such things properly and place them in the right light—which can also teach us a thing or two about conditions we are now living in—we will be compelled to acknowledge other more hidden and secret aspects connected with them. The important, hugely revealing fact connected with the composition of Thomas More's *Utopia* and with his whole life is interwoven, you see, with historical events at the time.

Now, my dear friends, we might also wonder what would happen if some indiscrete person were to pass on what has been said here today to a Jesuit, and what an *Advocatus Diaboli* might then say about it at some later canonization of Thomas More. He might perhaps raise grave charges against More. But his opponent, the good Advocatus, could reply that everything occult is the work of the devil. And if it could be shown that Thomas More drew his *Utopia* from occult depths, he might be said to be all the saintlier for having miraculously resisted the diabolical attacks contained therein.

But what I wished to say is this: the fundamental theme, the leitmotif if you like, of the lectures given here, is that spiritual realities and spiritual matters play into outer historical events, and that the nature of our fateful times, of present, gravely incisive events, asks us to understand this. Next time I will speak further of this.

Lecture 9

9 May 1916

As previous lectures have shown, I will try to use the time we have for these reflections to shed light from spiritual science on aspects of human life; and this is because we are living, of course, in a time when it is particularly necessary to hone our understanding of what is at work in human life and history. Now I have sought to suggest that in occult brotherhoods, fraternities that look back to all kinds of occult insights, the way in which the human soul is engaged and worked upon is different from what is usual, and also basically desirable in our era. Last time I spoke of the case of Thomas More, his *Utopia*, trying to show that what we call history is a *fable convenue* full of all kinds of legends, all sorts of views tailored and curtailed, but that we can inform it with truth if we take account of influences playing in to human life from supersensible worlds.

Now today let us first ask ourselves how teachings of resurrection, as I spoke of in relation to rediscovery of the lost Word, can act upon the human soul in certain rites and services common in occult brotherhoods. How is it that these work on the soul in a particular, distinctive way?

This is very closely connected with how the human soul is generally influenced in our time, and increasingly will be the longer we pass in the fifth post-Atlantean age in which we now live. We are still in the first third of this era at present. The way in which influences act upon the human soul in this fifth post-Atlantean epoch should therefore first be considered. During this epoch all human endeavours are focused on excluding certain things that were once innate and natural to people. If we look at a work of natural science from a period not so far back, a work, say, by Albertus Magnus[67] from the thirteenth and fourteenth centuries, you can see that this way of looking at the natural world is now very alien to modern people. Why is this? It is because in those times a person still held the view that certain elemental powers were at work in the world of nature around them, powers, if no longer beings, of a spiritual, etheric kind. The chief trait of modern thinking is the rejection of everything the senses cannot see. Nothing of a spiritual, etheric nature is acknowledged. We can only understand works such as those by Albertus Magnus in the thirteenth century if we realize that he still saw spiritual powers everywhere at work in his physical surroundings. In our modern, scientific age, the fact that we only absorb into our thoughts what we perceive in the outer world through our senses, what is available to sensory perception, exerts an important influence not only on scientific views but also on all human thinking and conception. This outlook filters down into the minds of ordinary folk. It is of course quite wrong to use the term 'spiritual science'* as it is used in ordinary discourse today in reference to aesthetics, art history, and even sociology. Spiritual science inevitably involves the spirit, or in other words everything that does not unfold in the sensory realm. But what history recounts does occur in this realm, even though it originates in thoughts, feelings and so forth. Such disciplines should not rightly be called 'spiritual sciences' but 'sensory sciences'. Thus the characteristic of our fifth post-Atlantean epoch, initially, is that human thinking only absorbs and acknowledges what originates in outward, sensory nature.

It would be wrong to think that one should attack the nature of this fifth post-Atlantean epoch, denigrating its coarse, materialistic

---

* Translator's note: 'Geisteswissenschaft', always translated 'spiritual science' in Steiner's works, can be used more generally in German to refer to disciplines that embrace the humanities.

ideas. This says really very little unless we can also, at the same time, counter such ideas with something equally real. You see, we can say that this fifth post-Atlantean era exists specifically to develop materialism, to discard from human thinking anything that does not enter us from the sense world. Only by giving ourselves up once in more than two millennia—which is how long this era lasts—to a worldly life that excludes elemental powers can we possibly attain our full freedom, fully unfolding from within us our true spiritual activity and efficacy. The excesses of materialism in this first third of two millennia have occurred only because we are still at the beginning of this era. The flood of sensory perceptions has inundated us and we have not yet succeeded in allowing the spirit to emerge by eliciting it within us. Through true spiritual science this spirituality must still emerge.

The previous epoch, the Graeco-Roman, had a different mission. At that time people were still tuned to perception of the elemental, etheric-spiritual powers in their surroundings, and, having perceived them, could allow these to work upon them. In the way people related to each other, too, it was assumed that we are enveloped in an elemental, spiritual atmosphere. During these 2160 years that preceded our fifth post-Atlantean era, the human body was prepared as an instrument for our present thought-oriented and purely sensory grasp of outer reality. The work accomplished upon the human being during the Graeco-Roman epoch was one that concentrated more upon the body itself. This shaped our body so that now, in our current period, we can think about the sensory phenomena we perceive. For example, when people taught others back then, either in the mysteries themselves or in institutions dependent on them, as all teaching centres and sites of worship were in the Graeco-Roman epoch, it was not a matter of telling people things that would then inform their outlook and convictions, as is inevitably so today, but rather to give them something directly that worked upon their bodies. If someone today undertook such a thing, trying to convey through his teaching something that works directly upon the human body, this would be impermissible and at odds with our modern zeitgeist. The human being today wishes to preserve his body from direct influence, and rightly so, for it is inherent in the nature of our time. Only a person's soul should be affected and influenced. Anything else is, basically, impermissible magical influence, although this was certainly still allowable in the Graeco-Roman era. At that time the human being's corporeal instrument was still softer, more flexible, pliant, and work still needed to be done upon it. Now it has grown harder, and teaching or instruction instead addresses the soul.

But to work in a formative way upon a human body that is still pliant, we cannot resort to things gained solely from the outer world of the senses. The Graeco-Roman epoch could not have fulfilled its mission with the contents of our modern science. If Copernican astronomy had been taught back then, or Darwinism, rather than preparing the human body for the fifth post-Atlantean epoch it would have become desiccated. It would have been shaped wrongly. And this was a quite different science, therefore, which instead of conveying a kind of photography of natural existence, as our modern science does, presented symbols. Instead of the kinds of experiments done today, empirical science, it offered rituals and a kind of sacramentalism. You see, with sacramentalism, rites of worship, symbolic-mythic accounts, one reaches into regions of human experience that are quite different from what we possess today in our natural laws, in the Copernican world-view, in Darwinism.

Now as I suggested, these brotherhoods retained the ancient symbols, symbolism, sacramentalism, ritual acts and services; and these are perpetuated in our day and can influence people in the way I intimated. One aspect of human nature especially falls under this sway, though it should not be exposed to much influence if we remain in the realm of what is permissible. Remaining in the realm of the allowable, one should clothe one's words of teaching or communication in such a way that they pass only into the other's ear, leaving a person free to form his own view and conviction in response. Everything should basically be done in this way. Thus our teaching or communication works solely into the physical body, and if all runs normally, this body will not be reconfigured in consequence, not altered from the shape and imprint it was taught in the fourth post-Atlantean epoch, the Graeco-Roman. But by using symbols, sacramentalism, rites and rituals, one works deeper, right into the etheric body. In other words, one directly influences the whole nature and direction of a person's thinking. In a sense one resorts in one's teaching or communication, as one elaborates something in one's surroundings, to an element that works into the other's etheric body, and thus directs his thinking in a certain direction.

Now this is what happens primarily in the occult brotherhoods I have been speaking of. But another, quite different kind of fraternity exists, one that should also be called 'occult' but pursues the same thing in a quite different field. In the way these work, they too knowingly reach deeper into human nature. Occult fraternities of this kind include the Jesuit Order for example. This order is certainly founded on occult insights, as I explained in the cycle of lectures I gave in Karlsruhe.[68] On that occasion I specifically described the exercises a Jesuit pupil is obliged to undertake in order to become a Jesuit. These exercises involve the person who is speaking or enacting rites of worship intervening not in the human etheric body but the astral body. All Jesuit schooling focuses on giving the Jesuit the strength to shape his words, the way in which he speaks, so that what he presents or what he does, steals its way into another person's astral impulses.

Now Jesuit influence is not limited to the presence of Jesuits in one place or another. There are channels in human life through which one can exert an influence even in places where one is prohibited from staying. And if people sense certain dangers in Jesuitism, they should not think that this will be avoided by forbidding Jesuits from dwelling in a particular location. This demonstrates a lack of awareness of what is at work, and awareness only dawns through the kind of knowledge that only spiritual science can offer. But it is not so easy to show how Jesuitism exerts its influence since this involves all kinds of unknown channels, which people are reluctant to credit. I would therefore first like to give one example of what Jesuitism does whenever it can pursue its impulses in a robust and unimpeded way, doing everything its methods allow to work its way into the human astral body.

A very good example of this is something that occurred at the transition between the fourth and fifth post-Atlantean epoch: the founding of the Jesuit state in Paraguay in 1610. How did this come about? Now, my dear friends, you know that after the discovery of America and the rush to exploit its resources and treasures, including gold, a period followed during which the Europeans who made their way there felt very happy in the New World, but the native American Indians much less so. Many accounts have been written of how this poor indigenous population were treated by civilized Europeans. And in one region of South America, Paraguay, where European culture penetrated in a way that rode roughshod over the native Americans, larger numbers of Jesuits appeared one day with the intention of treating the Guaranis, a native tribe in Paraguay, in ways that were, in their view, a good deal better than the treatment they received from other Europeans.

Now the Jesuits did not know the language of the Guaranis, nor did the latter speak any of the languages spoken by the Jesuits, and not Latin either. And therefore this did not work in the ordinary way in which people seek to influence things. What did the padres do, therefore, when they appeared in Paraguay in larger numbers? They navigated the rivers on barges and ships, reaching wild regions inhabited only by the native peoples. It was hoped that they would fall under the sway of spreading European capitalism there. And so the Jesuits sailed down rivers into the wilderness and tried above all to have beautiful music playing around them, music, song, and to mingle into this musical element, into their singing, all kinds of things with which they were very conversant through their own practices. Along with the waves of music and song, they spread something else: a ritual, sacramental element. And this resulted in the Indians approaching them voluntarily, gathering in large numbers; and before long the padres were accompanied by huge crowds of Indians in many different regions of the land, and were able to found villages, forming them into a kind of state and establishing their own forms of organization. From 1610 onwards, this renowned Jesuit state developed in Paraguay, the majority of whose inhabitants were the native Indians along with the Jesuits who governed and led them. Churches were built, one for instance at a location founded under the name of Saint Xavierus, that could hold four to five thousand people. In this Jesuit state everything was strictly governed and regulated, but everywhere under the sway of ritual and worship. Everywhere, in the smallest settlement, care was taken that music embedded in ritual should exert its effect in the form of services and worship, and that the day was carefully apportioned and human actions regulated by the ringing of the church bell. The time for this or for that was marked by the ringing bell. To mention just one example: rather than merely getting up in the morning, washing and then going to work in the fields, the church bell rang and this indicated the start of the day. One got up, gathered in the village square, and was received with music. In the middle of the square stood either an image of the Holy Virgin or some other saint, understanding of whom had previously been inculcated in the Indians through sermons delivered by the Jesuit priest. Here, first of all, a kind of service of worship was held. In prayer, the people gazed up to heaven. Then the whole train began to move forward, with the statue of the saint or the Virgin Mary carried in front. Thus they walked to the fields and then worked. After sufficient work had been done, they carried the image of the saint or Virgin back to the marketplace again and, as the bells rang, the people were dismissed. Everything was imbued with ritual, symbolic actions, even the work in the fields itself was accompanied by ritual actions in which certain Jesuit priests had been instructed. Everything was imbued and infused with ritual.

The whole interaction between the padres and the Indians was directed towards an influence on their astral bodies. All their astral bodies were correspondingly prepared and the whole Jesuit state in Paraguay was basically imbued with an astral aura in consequence of the symbolism, the sacramentalism, the ritual actions of the Jesuits, governed of course in a way that the Jesuits wished. And in some ways very striking things were achieved by this means. Remember, the indigenous people had previously been wild tribes preoccupied with hunting and suchlike; and within a short time they were made 'intelligent' in the sense the Jesuits understood it. These people soon became able to make everything needed by their Jesuit leaders. The padres in fact soon attracted the rancour of other European rulers there and needed an army. In a relatively short time they organized an army, some of whose officers were Indians, not all Europeans. They organized an army that successfully broke a blockade which England tried to enforce against Paraguay. Circumstances were simpler than today, but all this occurred. The Guaranis quickly learned to make everything the Jesuits needed such as muskets and cannons. They also learned to make European musical instruments, including organs; they learned painting and stone carving to a level that would have graced any church in Spain.

But now consider the astral aura in which all this was plunged! Those who interacted directly with the Indians and went about among them were only intermediaries of the Jesuits. The padres themselves lived strictly apart, held all the reins in their hands, governed and regulated everything, but were only glimpsed in their richly adorned and golden costumes at mass and ceremonial gatherings. The Indians, we can say, saw them only as theatrical apparitions in a cloud of incense. No wonder, then, that the Indians looked up to them as if to higher beings. And all this was part of the desired effect of working directly into their astral bodies.

The moral condition of this Jesuit state truly does not seem to have been particularly bad. It is said, at least, that in the most numerous instances the Indians, who had no need to fear that anyone would have reported them if they did something wrong, were so plagued by their conscience that they reported themselves for any misdeeds. And care was taken that any punishment meted out was one which the person punished could agree with and accept.

I do not know whether application of this principle in our society would lead to happiness. But people fail to understand to what extent ways of thinking have changed over the centuries. Remember that roughly at this time the Italian Campanella[69] describes a state similar to that imagined by Thomas More. Campanella certainly thought his idea was feasible, describing the state he conceived as something that could well be realized at that epoch. But his basic premise and condition for his state is that no one should be hanged if he has not agreed to be so. This is not a joke, and is seen as such only in our own time.

Another thing the Jesuits achieved in their state was to reflect on the problem of how much all should work to serve the needs of an enclosed human society. Everyone worked in the way I described, except for the Jesuits themselves who concerned themselves with government. And they found that a person need only work two days a week, for a relatively normal time on each of those days; and this would produce everything needed by the community. Thus the Jesuits only let the people work two days a week for themselves and everything produced during the other working days was surrendered to the state. This was used also as Jesuit propaganda throughout the rest of the world. Well, we can thank the Jesuits for the weekend too! For more than a century, therefore, the Jesuits found it possible to work everywhere in the world by using this principle of the Jesuit state—that people need work only five days a week, or at least four days. On Sundays they let people rest, except that they had to attend church and watch and listen to all the ceremonies. What the Jesuits garnered in this working week supported their economic activities everywhere else in the world.

But in the end the Europeans who dominated America, and were not Jesuits but were part of the growing capitalist surge, considered this Jesuit economy too backward. On 22 July 1768, mounted squadrons appeared on the scene in numbers sufficient to imprison the Jesuits. This marked the end of the Jesuit state. Thus it lasted from 1610 to 1768, and developed its activities as I have described.

I wished to describe this to you only to show what can be achieved by developing methods that influence the human astral body. Naturally these methods were easier to apply to the Indians than to other communities or societies, which would not have succumbed so easily to them. What would people around here do, do you think, if unknown people came sailing up the Elbe and tried to use music to control them? Back then it was easier to use such approaches since the people involved were relatively primitive. And the further back we go in humanity's evolution, the more susceptible the human astral and etheric bodies are to such influence and control. These wild tribes retained something of a former pliancy, primarily in relation to their physical bodies. If one wishes to exert such an influence one has to work upon the astral body; but the resonances of this astral body act in turn upon the physical body, and that is where the influence actually lies. When you speak to a European, you send words into his ear, but his brain resonates with them as determined by the person's whole education and the life circumstances in which he is rooted. This was not so in the case of the Indians. The Jesuits worked upon or into their astral body, and the brain resonated along with this. You can say that through these musical elements and other ritual acts the Indians were harnessed into all the resonances emanating from these rites, so that in a sense they became living parts of a common astral aura.

We Europeans are better off, are we not? You see, our heads have grown more dense, and are not so easily influenced. That is clear. But everything, my dear friends, is different in degree in every individual. And while one cannot work in the same way upon a highly civilized population in Europe in the same way as has been described, to a lesser degree it is still possible to work into a human being's etheric or astral body so that this effect vibrates on into the physical body. But an influence of this kind ought not to emanate from an individual; for even if he were to veil himself in a cloud of incense in either a physical or spiritual sense, the effect upon European people would no longer be very great. What the Jesuits did simply by leading their workers physically into the fields is not something that always has to be done physically. Where, as I said, the body has grown more dense than in the Indians this cannot be achieved with people physically, since people will not allow themselves to succumb to this. They reject such faith in authority and will not tolerate it!

But this type of authority practised by the Jesuits, invested in a physical human being, has been fading during the first third of the fifth post-Atlantean epoch. Yet as it fades, faith in authority increases correspondingly when the beings exerting an influence are less physical, or not physical at all, but merely work *through* a physical person. As we know there are ahrimanic beings whom the general population think of as the devil; and whereas the authority of a bodily person is avoided like the plague across the so-called civilized world, the authority of ahrimanic beings working through human actions is far from anathema. To modify a phrase from *Faust* only very slightly, we can say: 'The scholar never notices the devil, even when he has him by the collar.'

And these ahrimanic beings, acting amongst us invisibly, inevitably have their own methods and means that are different from those, say, of the Jesuits in Paraguay in the seventeenth and eighteenth centuries. The Jesuits could work upon the Indians' astral body, and their physical body was soft and pliant. Now one has to work differently. In particular, one has to take account of the fact that human thinking as such is influenced, that one enters the thought orientation of people and exerts a power that they do not notice. I don't mean that people are doing this; people are usually the vehicle for it, used by ahrimanic beings who enter the thought orientation of human beings, their ways of thinking. Then when people adopt a view, they think this is through their own conviction. Superficially this is true, but if you look deeper you find it is not. When a particular view or judgement is buzzing around in public life so that—if you will forgive the expression—it lubricates its way into people's feelings and sentiments, people believe that they have grasped it rationally. In truth they have only adopted it into their habits of thought. It has insinuated itself. And then people think of course that the idea or thought is their own, and not based on any faith in authority. But they completely fail to notice how it has insinuated itself into their soul.

How does such a thing occur? Well, it may happen for instance in the following way. As time goes by, through all sorts of habits of thought—for if you trace the historical development of such things you will find that they really do not emerge from rational insights—a view forms about what science is, about what a strict scientific method should be. In the same way this view about the nature of scientific rigour merges with a requirement that this scientific rigour must proceed from an arcane or esoteric location—from a university or similar. Whatever does not emanate from such a place does not insinuate itself so fully into hearts and minds. Into these habits of thought all kinds of names and nomenclatures insinuate themselves. Naturally there is no faith in authority, but nor do people believe in anything else either, except perhaps what a renowned person may have said about it. A current of views and judgements composes itself, compounded of all such elements. And this forms a real riverbed, a channel, for Ahriman—a river for Ahriman to sail up! Ahriman can now let his powers flow up it, for he cannot sail up into really conscious life and conscious thinking. If one stands guard at the gate of one's consciousness, Ahriman cannot enter. If we do not stand guard, but in the way I have indicated allow ourselves to be carried along on a current of thought habits, Ahriman can gain free entry everywhere, and do as he pleases with us. One has very little protection indeed against this if one has thrown one's whole self into this current, for instance if, from the earliest childhood, one has been inculcated with 'rigorously scientific' disciplines.

Let us assume, therefore, that someone has been trained from early infancy, brought up in accordance with a strict psychological method. Psychology has become very popular in our time. Eduard von Hartmann wrote a history of modern psychology in 1901.[70] At the very beginning of this work he speaks of something that modern psychology no longer mentions since it is seen as outmoded, unscientific. He says, for instance:

> Only in the first half of this period [the second half of the nineteenth century] do some theistic philosophers still adhere not only to the immortality of a self-aware substance of soul but also to a vestige of non-determinate freedom, though mostly

> they make do with positing this heartfelt desire of theirs only as an academic possibility.

Such a view has ceased entirely in recent times. It is self-evident that in modern psychology no attention is given either to the question of immortality nor to that of whether human freedom even exists. These are no longer even regarded as scientific questions!

I don't know whether you have seen the newspapers in recent days. The particular political slant of your paper is unimportant here; you can read many column inches in every newspaper of any persuasion about a lecture on psychology that was given at a very scholarly psychology society in Berlin. A Dr Loewenstein, a very scholarly psychologist of our time, was speaking there about the psychology of a personal column! One must of course be fully conversant with scholarly methods to be able to apply them to any and every field in a rigorously scientific manner. Just think what a rich field of scientific exploration is offered if one knows that a notice is being published in a paper in which someone says he is looking to marry: that he seeks a girl with quite specific qualities. Then one sits back and waits for the letters to pour in, which give expression to the psyche, the soul of a certain number of girls or women. What deep insights one can gain in this way into the life of the soul! Surely it is far more dignified to speak of such insights than to discuss the immortality of the soul in the old way, or human freedom. The latter subjects are discussed only by those who fail to understand the demands of strict science! One needs a certain flair for experimentation if one is to handle such matters in an entirely scientific manner of course. You see, the strict scientific method says that chance or random observations do not lead to—well I don't know if you've heard of the expression—'strong inference'. A strong inference is always the basis for empirical discovery. This means that cases should not be handled in a way that provides us with chance observations whose conclusions could be misleading. One must be an experimenter. In the same way that a chemist tries to discover nature's secrets through his experiments, one has to try to deduce the secrets of the life of the psyche, which can be revealed when marriage invitations are published in the papers, and girls write back.

But how does one become an experimenter? That is also something the papers explored in their many column inches on the subject. Someone is a scholar, a psychologist—not of course of the old school in which the soul's immortality is still discussed; he discusses the psychology of the personal column and experiments by posting his own marriage advertisement! As the paper relates, this is first done by announcing that one seeks a younger girl, with idealistic traits, who is not so very concerned about outward appearances and lifestyle. Then one gets the notice published and waits for all the replies, of which there are many. This scholarly gentleman received over two hundred replies to his announcement, and this of course gives us helpful glimpses into the respondents' psyches. It allows us to judge the effect of such an announcement on the soul. That is the first step. But to have a really 'strong inference' and in other words to see the problem from the other perspective, one inserts a second announcement in which one no longer seeks an idealistic wife but a smart, good-looking one, who cares a good deal about appearances. Again one receives over two hundred replies!

The scholarly chap then set to work in a thorough manner, tracing the history and development of marriage advertisements. It emerges that the first such advertisement appeared over a hundred years ago in a Hamburg newspaper. Just think what a contribution to scholarship this is! We even discover how long the advert was—much longer than nowadays, the length of a whole feature. Gradually there were more and more of them, offering a fund of source material for modern psychological research! The researcher, it is said, counted how many marriage advertisements appeared in two newspapers on two successive days, in order to obtain a 'strong inference'. He did not only do this once but repeatedly. This is all done statistically by counting up the findings from many sources and finding the arithmetical mean, thus by dividing. We must of course always resort to scientific measurements. As far as I remember, there were seven hundred such marriage announcements on two successive days in two newspapers.

Here we find therefore a very fertile field for scientific rigour. Actually I do not know if the scholar really stated what the newspapers reported him as saying; but according to them he said that this matter had a deeper significance. In his view, as reported, psychology had reached a certain level of scientific rigour and should now fulfil its mission in the world in practical ways at a time such as the present, when humanity faces such challenges. Apparently this scholar said that those who develop this field of psychology in relation to marriage advertisements will be furthering practical psychology, and can for instance serve the pragmatic needs of soldiers returning from the front in their search for a wife! Thus psychology, with its new academic and scientific standing, should become practically useful and draw on its experimental findings to discover the right way of formulating marriage advertisements, and advise returning soldiers on how best to do so.

This is no fairy tale, but has come to light in recent days, my dear friends, and shows us that people do not have a clue what is happening in their astral body since they do not even know they have one. The whole thing is only possible because of the presence of these currents sustained by ahrimanic forces and mingling with human habits of thinking, creating in people a view of scientific exploration that is applied to absolutely everything. One can forgive this if it retains a little humour. The scholar of philosophy who has just published a detailed treatise in the *Preussische Jahrbuecher* does at least bring some humour to bear on his subject—which is to see whether Greek literature provides any evidence that people back then suffered from lice infestation as we do nowadays.[71] He searched for lice through the whole of Greek literature, from Homer to Aristophanes; but at least he did so with humour, although the treatise is presented in a strictly academic and scholarly way.

These things do illumine what is happening below the surface of contemporary life, and are more important than one might initially think. It is important to know that in our time we need a spiritual-scientific stream which people do in fact fear to begin with if they cling to the habits of thought I have indicated. They fear it because it offers knowledge of the human being which awakens unconscious fears in people, since such knowledge can only be sustained if we do not allow our deeper humanity to suffer or lapse. Thus in a society such as ours we endeavour not only to disseminate spiritual science but to nurture feelings of fraternity and sorority. This must be cultivated too since otherwise human passions would be unleashed in too drastic a fashion. But on the other hand, to judge the nature of the times, we do need to cast our eye a little upon the nature of many human beings. In this realm we will always need to abide by a certain rule which I would compare with the confidentiality of a letter. If you find a letter addressed to someone else, you do not read it, do you? Likewise we do not gaze into the soul life and whole human life of another person without good reason. But a good reason can exist if we see that a certain individual has a particular importance in contemporary life. Then, in order to educate and inform our contemporaries, we will need to shine a light into the soul life of this individual, using the means afforded by spiritual science. You see, someone like Loewenstein, with his psychology of marriage advertisements, is able to spread the strangest views of science amongst those who certainly do not put their faith in authority, of course, but—how shall I put it?—do not have any other faith either, but, when someone appears dressed in the mantle of science, immediately succumb to this. We need to know that the human soul is a very, very complex thing, that the whole human being is very complex, and that we cannot acquaint ourselves with human nature if we do not fully engage with this complexity. Just think: we possess four aspects initially, if we overlook the higher levels, and these four are in interplay within us. The physical body can still retain some of the pliability and flexibility of the fourth post-Atlantean epoch, but at the same time have a certain receptivity towards everything modern thought life engenders. Thus a person can appear who, let us say, possesses this quality: an organism that on the one hand still possesses residual qualities of the Graeco-Roman era, but at the same time has a head that can elaborate the thoughts of modern times with some acuity, and reproduce them. This can certainly coexist in someone. Such a person will be considered very sharp, very clever. But through the distinctive quality of his body I have suggested, he may at the same time also be weak-minded. If we know that the human being is complex, it will not be contradictory to say that he is both weak-minded and bright or sharp at the same time. Spiritual science, you see, is something that gives us a light we can shed to find our way through the complex conditions and circumstances of modern times.

Truly, my dear friends, do not think that I have anything against people speaking very cautiously at present about circumstances in America. I have no objection whatsoever to maintaining political tact or caution, and to corresponding conduct in order to allow certain things to happen that need to. But this does not mean we must obscure our view of the truth. And this is why, despite the current circumstances, and in fact because of them, I recently drew attention in a public lecture to the leading statesman in America, Wilson,[72] and the kind of thought forms he is developing. I read out a passage written by him about his views on freedom—this was in a public lecture[73]—to show how far removed this, well let us not say 'American' but 'mechanistic' thinking is from what we have achieved in European culture. In the living nature of the latter, people such as Fichte or others who have affinity with him have laid down the first elements of a true philosophy of freedom. And now we can ask this: do the current political conditions mean that someone must come along and 'by accident', let us say, quote the very same sentences I quoted from this book on freedom, and then use them to describe Mr Wilson as someone who has here written something of greater significance than anything else written in the past two years, and to suggest that we in Europe would be very lucky to have such a figure amongst us who is the 'Fichte of America'? This is what has been said: Mr Wilson is America's Fichte! This comment has been published recently in the German-speaking world!

My dear friends, such phenomena are only possible because people are complex beings. And amongst ourselves we can certainly highlight special circumstances of this kind, for we need to have people in our circles who become fully conversant with life through what spiritual science offers us. As I said, one may have a body that is as pliant and easily influenced as a Graeco-Roman body, and which therefore has not attained the more advanced stage of modern corporeality; and then one may be sharp and clever, absorbing all the sorts of views that are expressed in modern society. Thus one is a very clever person, but at the same time weak-minded. Both at once. In fact, one may find particular resonance and response amongst our contemporaries who are, well, not submissive to authority but unsubmissive to it, if, furnished with a soft and pliant body, one acts as a kind of human phonograph that can amplify, distort and caricature all kinds of contemporary thoughts. To write the kinds of tasteless and stupid things I have just described, one does of course have to be fully immersed in modern culture. But to appear to be a clever person, and to exert an influence, one does not need to stand fully in this culture but only has to be quick-witted enough to absorb its forms of thoughts and then have a body as I described. And then, you see, someone like this can be a modern journalist—someone like Maximilian Hardens, who has exerted great influence for decades now.

One has to know what forces are working in modern culture, and how modern opinions are formed; and also how these can be traced back to human nature. But without absorbing spiritual-scientific insights into the human being, one has no means to do this. Only by such insight and knowledge are we prevented from being carried away on the stream I described, which engenders the habits of thought that make people believe they have long since overcome any faith in authority because they are now so wonderfully advanced. They place no faith in authority, apparently, and yet they believe every word that is printed in the *Zukunft* periodical!

My dear friends, by judging things in the light of spiritual science—though without allowing this to affect our practical conduct and of course not our emotions, but only allowing these insights to inform our views and judgements—we must become aware of the values that hold sway in our culture. Today everything is an unformed, chaotic mass. Nowadays of course we do not live in regions in which, like the Indians of Paraguay, we gaze upon gold-garbed priests surrounded in clouds of incense. No, we don't do that. But we have other altars: the newspapers and suchlike. And the clouds of smoke are less material of course, since incense is more substantial than the aura around modern authorities. Though this enveloping cloud is more spiritual, my dear friends, its scent is not as beautiful as the more material scent of incense!

That is the whole chaotic mass of what exerts great authority on people who think they have grown beyond it and freed themselves from it. But it is difficult to gain full appreciation for what can lead the human being away from what he otherwise so easily succumbs to. For this, one must gradually engage with all kinds of things. Yes, my dear friends, the difficulties are by no means small which spiritual science encounters as it seeks to penetrate life, as it must. It must encompass diverse realms of life, and can only advance through one after another, slowly and gradually working upon people. For instance, as you all know, and as karma elicits from us, we have tried to develop a kind of expressive art, which we call eurythmy. People can think what they like about this, but our prime challenge is to present it to people in a worthy manner. A few days ago we read that one of our members—our members!—appeared on stage in Munich, a tall, slim gentleman, who first recited poems in his own fashion, then, after disappearing, reappeared in white trousers and vestments, and, as the newspaper naturally mockingly relates, accompanied his further recitation with all kinds of contorted movements, holding a veil in his hands which he fluttered about. Then he vanished again to reappear once more in a blue dress edged with yellow, and managed to continue to recite despite a torrent of mocking applause. He announced his whole performance—as I said, he is a member of our Society—as 'Eurythmy recitation art'. Thus a member has himself rendered this eurythmy, which is so dear to our hearts, a public laughing stock. 'Eurythmy and Other Plagues of the War' was one of the headlines in the Munich press about this performance.

So you can see how difficult it is to bring spiritual science into everyday life if those who wish to help do so lack the right outlook. My dear friends, we need to reflect in far, far more serious ways than has so far happened on the impulses that must work within our spiritual-scientific movement.

Next time I will speak further of this.

LECTURE 10

16 MAY 1916

DURING the course of these reflections, I have often mentioned the need to consider from our perspective some of the connections between what we perceive and acknowledge through spiritual science and what is commonly regarded today, in science and human knowledge, as the only correct view. We can imagine that the course of cultural evolution in central Europe over recent centuries might have been somewhat different than it has been. We do not violate the comprehensive laws of karma by imagining that something which happened in the world could also have occurred differently. The law of karma—and we will speak further of this next time—by no means excludes the possibility of freedom prevailing in the world. Fatalists who think that everything that happens had to happen in the way external sensory observation—and thinking based on this—perceives it are at odds here with those who, in accord with spiritual science, speak of karma on the one hand and on the other of what occurs in the outer world. You see, whenever something occurs in the external world something spiritual also always occurs. The two streams flow into one another, and the karma law applies to this confluence, so that something could easily happen differently in the outer world and yet what is necessary would still occur. I say this only to preface some further remarks on central Europe's cultural development and to show that it could conceivably have taken a different course from the one apparent to outer observation.

In most circles today, of course, Schiller and Goethe are revered figures; and in very recent times, too, some have come to regard Fichte as a great mind, although most people do not bother to acquaint themselves even with Fichte's most basic ideas. They restrict themselves instead to things they absorb but have no possibility of understanding since they do not engage with Fichte's basic ideas. Nevertheless, the broadest circles of people revere Goethe, Schiller, Fichte and others. This reverence is offered without real efforts to acquaint oneself with the figures to whom it is given. This is true too in regard to Goethe and Schiller, since fully fathoming these great figures, acquainting oneself with what truly lived in their minds, is something we still await. We can only hope that such understanding will emerge from the gravity of our times. There is certainly already a yearning in people to understand Goethe, for instance. In the broadest sense, the general population harbour a longing and yearning for the spirit, as I said in one of my recent lectures. But here it is important how spiritual and cultural leaders handle their leading role. *Faust* is apparently one of the most widely read books at present! We can be certain that those who read *Faust* today, amidst the turmoil of these times, will, when they ponder on what they have read, find themselves thirsting for insights drawn from the world that lay open before Goethe's spiritual vision. But the theoretical explanations and exegeses of those apparently professionally qualified to give them will strike such readers as execrable. We have renowned philosophers of course, such as Kohler[74] and Eucken.[75] The *Faust* readers who would find 'Kohlereuckenism' abominable might very well hearken attentively if they gained access to spiritual science, to what it has in common with Goethe and the creative sources that he drew from.

The spiritual, cultural development of the nineteenth century could also have absorbed and integrated what underlay the whole vision of Goethe and Schiller, and the others who surrounded them and shared their outlook. But things took a different course. One need only go into a bookshop today—this is a fact—and ask for Goethe's scientific writings to find that the lad behind the desk is advising you to purchase Boelsche[76] instead, since Goethe is out of date!

Why did things develop differently from how they should have done if the seeds slumbering in the great soil of classical knowledge had germinated and sprouted at the turn of the eighteenth and nineteenth centuries? From such seeds, spiritual science would have followed in direct lineage. I will explore this in detail in the book, which is soon to be published, entitled *The Enigma of the Human Being. The Thinking, Vision and Reflections of Key German and Austrian Figures.*[77] Why did the seeds of the world-view of Goethe and Schiller, and what they contained, not find acceptance and acknowledgement? It is because people are afraid of this, and afraid for the following reason. Nowadays people find it convenient to acquire knowledge of the sort that is presented to them and which they then—what is the phrase?—mug up on, and later regurgitate in turn, priding themselves on being an 'authority'. Spiritual science requires a more thorough, intensive kind of thinking than most modern academics are capable of accomplishing. And the fear of having to learn something, of developing a greater capacity, is what creates a hindrance to them doing so. The fear of difficult ideas and concepts erects obstacles for them. Our modern form of reverence for Goethe and Schiller is more fitted to veiling and obscuring what Goethe and Schiller gave humanity than explaining or clarifying it. Why? Because a common modern outlook does not wish to engage with what has to be understood out of the same spirit that these figures themselves possessed. This same outlook emerged in the time of Goethe and Schiller, in those great days when the mind of Goethe dominated Jena, when Schiller was teaching, when Fichte, Schlegel and Schelling were teaching, along with other figures of whom we have spoken so much this winter and whom I will discuss in the forthcoming book.

What these minds had to say about various aspects of life is always of course embedded in a particular context, in which it must be understood. We must try to fathom the whole spirit of their being. The legacy of Goethe, Schiller, Fichte, Schlegel, and so on, has the form it does today because they were vanquished, basically, by those of like mind with the man who appeared in the time of Goethe and dared, in one of the worst examples of pamphleteering, to decry pupils of Goethe, Schiller, Fichte and Schlegel as idiots, fantasists and dreamers, as people at odds with life. It is always possible to ridicule things that engage in a serious quest for truth. Of course, any serious quest for truth may sometimes also display one-sided aspects. But to focus on these alone, accentuate, isolate and ridicule them, in order to render the whole outlook and endeavour suspect, is of course an easy way to draw a 'big crowd'. The man I'm thinking of—Kotzebue[78]—has been forgotten now. But the many Kotzebues—the tyrant is dead, long live the tyrants—are still alive and well throughout our culture. In many of the sayings by Schlegel, Fichte and also Goethe and Schiller, we can find things that herald our spiritual science. But one can also always take things out of context to cast suspicion on these minds, to make it seem as if what they said was stupid or foolish, and sought to hinder real human progress—or rather what the philistinism that clings so fiercely to sensory reality alone regards as progress.

Kotzebue—let us remind ourselves of this today—has been forgotten, but the Kotzebues are still with us. Let us recall this figure, Kotzebue, for a moment. He wrote a dramatic pamphlet in which he presents a student who returns to his family and his philistine origins—though I would not wish to denigrate them—after studying in Jena the supposedly noxious ideas of Goethe, Schiller, Fichte and Schlegel. He is depicted as a kind of idiot, and at the same time as a 'Hyperborean ass'. The pamphlet is entitled *The Hyperborean Ass or Modern Education*. Karl von Berg, the student, is expressly said to have been a student of Goethe, Schiller, Fichte and Schlegel. Let me just read a few scenes of this piece to you. The student Karl von Berg returns home after absorbing the teachings of Goethe, Schiller, Fichte, Schlegel and others at that great era of cultural life in Jena. His mother welcomes him first. Naturally one cannot blame her for being a little anxious that her dear son may have lost his piety in such circles, especially after all that has been whispered about them in her ears. After her son arrives home, Frau von Berg says to him:

> Frau von Berg: Once again I embrace you in my motherly arms (she embraces him). Thank God that I have you once again! You, my hope, my pride, my all! Are you still the one you were? Oh yes, I am sure you are! Whether you have learned much or little, your anxious mother would rather see you pious than scholarly. When you left me you were virtuous, and virtuous you return to me again, do you not?
> Karl: Dear mother, there is no virtue but consistency.
> Mother: What? If that were so, the worst villain could be virtuous!
> Karl: If he acts with consistency . . .
> Mother: Oh woe! What are you saying? Are you still religious?
> Karl: Religion is mostly only a supplement to or even a surrogate for education.

Let me note expressly here that this literary trickery takes literal phrases from the works of those it attacks but of course completely out of context.

> Mother: And nothing more than that?
> Karl: Nothing is religious in the strict sense that is not a product of freedom.

Actually, a beautiful phrase!

> Mother: I cannot argue with you, and I wish only to be reassured. People have related some things to me about the fashionable modern systems of thought. (She places her hand on his shoulder and speaks fearfully.) But Karl, do you believe in God still?
> Karl: I myself am God.

The God indwelling us of course.

> Mother: Oh woe is me. He has become like poor Wezel in Sondershausen!

'Poor Wezel in Sondershausen' was a poet of the time who went mad.

> Karl: Every good person increasingly becomes God. To become God, to be human, to educate oneself, are expressions that all mean the same.

All this is taken word-for-word, and out of context, from the works of these figures!

> Mother: What? I was afraid that he no longer believed in God but find he believes there are millions!
> Karl: If every infinite individual is God, there are as many gods as ideals.
> Mother: He has lost his Christianity!
> Karl: The scientific ideal of Christianity is a characteristic of the Godhead with infinite variations.
> Mother: Are you speaking of a rondo?
> Karl: God is not merely a thought but at the same time also a cause, as are all thoughts that are not merely imaginary.
> Mother: But tell me, what religion do you actually hold to?
> Karl: It is a very natural, almost inevitable wish to seek to reconcile all species of religion within oneself.
> Mother: All?
> Karl: All.
> Mother: Ah, I cannot dispute with you. But I beg you, speak to our priest, he is a brave and rational man.
> Karl: I do not wish to. Religion is as great as nature itself and the best priest has only a portion of it.

All this word-for-word!

> Mother: I assure you, he has all of it.
> Karl: Besides which, I myself am a priest.
> Mother (astonished): Both God *and* a priest?
> Karl: The relationship of the true artist and the true human being to his ideals is certainly religion. He for whom this inner

worship is the goal and preoccupation of his life is a priest; and therefore I am also a priest.
Mother: Son! Son! What is to become of you in this and the other world?!
Karl: People speak always of this and the other world as if there were more than one world.
Mother: Oh woe, you are caught in Satan's net.

As you can see, the Protestant priest in Hamburg who wrote to one of our members—I have read the letter—to state that I myself am Satan is not alone in his views!

Karl: Satan is a German invention, for the German Satan is more satanic than the Italian or the English one. He is a favourite of German poets and philosophers, and must therefore also have his good side.
Mother: Satan has a good side?!
Karl: What I don't like about Christian mythology is its lack of satanists.
Mother: Ah, my God! Isn't *one* Satan sufficient for us?
Karl: Mother, I beg you to cease these elegiac laments; they are expressions of feelings of woe at the thought of the inanity of conditions ranging from banality to lunacy.
Mother: Thanks goodness that I do not understand your blasphemies.
Karl: You wish to stop me in my chosen course? It is a vain attempt. He who has made endeavours, whether foolhardy or noble, to intervene with others in the advance of the human spirit . . .
Mother: Intervene? In an advance? What does this mean?
Karl: . . . must keep moving onwards or will be no better off than a dog in a treadmill who refuses to move his paws forward.
Mother: Oh, I beg you, turn your paws backwards! The great confusion of your mind may lead you to despair and suicide!
Karl: Suicide is only an occurrence and rarely an action.

Taken out of context of course!

> Karl: If it is an action, there can be no talk of right or wrong, but only of appropriateness.
> Mother: It is neither right nor appropriate.
> Karl: You are wrong, it is never unlawful to die voluntarily, and often less decent to live longer.
> Mother: What must I hear! Oh woe! How bitterly are my hopes deceived!
> Karl: Calm yourself, mother, you will soon think as I do.
> Mother (horrified): Never in a million years!
> Karl: It may be that, like Rousseau, you think that any good, fine free-spiritedness is less suitable for women than men?
> Mother: It is fit neither for the one nor the other.
> Karl: Yet that is only one of Rousseau's endless number of general platitudes.
> Mother: Foolish person! It is shameful to speak of Rousseau like that. But, great God, if shameful were all you were it would be better. I leave you deeply downcast. I am only a woman and have only my feelings to oppose you with. Your uncle can speak as man-to-man with you.
> Karl (alone): The narrow-minded person cannot grasp that all others are not the same as he is.

And now, from a subsequent scene, we find Karl in conversation with his uncle, the baron.

> Karl: The human being is an earnest beast.
> Baron: A beast? Shame on you. I can see you have studied too much and have grown lonely. I will take you into good company.
> Karl: The societies of the Germans are earnest, their comedies and satires are earnest, their critiques are earnest, their whole beautiful literature is earnest.
> Baron: Oh, there are certainly enough fools amongst the Germans.

> Karl: Folly is an absolutely wrong tendency, a complete lack of historical awareness.
> Baron: Listen to me, nephew, keep all this rubbish to yourself and let us speak sensibly to each other. I have a project in mind for you.
> Karl: A project is the subjective seed of a developing object.
> Baron: Whatever you say, lad, but you will have to exist and earn a living.
> Karl: There can be nothing more arrogant than to exist, let alone to exist in a definite, autonomous way.

So now we have arrived at great existential questions, haven't we!

> Baron: What the devil do you mean? How do I exist then?
> Karl: You? You do not exist at all.
> Baron (taking a horrified step backwards): Not at all?
> Karl: Most people are only entitled pretenders to existence. Few actually exist.
> Baron: Goodness, you are either mad or hare-brained.
> Karl: Foolishness is only distinguished from madness by being voluntary like stupidity.

And one further little passage, a scene between Karl and Malchen.

> Karl runs towards Malchen and presses her ardently to his breast.
> Karl: O my Amalie!
> Malchen: A moment, a moment, dear cousin! You are crushing me.
> Karl: It lies in a man's nature to possess a certain loutish enthusiasm that easily becomes almost coarsely divine (he tries to embrace her again).
> Malchen (bashful and resisting): Not so unbridled, dear Karl.
> Karl (smiling as he looks at her): It really is a strange position to be in as an innocent girl.
> Malchen (astonished): What? A strange situation?
> Karl: Certainly, but women must no doubt remain prudish as

> long as men are sufficiently sentimental, stupid and bad-natured to look for eternal innocence and lack of education in them.
>
> Malchen: So you do not wish me to be innocent?
>
> Karl: You are a flourishing girl and therefore the most charming symbol of pure, good will.
>
> Malchen: An odd compliment!
>
> Karl: We will marry.
>
> Malchen: Perhaps.
>
> Karl: It is true that women lack a sense of art, a disposition for science and abstraction, and true too that wilful malice along with naive coldness, ridicule and lack of feeling are inherent in their sex . . .
>
> Malchen: How flattering!
>
> Karl . . . but nevertheless I have decided to attempt it.
>
> Malchen: Attempt it? How very kind.
>
> Karl: Almost all marriages are merely concupiscence, provisional attempts at real marriage.
>
> Malchen: Sir Cousin, I do hope that I misunderstand you.
>
> Karl: We could of course enlarge on our attempt, for example with a marriage à quatre.
>
> Malchen (almost struck dumb with astonishment): What?
>
> Karl: It is hard to see why anyone would really object to a marriage à quatre.

Again, all taken completely out of context!

> Malchen: You mean you would be capable of sharing your beloved?
>
> Karl: I will attempt to possess her as if I did not possess her.
>
> Malchen: A pleasant prospect!
>
> Karl: That is the duty of a true cynic.

One last passage. The sovereign now appears and engages in conversation with Karl.

> Sovereign: I love history.

> Karl: The historical style must be lofty by virtue of naked dignity, noble haste and grandiose good cheer.
> Sovereign: What bombastic words! Have you been preoccupied perhaps with state administration?
> Karl: If only the actions of lawgivers, executives or judges did not often contain a wilful quality which appears to exceed the bounds of their entitlement.
> Sovereign: What should be done about this?
> Karl: Is their authority not borrowed from constitutional power?
> Sovereign: It may be so.
> Karl: And therefore should this power not inevitably possess a veto?
> Sovereign: Ah, now I see where you're going; and I advise you, benevolently, not to involve yourself in state administration. Or at least not in my country, where peace and morals hold sway.
> Karl: Morals? I do not think so. For the first sign of morality is opposition to positive legality and conventional lawfulness.
> Sovereign: That sounds very like the new, universally destructive principles.

Even if such opposition to the great spiritual upsurge in those days, and what could have arisen from it, did not focus narrowly on any specific area, nevertheless this oppositional spirit did prevail. And it is really true to say that the seeds planted at the time still await germination. They will only germinate if people lose the fear, due to their comfort-loving mundanity, of what can flow to them from worlds of spirit. The first condition for this will be—and I have often said this—that they acknowledge how necessary it is to be true, absolutely true in life, and really to have the courage—forgive me if I use this word, but it figures in the passage I read—for consistency, to draw the conclusions of what one perceives to be true. Truth lies not only in the nature of the views one asserts but also already in the very way we use words. We can see this very clearly if we consider the resistance which arises in the outer world nowadays in the realm that ought really to lead people to comprehend Christianity and the Mystery of Golgotha in the way essential today, so that a person can bring into full accord with the most contemporary knowledge and insights what he can sense and feel about the Mystery of Golgotha. We can say that certain figures in the outer world today are most furiously antagonistic to what spiritual science has said about the appearance of Christ Jesus and his descent to the earth.

To comprehend the Epiphany, the manifestation of Christ Jesus, my dear friends, we had to invoke all three worlds. First we have the Jesus who bears the great individuality of Zarathustra within him. Growing to the age of 12, he then departs from his body and passes over into the body of the other Jesus boy, who has developed a soul that has not undergone all of earthly evolution but—as I have previously said—was withheld and remained behind, in a sense, in the substance of the earthly human soul by virtue of one portion descending into human bodies while another remained above. This latter only entered the body to which the second Mary gave birth as the second Jesus boy. And I have drawn your attention to what spiritual-scientific knowledge teaches us: that at the moment he was born this Jesus boy did something impossible today—he spoke, he uttered what he is. This Jesus boy continues to grow with the soul of Zarathustra until the age of 30, when the Christ individuality incarnates in him and then lives in this body that has been prepared by the spirit of the great Zarathustra: prepared by that soul who did not undergo earthly evolution along with all other human souls but remained behind at a time before earth had as yet descended to its current state of materiality. The Christ individuality now lives in this body for three years. We necessarily invoked three worlds to comprehend this great, the very greatest figure, and this greatest event in humanity's evolution: the highest worlds of spirit from which Christ descended; the world that exists before our earth came into being; and the world through which human beings have evolved, and to which Zarathustra belongs albeit as an outstanding incarnation, yet nevertheless one that must be counted among ordinary human incarnations.

I have mentioned in a little book that is also to be published now, *The Mission of Spiritual Science and its Building in Dornach*, that when one listens to people who offer a judgement about such things one discovers what fear they have of comprehending it. They say such things are 'unchristian', and instead cite what they themselves believe about Christ. If one expresses the view that they ought to be pleased if we believe the same as they do yet seek to add something further to it, one finds they are not actually pleased; they do not permit one to add anything to what they think they know. It becomes apparent here that people are not in fact concerned with perceiving the truth but only with wielding their power. They do not wish to allow Christ to be presented in his highest glory if vision of this glory requires them to learn something they are not comfortable with.

Such people who not only call themselves Christians but who even officially represent Christianity as priests or clergy dismiss the Christian nature of spiritual science; but at the same time we must consider another aspect, which is that there are people today who claim the right to practise as Christian clergy without in any way acknowledging that Christ, or as they put it Jesus, entered human evolution in a way that was different from every other human being. Today there are certainly Christian priests and clergy who do not think they need consider that Jesus' birth was in any way special, regarding him rather as a kind of higher Socrates, as one of the noblest human beings, perhaps the noblest, but nothing more. There are famous theologians who speak of belief in the Resurrection emerging from whatever happened in the Garden of Gethsemane, who wish to adhere to belief in the Resurrection without knowing what actually occurred. Many years ago during a talk at the Giordano Bruno Society, I called it 'baroque' for people to think in this way: not to concern themselves with what may actually have happened in the Garden of Gethsemane, but to adhere still to the belief that the Resurrection occurred there. I called this mode of thinking baroque and paradoxical, and mentioned that it figures in the book by Adolf von Harnack[79] entitled *The Nature of Christianity*. The president of the Giordano Bruno Society, a professor, came up to me afterwards and objected that Harnack cannot have said such a thing, that it would have been like the Catholics who, irrespective of the nature of the cloth that hangs in Trier [Treves], claim that they must maintain their faith in it since it is regarded as Christ's tunic! The professor said that Harnack could not have written this in his book. Naturally you can find it there. This man had read *The Nature of Christianity* but had overlooked the passage in question because he wished to bury his head in the sand about what was in it.

We experience such things today in relation to the way people relate to the spiritual world. And likewise there are numerous people who come to us repeatedly and say that what we propound is very abstract. They want a simple, ordinary human Jesus of Nazareth, whereas we offer them three Jesuses! The most enlightened theologians have embraced the 'simple man of Nazareth'. But now we must ask this: can we still regard as Christians people who actually refuse to comprehend Christ in the way that he must be comprehended in our time?

Let us assume for a moment that someone came to us and said that belief in these ideas of Jesus as, firstly, Zarathustra and secondly as the one who absorbed the soul substance of humankind before this descended to the earth, is something that contradicts the convictions he has formed in accordance with his view of the world. But he holds fast to one thing, which accords with his world-view: that the being who lived in Jesus entered the world in a supernatural way and not as other people enter the world; that this being did speak at the moment he was born, unlike others, and prophesied that he would not die in the same way as others. Let us assume that someone approaches us and says that he can believe this. Then we would say: Well, yes, Christianity has been disseminated through the most diverse currents of outlook, and this person has only absorbed the aspect of Christianity indicated in the Gospel of Luke—the Jesus boy from the Nathan line of the House of David. If we assume that such a thing were specifically expressed in a religious text, we would say: Well, yes, the belief of the person who says this has been influenced by a tradition that has been muddied, and must be clarified again through spiritual-scientific insights into the second Jesus boy. I will read out to you such a passage in a religious text,[80] relating to Jesus; and I beg you to judge the value of it for yourselves.

> Herewith the mercifulness of your Lord to his servant Zacharias.

You know the figure of Zacharias from the Bible of course!

> Thereupon he called upon his Lord in secret, and said: My Lord, behold, my limbs are weak and my head shines grey with age,
> And never did my prayers to you go unheard.
> And behold, I fear for my tribe after me, for my wife is barren.
> So give unto me a successor to inherit me and the House of Jacob, and make him pleasing, my Lord.

This means 'make him pleasing to you'.

> O Zacharias, behold, we proclaim a boy to you, John by name,
> A name we have never previously given.
> He spake: My Lord, how shall I have a son, seeing that my wife is barren, and I am become old and frail?
> He spake: So let it be. Your Lord has spoken: This is easy for me, and you too I once created ere you were anything.
> He spake: My Lord, give me a sign.
> He spake: Your sign will be that you, albeit healthy, will not speak to the people for three nights.

It is very similar to the Bible!

> And he went out to his people from the chamber and gestured to them . . .

He gestured because he was unable to speak.

> . . . Praise the Lord both morning and evening.
> And we spoke:

That means, the faithful.

> O John, accept the power of the scripture; and we gave him wisdom when that he was a child,
> And sympathy from us and purity; and he was pious and full of love for his parents and was not haughty and defiant.
> And peace be upon him at the day of his birth and on the day he dies, and on the day of his awakening to life!

This, therefore, was the teaching about John. And now it continues.

> And remember also in the Book of Mary. When she retired from her relatives to a certain place towards the East
> And hid herself from them, then we sent our Spirit to her,
> And he appeared to her as a perfect man.

Just as in the Bible! A remarkable document, don't you think?

> She spake: Behold, I take my refuge before you in the Merciful One, so may you fear him.
> He spake: I am but a messenger of your Lord, come to grant you a pure boy.
> She spake: How should I have a boy, seeing as no man has touched me, and I am no harlot?
> He spake: Let it be so! Your Lord has spoken, saying: 'That is easy for me'; and we desire to make him into a sign for humankind, and a mercy from us. And thus it has been resolved.
> And so she conceived him, and removed with him, retiring to a distant place.

Here you have the spiritual conception of Jesus.

> And the pangs of birth overcame her beside the trunk of a palm tree. She spake:
> O that I had died before this, and been forgotten and consigned to oblivion!
> And below her there cried a voice: Do not be afraid; your Lord has let flow a brook beneath you;
> And shake only the trunk of the palm tree to you, and fresh, ripe dates will fall upon you.

> So eat and drink and be content, and when you see anyone,
> So speak: 'Behold, I have promised the Merciful One to fast; today therefore will I never speak to anyone.'
> And she brought him to her people, bearing him. They spake:
> O Mary, indeed, you have done a remarkable thing!
> O sister of Aaron, your father was no villain, nor your mother a harlot.
> And they pointed at him. They said: How should we speak with him, a child in the cradle?
> He (Jesus) spake: Behold, I am the servant of God (Allah). To me he has given the scripture, and has made me a prophet.
> And he made me blessed, wherever that I am, and commanded me to prayer and alms, as long as I live,
> And love to my mother; and he made me not haughty and unblessed.
> And gave me peace upon the day of my birth and the day that I die, and the day when I am awoken to life!

As you remember, I described this by saying that he uttered something only his mother could understand . . . And then this text continues:

> This is Jesus, the son of Mary—the Word of truth that you doubt in.
> It is not fitting for God (Allah) to engender a son. Praise him!
> When he resolves upon a thing, he speaks only to it: Be! And it is.
> And behold, God (Allah) is my Lord and your Lord; so serve him; this is a right path.
> Yet the sects contest with each other; and woe to the unfaithful at the mighty day of witness!
> Make them hearken and see a day when they shall come to us.
> Yet the unjust are in manifest error today.

Thus this text speaks of Jesus, who in this case is recorded only in one figure and form. Surely we can say of this document, this record, that anyone who believes it believes considerably more than many who in our time not only speak the name of Christ, but are even official teachers of Christianity? Surely someone who firmly believes in this document is a far more faithful adherent of Christianity than many who call themselves teachers of Christianity today? And please do not imagine that this document I read—I am not sure if you know it—is regarded by only a few people, a small sect, as real testimony of their faith. The passage I read came from the Qur'an. I read you the nineteenth sura from the Qur'an, and every authentic Mohammedan believes in Jesus to the extent that is contained in this nineteenth sura. But this shows us that a great many of those amongst us who call themselves Christians know and believe less of this Christianity than would allow them to be called 'heathens'. In our day we have to look truth squarely in the face. Anyone who does not even believe that these events can only be understood through the spirit are not even 'heathen', much less Christians, and they do not speak the truth when they call themselves Christians. A 'heathen', as they should acknowledge, believes more in Christianity than they do.

It seems to me, my dear friends, that these are indeed serious, really serious matters, and that those who dedicate themselves to spiritual science are obliged to study them in the spirit of truth. You see, untruth is not only what appears a self-evident untruth in any assertion, but also any matter referred to in terms that invoke false ideas about historical developments. We must speak the truth not only in what we claim or assert but also in our whole being and bearing.

And thus it often happens that people who do not even deserve to be called heathen deny spiritual science its Christianity. But from another direction, too, spiritual science is opposed everywhere by inadequate knowledge, truly inadequate knowledge. Today I want to refer to one more instance. We speak of how our earth evolved from Old Moon. What we nowadays call our mineral realm was not yet present on Old Moon, and only gradually crystallized. Within us as human beings we possess the animals and plants. All of you have the mineral kingdom within you too—you are pervaded by it, are only perceptible to present sensory vision by virtue of this mineral realm within you. Looking back to the period of Old Moon, we must conceive the forerunners of humankind as not yet having these mineral constituents. Read *Occult Science*, and you will see what this Moon kingdom looked like, still as yet without the mineral realm. You can read there how all was soft substance, watery and fluid, and how what grew out of this watery medium only floated and swam around in it in a sense. It must therefore be assumed—and I have spoken of this in past reflections—that what evolved from the Old Moon condition as our primary organ was in a sense floating in fluid there; and on Old Moon a different kind of perception must have lived in a humankind that had not as yet developed the rest of its body. The brain existed only as a kind of appendage, floating and swimming about in the fluid with a quite different capacity for movement than it now has. On Old Moon, the tones of the music of the spheres were still audible too, the ringing and resonance of the music of the spheres. Now, how would things have been at that time? Tones audible without, then these tones reverberating in the Moon water through an instrument from which our larynx developed into what it now is; these tones resonating with the Moon brain in its ancient form as it swam upon the waters. Thus you can conceive of the music of the cosmos surging in the cosmic ocean, transposing itself into the pictures of Imagination through an instrument which later developed into our larynx, and surfacing in living imaginations in the dream consciousness of ancient Moon.

If that was really the condition on Old Moon, we should inevitably find signs of it in human beings today, would see they had evolved from such a state. Now, my dear friends, do we discover such signs? The music of the spheres has fallen silent today, has it not? What evolved from the organ that took in the music of the spheres during the Moon period gave rise to our larynx, embedded in the lung system. Our brain is now enclosed in a firm sheath. Does it still show any indication of its state on Old Moon, when it was floating, swimming in fluid? What people usually learn by studying the brain does not allow them to focus on what is really involved. But it would be possible for people to reflect on the following lines—and, in fact, to give people their due, some of them have. This brain of ours weighs 1350 grams, and has blood vessels supplying it. Now these blood vessels would be crushed by the weight of 1350 grams. If you placed the whole weight of the brain upon them, there is no question of them remaining undamaged. Within our skull, though, they are not crushed and this is because the weight of 1350 grams does not press upon them. Why? Yes, let me remind you of what you may once have read in books on physics—that an ancient Greek scientist cried out 'Eureka, I have it' when he was getting in his bath and found that his body weighed less in the tub. Every body becomes lighter in a fluid or gaseous medium in proportion to the weight of the gas or water in which it is contained. Otherwise an air balloon would not rise into the sky. And in water every body loses as much of its weight as the weight of water that is displaced. Now our brain swims in cerebrospinal fluid of course! The cerebrospinal fluid buoys up our brain and also runs down through the spinal column. Our brain floats in fluid and thereby loses so much weight that it only exerts a pressure of 20 grams. In other words, the brain weighing 1350 grams presses down with only 20 grams because the weight of fluid is so great: 1350 grams less 20. The brain really does float or swim in fluid, and is still in a situation that resembles its state on Old Moon. Within our skulls it still imitates the form it once had then, though it has been transformed and is now enveloped, surrounded, by the rest of the human sheath that has emerged from earthly laws here.

And even the communication with the outer world is still there. When we breathe in, our diaphragm rises, but besides doing this it also at the same time exerts pressure on the whole venous system here and the ganglion system, and because of this the accumulated fluid in the spinal column is pushed upwards into the brain. Thus when we breathe in, the cerebrospinal fluid in the spine rises into the brain. When we breathe out the opposite happens: the diaphragm sinks again, the fluid runs down from the brain into the spine. Just imagine: basically we are still in continuous relationship with the outer world's wave movements. With every outbreath the cerebrospinal fluid sinks and with every inbreath it rises—a rising and falling of the cerebrospinal fluid in which the brain floats. Here we have a complex process which makes the human being today more than he was on Old Moon; as the human being who creates mechanical tools he is now able not only to have imaginations but also to think. What continually occurs within us has been pushed down into the subconscious. Yes, my dear friends, this is happening all the time: we continually have imaginations but these are overlaid by our waking thoughts in the same way that a stronger light outshines a weaker one. These imaginations are continually there and are related continuously to inbreath and outbreath. And only because the more solid brain, full of mineral substances, counters these imaginations are the latter sublimated when the solid brain mass weighs down upon the substance of the imagining cerebrospinal fluid; our conscious thoughts are in a sense sublimated or extracted from these imaginations.

There is no scientific truth which, when properly illumined, does not fully confirm what spiritual science draws from deeper realities. Yet we need to think in a quite different way from modern scientists and, especially, their proponents. There is no contradiction between spiritual science and science. The scientific facts fully confirm spiritual-scientific findings. But those whose profession it is to know things are afraid of such truths. People in general have a blind fear of complex thoughts, of thinking altogether. We have so many foolish theories really only because nowadays a person can learn in a comfortably indolent way, and, having read a little in the literature, can become an acknowledged 'expert' in his field, and not only an authority but even lay claim to great scientific discoveries. Once a person has acquired a few concepts and learned a few facts, he can make a career as scientific innovator. In fact he need know nothing of any real scientific value, nor of real mental and spiritual processes. Precisely because he knows nothing he is able to combine a few observed facts with 'strict scientific rigour' rather in the same way as the psychologist I described investigated marriage advertisements. As you know from our last lecture, this has been heralded in the Psychology Association as a real innovation in modern science! Everything, whether a marriage advertisement or the human soul, can all be approached with the same 'scientific rigour'. And then it is all, as the saying goes, much of a muchness whether one becomes a psychologist of marriage announcements or a psychoanalyst. And our modern faithful, who naturally reject all authority, hear about a lecture in the august Psychology Association about the psychology of marriage advertisements, and of course regard this as 'strictly scientific'!

These things insinuate themselves as subconscious impulses into human souls. That's what happens in this field, and likewise in the realm of 'higher culture'. If people wished to understand what spiritual science can say about the Mystery of Golgotha, along with everything connected with this, they would see how this Mystery can be illumined by invoking the three worlds; they would recognize how it can really become the central focus of all our spiritual strivings and feelings in the modern world, in a way appropriate for this world. But because far too many creep so cautiously around Christianity today and do not even have as much Christianity as a heathen, it is hardly surprising if the official representatives of Christianity dismiss real understanding of the Mystery of Golgotha. But let us hope that the grave signs of our times will engender in a great many people longings that can only be stilled through what a real science of the spirit can offer. There will be ever greater numbers of people who no longer pay heed to superficial or journalistic references to the spirit, such as Eucken indulges in, nor submit to the authority of those who say that the Resurrection itself is of no importance, and that all that matters is that people believe in it. This will wash over them without effect.

To live in truth, to wish to be true in one's whole being, will be the watchword of the future. And into a humanity that seeks to live in truth will shine the Mystery of Golgotha so that, if a spirit were to gaze down from distant stars, he would perceive in it the meaning of earthly evolution. But he would also say, 'Humankind has grasped the meaning of earth, for this is the same as comprehending the Mystery of Golgotha.'

I will speak more about this next time.

LECTURE 11

23 MAY 1916

LAST time we found, to our surprise perhaps, that a great number of those who officially represent Christianity in the West have less belief in Christ Jesus, accord him less truth, than any faithful Mohammedan, any faithful adherent of the Qur'an. And we saw that we can better understand the Jesus of the Qur'an through insights we gain about the figure of Christ Jesus when we contemplate the teachings of spiritual science—which tells us that the Zarathustra soul dwelt in the body of the Solomon Jesus boy until he reached the age of 12. We know that this Zarathustra soul then passed into the body of the Nathan Jesus boy, and that, in the thirtieth year of the life of this Jesus, the Christ spirit took possession of what had thus developed.

As we saw last time, if we consider the idea of Jesus in the Qur'an, it inevitably concurs to some degree with the Nathan Jesus. You even find in the Qur'an a reference to something I drew from purely spiritual-scientific sources and needed to tell you: that the Nathan Jesus child uttered words the moment he was born. And thus the view of Jesus entertained by many theologians who profess themselves to be 'free spirits' does not even permit them to call themselves 'heathen' let alone Christians. In our midst there are many who proclaim teachings whose view of Jesus is at a lower level than that of Mohammedans. Last time I wanted to highlight this surprising fact. For many it might perhaps show that the mission of our western culture, in so far as it seeks the spirit, must be to increasingly contemplate the deeper nature of the Mystery of Golgotha. If we combine all our knowledge and insights from the diverse worlds and apply this in the most assiduous way, we can then begin to glimpse something of what the Mystery of Golgotha has meant for evolution on earth, and what the nature of this event really was. We have in the past spoken of how little headway we make in spiritual science if we think schematically, and how necessary it is to illumine these things in ever more detail from the most varied perspectives. This can tell you how beneficial it also is to look more closely from certain angles at what meets us when we reflect on Christ Jesus, firstly in terms of the line of Solomon, and secondly in the indwelling of the Zarathustra soul in a body descended from that line, and then also to consider things that can illumine the figure of the Nathan Jesus and so forth. Today therefore I would like to start by speaking of Solomon himself, and matters connected with him.

If we only consider what is contained in the teachings of ancient Judaism, in its concepts and ideas—I mean what one finds in the Talmud or other scriptures apart from the Old Testament, which is different in this respect—we will gain inadequate ideas of the whole thought world of Judaism. In particular we gain an inadequate sense of ideas that relate to a figure such as that of Solomon. The concepts and thoughts contained in Judaic teachings are referred to as Halacha, as opposed to Haggadah, which means its legends, pictures and tales. In reality, such tales and legends, such pictures, can be traced back to visions in the world of spirit, to what was perceived or learned from the world of spirit through clairvoyant vision. These legends and tales of the Haggadah are rooted in imaginative vision.

Today I want to take a short passage from this Haggadah[81] as the point of departure for further reflections. This passage describes an important moment in the life of King Solomon, and runs as follows:

> Rabbi Yohanan says: 'The feet of man are a pledge that they will bring him to the place where he is required.' The tale is told of those two Moors who belonged to the circles surrounding

> Solomon: Elichoref, Achiyah, the sons of Shisha, who were scribes of Solomon. One day Solomon saw the angel of death, who was downcast, and he spoke to him, saying: 'Why are you so downcast?' At this the angel of death replied: 'Because the two Moors here are required by me.' At this Solomon gave his two Moors to the Seyrim . . .

Seyrim are demons which, in imaginative vision appear in the form of goats, and can fly through the air.

> At this Solomon gave his two Moors to the Seyrim and sent them to the city of Luz. When they arrived there [the two Moors, that is] they died. The next day Solomon once more saw the angel of death. He was laughing now, and Solomon said to him: 'Why are you laughing?' And the angel of death replied: 'You sent them precisely to the place where they were required by me.' Immediately Solomon lifted his voice and spoke: 'The feet of man are a pledge that they will bring him to the place where he is required to be.'

In other words, Solomon had an experience of the angel of death which affirmed for him what Rabbi Yohanan stated as a general truth: 'The feet of man are a pledge that they will bring him to the place where he is required to be.'

Now you will admit, my dear friends, that much remains obscure in this tale from the Haggadah, and many questions about it remain. First we hear that the feet of a human being are a pledge that he will be given up to the location where he is required to be. Why does the tale mention the feet especially? You see, in old, pictorial legends of this kind, nothing is arbitrary, but all has its deeper significance. So that is the first question we can ask. Another must be this: why was the angel of death sad when he appeared before Solomon to tell him he must fetch away his scribes? There is really no explanation in the immediate context of the story to explain this. It would of course be trivial to think that the angel of death was sad because he had to fetch the two. That is his task, after all, and it would be incomprehensible to think that he was sad about it. Solomon asks him, 'Why are you so downcast?' But what is the meaning of this question? The angel of death replies that it is because the two Moors, the scribes of King Solomon, are required by him, and he must fetch them. Yet Solomon gives them over to demons, who bear them away to the city of Luz. Well, the city of Luz is something easier to explain: it was a place that had, strangely, ordained that no one was permitted to die there. Those close to death were therefore carried outside the city boundaries. It was the only city that had this custom in those days. One might think that it is simply this fact that is being described. But no, it is just a part of the story: Solomon hears from the angel of death that his two scribes must die and it is suggested that he sends them to the city of Luz because he thinks the angel of death cannot fetch them from there. This tale from the Haggadah appears in many places in Hebrew tradition. Other such passages tell us that they fell from their mounts just outside the gates of the city and so never arrived there, and the angel of death was still able to fetch them. Then, next day, the angel stands laughing before Solomon; and it would be very easy, though trivial, to say that he is pleased he succeeded in fetching them to death, and is laughing for that reason. Solomon now recognizes the truth that Rabbi Yohanan seeks to impart: that the feet of man really are a pledge that he will be brought to the place where he is required to be.

Usually there is nothing at all arbitrary in such tales. It is even important that the two scribes, the two Moors, are sons of Shisha who was himself the scribe of David. There is a suggestion that these two scribes of King Solomon were very special. We must consider all this if we wish to grasp the whole gravity of questions that can surface here, in a key moment of recognition in the life of King Solomon.

Now let us remind ourselves, too, that King Solomon was called 'wise' not only because he was clever in the modern sense but because he had real insights into the world of spirit, and this world was open before him. Solomon was to learn the truth recounted also by Rabbi Yohanan, related to the human feet.

You see, if we consider the human being and compare him with the animals, we find a key distinction in our upright spine, in the fact that we stand vertically upon the earth while the animal is horizontal to it. I do hope no one will object that kangaroos or suchlike stand vertically, for naturally these are exceptions, and can be explained if we go into these things in detail, which is not what I intend to do at present. The fact remains that the chief distinguishing mark of the human being as regards outward shape is that he stands upright while the animal's spine lies horizontally. if we extend the line of the animal's spine this line will not in fact be entirely straight but curved a little. Overlooking the s-shaped curvature, the arc of this line passes slightly downwards. If we extend this average curve of the animal's spine, we will find that it can give us a circle that encompasses the earth. Really a girdle round the earth! In other words, if we draw a circle parallel to the earth's curve, it will pass through the spine of animals. If we were to do the same thing for the human being, this circle would naturally not encircle the earth but—if you picture it very clearly—you would find that it has a centre. In the case of the animal, the centre would be the centre of the earth, whereas in our case it would be the centre of the moon. Why? Because, back on Old Moon, the human being passed through the evolutionary stage which animals today are passing through in relation to the earth, and this remained with him as a legacy from that period. He is connected with the vestiges of Old Moon in the same way as the animal is connected with the earth.

Thus the human being is connected with the vestiges of Old Moon in the same way as the animal is connected with the earth. The human being therefore has detached himself from his planet, and is not as bound up with it as the animal. As far as his outward, physical being is concerned, he has sundered himself from his planet in as much as one aspect of his being has detached itself from this planet. Instead of the circle I spoke of encircling the earth, it enters the earth and this gives us our standing relationship to the earth, the position of our feet relative to it. This means that we are connected to the earth by virtue of a power that is expressed in the relationship of our feet to the ground. Our whole passage from Moon to Earth evolution is related to the fact that our hands were sundered from the earth while our feet still connect with it. If we understand the human form as it has developed in the transition from Moon to Earth evolution, we have to recognize that we belong to the earth in so far as the earth was able to draw one part of us down towards the feet, pulling us towards itself in the whole shape of the feet.

What gives the earth a pledge that the human being comes to earth? The mystery of his foot position gives it! The word we find in Hebrew in this passage 'The feet are a pledge . . .' is exactly the same that is used, for instance, in financial affairs when a pledge of some kind is given for capital. The phrase means that the feet are held back from human evolution as a pledge for the fact that in one aspect of our being we stay connected with the earth. Thus the phrase does not mean that the feet themselves carry a person to the place of his death. The whole secret of the human form lies in this phrase, and was recognized by Solomon through his capacity to see into the world of spirit. What I have now characterized in words was therefore something revealed to Solomon when he saw the vision of the angel of death. In this example, we see in turn that human beings possessed a wisdom which, on one occasion recently, we have called 'primordial wisdom', which was lost in order to give human beings the opportunity to achieve this wisdom once again in freedom out of their own resources during Earth evolution.

The next enigma in this tale can be the fact that the angel of death is first sad and then laughs. Laughing and weeping are not considered by most people as a question of knowledge worthy of consideration; and when they are, it can sometimes be very disconcerting to see what is said about them today, in an era when, as we heard, even marriage advertisements are thought fit for serious psychological investigation. And yet there are opportunities near at hand to consider the nature of laughing and weeping, for the population at large does have popular wisdom on the subject. If you go to the country you will find a widespread view that if someone is walking along the road and starts laughing, all is not right with him. This points to a deeper insight, a sense that people do not laugh when alone if they have all their wits about them; that laughter is something you do in others' company. Of course there are always exceptions, but by and large it is true. And so, my dear friends, laughter is something we really only do in company. This is not so much the case with weeping. Indeed we may well seek out solitude if we wish to cry fully and properly. The authenticity of those who like to weep in company may be in some doubt. A farmer does not reflect long and hard if he sees someone laughing alone, but he thinks instinctively that there is something wrong with the person in question. Why is this?

To understand phenomena of human life such as laughing and weeping, my dear friends, we really do need to draw on spiritual science. You see, what lives generally in people's awareness does not even hold entirely true in relation to material existence. I have often spoken of how people generally believe a person contains no more than what lives within his skin. This is the general view, but one that is actually itself only skin-deep.

Think for a minute what is inside this skin of a person—it includes air! But while it is inside one moment, the next it is outside again. In other words, it simply is not possible to completely sunder what is inside our skin from all that our whole human existence is embedded in. The earth's atmosphere basically belongs intrinsically and absolutely to our whole nature, entering and leaving us continually. And therefore it will scarcely be a surprise if we extend this idea of the physical human being and his relationship to the wider atmosphere to the whole of our human nature. When we wake up in the morning, we take into ourselves something that is outside during the night. In every moment we take into ourselves the material air that is outside us. Then it is in us. When we wake up, similarly, we take into us what is outside us during the night. When we fall asleep we breathe out our I and astral body in a sense. The physical relationship which we have with the atmosphere is one we can also imagine having with the world of spirit, which corresponds and belongs to the earth. The difference is only that the air we now have in us and later will have exhaled is immediately dispersed in the outer world, whereas the I and astral body we breathe out, as it were, when we fall asleep retain their form, and return to us as they were breathed out. But just as we are connected with the atmosphere around us through the air we contain within us, and keep breathing in and out, in and out, so there is also a tide of life that ebbs and flows between us and the other world, the world of spirit. We should not think that our I and astral body simply slip inside us and then stay there. They are related to the wider world of spirit just as the oxygen we have within us is connected with the whole surrounding atmosphere. Through our I and our astral body, therefore, we are continually in reciprocal connection with the spiritual world.

Let us assume for a moment that something strikes us as funny. What is the reality of this? It is very similar, in fact, to the physical condition that would arise if, instead of breathing in a normal quantity of air, we left a little outside us and dispersed it through our surroundings. When something strikes us comically we extend our I and astral body outward from us, pouring this I and astral body into what we find comical. So when you laugh about something, you are really spreading your I and astral body over it. This is a spiritual process which does not involve such a repulse as when this astral body, in a different feeling, also pours into our surroundings, taking with it something from the physical body. I mean when we stick out our tongue, as do badly behaved children! When we laugh, our tongue stays inside our mouth, but the astral body is in a similar condition in that it is drawn out sufficiently to envelop in a mist whatever makes a comical impression on it. Laughing is based on an expansion and spreading out of the astral body, and this even affects the ether body too. That is what happens when we laugh.

In weeping we find precisely the opposite process: the astral body compresses itself with the etheric body, compressing also the physical body in this contraction, and expressing tears. This is much easier to understand. But you can see that laughing and crying, and naturally also being sad which belongs to the latter—for sadness is the same process without the actual tears—that laughter and rejoicing, and sadness, are due to expansion on the one hand and, on the other, compression, contraction of the human being's invisible nature, and are due therefore also to the action and potency of this invisible nature.

And so now you can also understand what Solomon saw. Naturally he did not see the angel of death as a physical body, but as a spiritual being. He saw how the angel of death expanded and spread out on the second day, whereas it had contracted on the first. Here you have something that can show how spiritual beings act, how they accomplish their actions. In our case, laughter and weeping, happiness and sadness are in a sense an accompaniment and correlate to life, by means of which we merely express our inner state, showing its mood and condition. Mostly our laughter and weeping accomplishes little for other people—we do not accomplish anything much through them. But the moment we approach certain spiritual beings who must work far more than us through their own self and condition, expansion and contraction is the very meaning of what they accomplish. And when the angel of death arrived to fetch the two scribes, he needed to hold his powers together, to compress, condense himself, to gather his powers through this inward concentration in order to begin his work. This is expressed as sadness, which is just a way of suggesting that he compressed himself. The next day, having accomplished his work, there was a corresponding elasticity and expansion. In other words, the sadness and cheerfulness of the angel of death convey a reality of spiritual life to us.

Only someone intent on thinking in trivial terms will take offence at such efforts to look beyond mundane explanations of this sadness and happiness of the angel of death, and instead see them as rooted in deeper spiritual realities. When Rabbi Yohanan discoursed, people still retained a certain feeling of the inherent nature of worlds of spirit. And in the seriousness with which this tale is recounted we can see that Rabbi Yohanan was drawing on it as a way of enlightening people about the nature of spiritual worlds.

In the late Middle Ages, however, when the fifth post-Atlantean epoch was approaching as we described, Jewish exegesists of the

Haggadah began to include people whom representatives of our 'enlightened times' would welcome with open arms. For instance, there was a Jewish exegesist regarded as a great scholar in this progressive time—though not in the older times when people still believed in the realm of spirits. This man said that we should relinquish old, superstitious explanations of the tale and relate it all to the city of Luz. It is known that Solomon, in his day, sought locations for settlements that had good air and a good climate—places suitable for summer residence. Modern, liberal scholars would certainly greet this Jewish exegesist as one of their own! If we know that the city of Luz had such a climate and that it was founded by Solomon for this reason, then we easily discover the supposed rationale for the tale. We need only imagine that the two scribes were, well, not of a 'nervous' disposition, since this complaint would have been unheard of then, but something of this kind—were no longer fully healthy, and that Solomon in his wisdom (which was naturally, in the view of a modern person, a much greater wisdom than vision of the world of spirit) had recognized this. The two scribes are therefore sent to Luz to enjoy the fresh air of its summer climate! But these two died there, not withstanding the fine climate. And this was viewed in those times as a kind of punishment or judgement. Well, in the Middle Ages this was still a reasonable idea; and this explanation was one that arose fairly early, as the fifth post-Atlantean epoch was approaching.

But why is the city of Luz mentioned in the legend? And what is the meaning of the whole event involving Solomon? Well, first we must remind ourselves always that Solomon is someone connected with the world of spirit. I said it was significant that his two scribes were the sons of Shisha, who had been King David's scribe. Thus they are figures of some status and importance. In those days, to be a scribe meant something different from today. For example, in Egypt, scribes, as I have mentioned previously, were required to reproduce the hieroglyphic script with great inner devotion. If someone wrote a sign wrongly they would be condemned to death since the script was a sacred matter. And the scribes of King Solomon, too, were people in communication with the spiritual world; they were connected with it, and, we can say, were part of the community of those who shared with Solomon his knowledge of worlds of spirit. The city of Luz occurs in the tale only to indicate that these scribes possessed a quality of connection with the spiritual world that endowed them with a sense of immortality already in their earthly life. It is a way of telling us that neither these scribes, nor Solomon himself, passed their earthly sojourn without knowing of their soul-spiritual core, which passes through the portal of death. This was not just a theoretical knowledge but to some degree they were initiated into these secrets. For this reason the angel of death needed to connect in a certain way with King Solomon. That is, since the two scribes were aware of their immortality and, since Solomon himself, especially, was aware of this, the angel of death had to approach what he must now undertake in a way that consciously involved Solomon in their death. The tale does not convey an effort on the part of Solomon to protect his scribes from death by sending them to Luz. Instead it seeks to show that death here occurred in full awareness, that full account was taken of it. This is the main emphasis: that Solomon was aware that his scribes would die. And saying that he sent them to the city of Luz is only a way of suggesting that Solomon saw the ahrimanic power, which is embodied in the angel of death, approaching in the form of its agencies, the goat-demons.

Thus the tale seeks to give us a vivid sense of the conscious unfolding of the process it describes: a death occurs which the wise initiate consciously observes. That is what Rabbi Yohanan wished to suggest. And the whole process was transformed into a knowledge possessed by Solomon, so that he now knew how the human being is connected with the earth and the world of spirit. The tale recounts the emergence of knowledge of the supersensible in King Solomon. We only understand the story as it should be understood if we take it as a retrospective account of a process clairvoyantly witnessed by King Solomon. Rabbi Yohanan stated that human beings are bound to the earth through the form of their physical body. The way in which the form of the feet and their position relative to the earth connects them to the earth expresses a one-sided relationship in so far as only the feet are a pledge for the fact that humankind belongs to the earth. But the human being's upright stance is a pledge for the fact that the essential core of his being is given up to the world of spirit. In order for Solomon to be able to believe this, he was granted conscious vision of the death of comrades precious to him.

You see therefore that we only grasp these things with concepts and ideas which are themselves drawn from the world of spirit. And many old legends—as they are called—can only be understood by approaching them with spiritual-scientific ideas. But there is great significance in the recounting of this precise fact about King Solomon, for it tells us that Solomon's wisdom consisted of the capacity to look into the spiritual world, in which the secret of death is first unveiled. And when we learn of the ancient mysteries that the first stage of initiation involves a person experiencing his approach to the portal of death, then what we discover in this legend is really nothing other than that Solomon was one such initiate, and had come to this threshold. In the line of generations descended from King Solomon, we have in a sense the physical preparation for this clairvoyance which approaches the threshold of death. The body of Jesus is thus descended from the Solomon line of the house of David, and the soul is that of Zarathustra. And now let us be very clear what the importance is of the Zarathustra soul, why the soul of Zarathustra indwells a body that is descended from a figure who possessed clairvoyance.

I have often spoken of what came from the soul of Zarathustra. Today let us only consider the aspect that primarily later led to the teachings of Zarathustra, and then chiefly passed on into the teachings of Mani and Manichaeism. One of the profoundest questions which the enigma of the human being poses for us is certainly the relationship between the good, sunny qualities in human life and the evil, shadowy sides of our nature. We know how much of this we can understand when we gain insight into the influence of Lucifer and Ahriman. But this doctrine of Lucifer and Ahriman in a sense leads us back to Zarathustra—to his two spiritual potencies as distinct from the good, progressive deities. In the teachings of Zarathustra we already find the figures of Lucifer and Ahriman as a reality of the world of spirit. But there was something that could not enter this teaching of Zarathustra, my dear friends, because of a certain insight it had into the workings of Lucifer and Ahriman. Something could not form part of these teachings, and in subsequent ages this became an insuperable obstacle for humankind. If one no longer understands the interplay between Lucifer and Ahriman in the world in the right way, one no longer fully understands the world either: good remains an enigma, as does evil. From this perspective let us now look at a later doctrine which is distinguished by the fact that its proponents no longer knew how to encompass the ancient teachings of Zarathustra. This is the doctrine of predestination, and all that is connected with this in Mohammedanism.

On the one hand, this teaching of predestination clearly states that everything which happens is determined in advance. Everything has been as it were predescribed in the ur-text of the most ancient primordial times. I cannot step out of my door without this having been determined in advance. The time of my death is fixed in advance. Everything is strictly predetermined! For a strict Mohammedan nothing happens in life that has not been written down previously in the book of God. But at the same time, whenever a Mohammedan speaks of what might be about to happen, what he hopes will happen, he says, as we might say in Europe, 'If God wills it!' He will not forget to use this phrase in relation to matters that seem important to him: 'If God wills it.' If you ask a western person, or a Mohammedan himself, how these two things can be reconciled—that everything is predetermined and inscribed in advance, and so it can make no sense to say 'If God wills', since if predetermination is true, then there is nothing left to will—they will both say that this is an insoluble contradiction.

It is indeed. If you read all of western philosophy, Spinoza, Descartes, Kant, Fichte, Schelling, Hegel and so on, you will be able to trace in their works the continuing repercussions of this insoluble contradiction, which surfaces in especially blatant form in the doctrine of *kismet*, of predestination in Mohammedanism. Here therefore we have a teaching which in this respect is different from that of Zarathustra. The teaching of Zarathustra would not see a contradiction here, because it encompasses Lucifer and Ahriman. And now, you may recall our reflections here in which we considered how these things are reconciled. From this we can acknowledge a primordial teaching in humanity's evolution that did not give rise to any such contradiction, yet this transformed into another that cannot get round the contradiction, except by ignoring it unthinkingly. This contradiction, my dear friends, is merely similar to many others, though it is one which most closely affects life. It resembles a great many other contradictions that we repeatedly encounter. Anyone who refuses to acknowledge that life is full of contradictions is completely ignoring one side of reality. Life is full of contradictions if we consider it from the standpoint of human reason! And this indeed is what we must do—draw on human reason. In other words, it was necessary for a time to dawn when the human being found himself enmeshed in contradictions. The Zarathustra era was to be succeeded by a time when human beings learn through contradictions, are by this means spurred on to discover their true inner life. Among the many things that earthly evolution should impart to humankind, the many trials we pass through, is this awareness of living in contradictions.

Now let us reflect that the fourth post-Atlantean epoch was a kind of midway point of earthly evolution. In this fourth epoch, what the earth should primarily impart to us had not yet emerged, and would do so only in the middle of the fifth epoch; and the nature of the contradiction relates to this. Contradictoriness is inherent in the earth element. Why was this not already present in Zarathustra's teaching? Because he still enjoyed the legacies of ancient times! In the fourth post-Atlantean epoch human beings were already fully immersed in mundane reality, in earthly things. If people were to gain nothing for their inner powers of reason and understanding than what can be derived from the earth, they would not be able to get beyond the contradictions either; and then the remainder of earthly evolution would pass with the human being inwardly devouring himself in these contradictions, which would destroy his soul. You see the spiritual element that can only develop through our earthly sojourn inevitably involves contradictions.

What had to happen for the human being to be led forth again beyond contradictions? Something that belongs to the earth but has not passed through humanity's earthly evolution had to enter it. Something had to enter that had remained behind in ancient Lemurian times when the human being descended; and this was the being of the Nathan Jesus. The Nathan Jesus stands close to humankind because, we can say, he remained latent and did not engage in earthly evolution; and yet he is free of human contradictions because of this very fact, and only entered the earthly realm when humankind had brought its contradictoriness to a culminating point of evolution, in the fourth post-Atlantean epoch. At this moment he appears as a remedy to the contradiction that inevitably evolves in human nature as we pass through our earthly sojourn. Truly, for their spiritual evolution human beings must have access to the old legacy from Zarathustrian culture; but in addition to this they must acquire the contradictory nature they experience on earth. This is why the Zarathustra Jesus, the Solomon Jesus, had to be complemented by the Nathan Jesus. And those, like the Mohammedans, whose religious confession is otherwise pervaded by this terrible contradiction between predestination and 'if God wills', also at the same time gained the revelation and blessing of the Nathan Jesus. Where, eventually, they find sufficient developmental capacity to comprehend this, they will acknowledge that recognition of the nature of the one whom the Qur'an reveals to them can enable them to discover how predestination and 'if God wills' are reconciled.

In our current stage of evolution, the Mohammedan has not yet achieved this, but in a sense he bears these developmental seeds within him, and they are present, albeit only germinally. Christians should have got further, and should comprehend what they possess in the being who passed through the Mystery of Golgotha, and how the powers of earthly evolution really have united in him. They should understand that humanity's primordial legacy has come to them through the nature of Zarathustra, while the direct gift of human essence entered in the Nathan Jesus.

This is as far as we will go in these reflections for now. But from this you can once more discern how everything is united and reconciled. You can see how things that coexist side-by-side in life do so for good reason. In the Qur'an we find predestination standing side-by-side with 'if God wills it'; but at the same time a remedy is there, the Nathan Jesus. You see, my dear friends, how we approach the real, intrinsic nature of human life, and attempt to broach this in its loftiest forms by drawing on spiritual-scientific concepts. We live in a time when the old forms of knowledge are fading. There are only a few now who still retain this old mode of knowledge, the instinctive knowledge that is a legacy from clairvoyant times. These few are mocked and ridiculed. And the other form of knowledge just beginning to emerge, a knowledge of the rational mind, is regarded by those who trumpet its glories as being in full bloom. Those who see things in their proper light, however, know that such knowledge is just beginning, and is still very inadequate. Realities outstrip this knowledge. In ancient times, when knowledge was endowed by the gods, things were different—it was adapted to and in tune with reality. People now have no inkling that realities speed ahead of them while their knowledge hems them in like a dress that is far too small and tight. As realities emerge, therefore, human beings are as yet unable to use them sufficiently and learn from them what they need to.

In recent years a very rigorous scholar drew on advanced economic ideas to demonstrate that no war in the modern era can last longer than three to four months at the most. He used 'strict scientific methods' to prove this. What can rational people learn from this, now that the war has already lasted two years? They could see that this theory is inadequate to explain the facts. But people do not draw such conclusions so readily. They hold back from doing what they should—questioning why someone with all the tools of modern economic theory can prove that a war cannot last longer than three or four months, and yet his theories are clearly not adequate, cannot encompass reality. This is an unpleasant discovery. The man in question has been well schooled in modern disciplines. To be really consistent in one's thinking one would, ultimately, have to acknowledge that all schools of economics, university economics departments, should be abolished! Since this really cannot be done, it has to be accepted that economics must continue in modern life in the form it has. Continuing as it is, it will certainly offer many more such 'strict and rigorous' proofs, with dire results. And yet if one drew further-reaching consequences, examining whether perhaps other theories would prove equally inadequate to circumstances or not, who knows what might follow from this? And this cannot be countenanced of course, and so all these things continue to be regarded as true.

You see, my dear friends, some courage is required to think things through to the end, and people do not always have this courage. And yet this is what is needed to some degree. It may well be that even then things won't all suddenly change. Think of all the pensions that would have to be paid to the professors without jobs if these economics departments were abolished! But even if things can't change radically from one day to the next, they could slowly find better channels if a group of people, at least, had the courage to think properly, think correctly, and allow what is right in this context to filter through wherever it can. This would be important. In such things one always starts with oneself and tries to think correctly to the degree this is possible. You see, life progresses not by itself but through human endeavour. And though many take comfort from the thought that things won't change all of a sudden since 'nature takes no sudden leaps', the world doesn't suddenly take a step forward, this is not true: the world constantly takes sudden leaps. What would happen do you think if a green leaf were to keep saying, 'I am forbidden from taking sudden leaps'? The leaf would become a very slightly different green leaf, but it would never become a rose, as it does, for the rose emerges from a sudden leap! Nature takes leaps everywhere. And the same is true in human life. Things do not develop comfortably without a leap into the unknown but everywhere new developments emerge—new, sudden leaps—and we must remember this. We can already achieve a good deal by judging things correctly, untinged by predilections or desires about how we wish them to be. You see, thoughts are already living powers.

But in our time people do not manage to form healthy, forthright, positive judgements about things. Instead they accept things as they are without real inner participation, without inner involvement and feeling. For instance, would it not be right and natural for someone who speaks about literary matters, about the literature of a nation, to understand a little of what he is talking about? But this is not universally the case. Recently we have been very thoroughly instructed in the meaning of German literature by a man who knows nothing about it. He is not even a professor of literature but the president of a republic, and has not had an opportunity to learn a subject which he felt called upon to lecture about to a whole nation. A political advocate lectures us on literature! A poet instructs us in politics![82] Both these things have occurred recently, one after another. We must reflect on such phenomena and form our thoughts accordingly. It seems to me that we are far too indifferent and unconcerned nowadays. And theosophy is not there to persuade us to be even more indifferent in a way that is often regarded as 'calm' or, using the word quite wrongly, 'composed'. Composure is something one has to strive for and should by no means make us indifferent to everything. Modern life is asking us to have some fire and energy in our recognition of what is good and in our abomination of what ought not and must not be. This is necessary if evolution is really to progress in the way that the benevolent spirits of humanity desire.

We will speak further of this next time.

Lecture 12

30 May 1916

As you will have seen from various reflections this winter, someone who has a close relationship with spiritual science will need to make his ideas, in so far as they flow from spiritual-scientific insights, ever more tangible and real, or in other words connect these ideas with ever more specific and complete realities. In speaking of the in some senses benevolent spiritual powers of the various hierarchies, we know that certain beings of these diverse hierarchies remain behind at a former stage, and therefore do not unfold the activity they would have done if they had advanced; instead the activity they develop is one that would correspond to a former stage of the evolution of the cosmos. On a large scale, therefore, we can identify luciferic and ahrimanic beings who today engage in activity that normally progressing beings once engaged in during the Old Moon stage. From many different perspectives we have described the significance for the whole cosmos and its evolution of the fact that such luciferic-ahrimanic beings and powers are interwoven with this evolution. Now, in a more intimate circle, we must really accustom ourselves to discerning these luciferic and ahrimanic elements. But to do so correctly, we must shape our feeling world correspondingly, for if, as many amongst us unfortunately still do, we immediately feel in response to Lucifer and Ahriman that we must keep them safely at one remove from us, keep them at a distance, this will of course always lead to excessive unease and anxiety whenever we speak of

Lucifer and Ahriman in this more intimate context. And yet to fully understand world phenomena as we need to if we are to meet life with understanding, we should certainly become able to perceive luciferic and ahrimanic attributes in this smaller circle.

You see my dear friends, centuries before the Mystery of Golgotha occurred, there was majesty and grandeur in the ancient teachings that emerged from India, and were recorded in the Bhagavad-Gita and in other oriental scriptures. At the time this was something great and mighty, of huge significance. You will be able to see from the lecture cycle on the Bhagavad-Gita given in Helsingfors[83] [Helsinki] that our spiritual science in no way seeks to diminish the grandeur and majesty of such things. There indeed I pointed to the great and profound truths contained in the Bhagavad-Gita. For modern humankind it is a very good thing to immerse oneself in this way in something that was of huge importance and significance at that time. But then came the Mystery of Golgotha upon humanity, and only through this in fact do we gain a really historical view of earth's evolution because, if we understand it rightly, we can then distinguish between the time that preceded this Mystery, and prepared for it, and the era that followed it. The Orient does not actually have these concepts of evolution at all, of historical development, since it cannot gain any real understanding of the Mystery of Golgotha. As far as the Orient is concerned, there is only a generally valid truth for all times, rather than any evolution of the truth.

Now in our time a great many people find it difficult to conceive of the evolution of knowledge. This is because we have not yet fully imbued ourselves with the meaning of the Mystery of Golgotha. If we assume therefore that someone in our time wished to speak in roughly the same way as the author of the Bhagavad-Gita spoke, or the Buddha in his time, this would mean that he was seeking to do something that was right for an era centuries before the Mystery of Golgotha. And it could therefore be said that the person in question would have been acting rightly if he had done this at the time the Bhagavad-Gita emerged, and this would, at that time, have been a right and proper deed in accordance with evolution. But if he appears today and speaks in the same manner and sense in which the Bhagavad-Gita was written, he is carrying into our own time something that ought to have been developed back then and therefore his whole way of thinking would extinguish everything that has arisen in evolution since that time.

In fact I am not speaking here in the abstract but wish to refer you to something very specific. In 1912 a book was published entitled *The High Goal of Knowledge. Aranada Upanishad* by Omar al Rashid Bey. Let me expressly mention that Omar al Rashid Bey is not from the Orient and has nothing to do with Mohammedanism, but affiliated himself with it for purely external reasons. We will leave to one side here why he embraced this culture. In fact he is a German and sought to do something you cannot do without joining Islam, which he therefore did. Omar al Rashid Bey also became a Brahmin and wrote this book, *The High Goal of Knowledge. Aranada Upanishad*. His wife Helene Boehlau,[84] published it after his death. Let me note here that I have nothing against the excellent tales and novellas that Helene Boehlau wrote previously. There is no need to tar all of an author's works with the same brush. But the preface which Helene Boehlau, now under her married name of Helene Boehlau al Rashid, wrote for this work by her husband would have been better left unwritten. In *The High Goal of Knowledge*, published in 1912, we do really discover something that could legitimately have been written centuries before the Mystery of Golgotha, and, appearing now, is therefore most eminently luciferic.

A book by me, due to be published soon,[85] contains many of the ideas I presented in public lectures over the previous two winters. But it will also highlight the distinction between the more modern outlook of idealism, which has fully comprehended its place in the world since the Mystery of Golgotha, and the philosophy of ancient India. The book will show how the former has moved on from the latter. You see, my dear friends, the teachings of Fichte, Hegel, Schelling and others I name there go far beyond what is contained in oriental wisdom, in Brahmanism. People do not yet generally acknowledge this progress, this advance, for two reasons, the first of which is, as I describe in my book, that they generally find it difficult to concern themselves with these things. The second is that nowadays, once we have gained some knowledge, we have absolutely no talent for appearing lofty and noble to ourselves and others in the way the Oriental is capable of. You can read this book, *The High Goal of Knowledge. Aranada Upanishad* from cover to cover and you will find that it not only conveys knowledge that the author thinks should be acquired, but continually also adds that this is knowledge imparted by the highest masters of wisdom and that such knowledge is very lofty—so much so that only chosen people can understand it.

Yes, my dear friends, we need only consider how, given the Orient's talent for veneration, someone like Fichte would have been revered, and you will see what we lack in the West. We do not have a gift for looking up to something of grandeur with the same underlying feelings with which the Oriental for instance gazes up to his Buddha or his Shankaracharya.[86] But it is seductive—and here we can even say luciferically so—when someone speaks in this vein. Firstly we find it very appealing when someone writes a *High Goal of Knowledge*. That's quite a title, don't you think, and acts suggestively. Everyone will be eager to acquire such knowledge by reading the book's 173 pages. But apart from this, when the book expressly accentuates that this knowledge is being imparted by the wisest of the wise to you alone, as worthy recipient, and you must therefore be an important person if you are receiving the knowledge preserved by these wisest of the wise, the feelings of incense-wreathed self-elevation can get out of hand, especially when such a book closes with these significant words:

> Peace be with you, O worthy one!
> I have spoken to you of the final goal of knowledge—have said as much as it was fitting to your understanding to say—for earthly good and the redemption of the world—stammering words for a questing soul. From the plains, the first hills have been ascended, the mists are clearing. Before you now shine the

> heights of Himavat. Open your eyes to the divine light—you see truly—and all earthly wisdom is shown to be worthless—the all-blinding nature of appearance has been swept aside—maya is extinguished—a dream—and what awakens in you is greater than all worlds—attainment of the high goal of knowledge, attainment of perfection—perfection in the Godhead.
>
> Thus resounds the adhyaya in the aranada Upanishad: awakening; the ultimate is wordless: Nirvana.[87]

'The ultimate is wordless'! And to accentuate this especially, Helene Boehlau al Rashid tells us in her preface that we should take this wordlessness in its deepest sense. In her pupilship to the content of this book, she states that she now acknowledges that human words are inadequate to express the things of greatest profundity. In other words, of course, the book contains much profounder matter than it actually expresses! The wordless knowledge, to which ultimate appeal is made in the book, must naturally be especially profound! If one already considers what it states to be endlessly profound, what it does *not* say must be all the more so. And yet, my dear friends, it is one thing to write and think such a thing, and quite another to hold fast to it. The words themselves are not the ultimate, wordless truth. But the book does start with a hugely profound vision, one rendered in a way that is fully in keeping with the ancient oriental mode of wisdom and utterance:

> If I stand *here*, and another stands *here*, he stands to my left. I say truly that he stands to my left. But when another stands *there*, the same person stands to his right, and thus left and right are not absolute designations. If I define his position, I say 'left'; when the other defines it, he says 'right'. And so right and left are maya.

How could one possibly give a better idea of maya than to say left and right are only relative terms, imposed from without! And the book continues with roughly this level of 'profundity'; for its depth is primarily assured by continually stating that its statements are unfathomably deep.

But the book raises itself to other matters too. You may know, and will easily realize if you read the book I am soon to publish, that the thinkers who cultivated a modern philosophical idealism were primarily concerned to experience the I, and to dwell within it. This is what is required since the Mystery of Golgotha. But oriental wisdom was concerned by contrast not only to experience the I but also vanquish and extinguish it. And now Omar al Rashid Bey, a German not an Oriental, renews this ancient Indian wisdom by saying, 'He who seeks salvation in the "I" hearkens to the command of selfhood: self-seeking is his god.'

Yes, my dear friends, apparently whoever *seeks* his salvation in the I, makes selfhood, self-seeking his highest command and god. In fact self-seeking, egoism, precedes discovery of the I. As long as we are still seeking the I, we develop selfishness, from which we are only liberated by finding the I. Once we have found it, we can no longer be tormented by self-seeking, by egoism. In discovery of the I lies the only true means to overcome self-seeking or selfishness. And today, after the Mystery of Golgotha, anyone who still seeks to flee the I, who still says the kinds of thing that were said ages past in ancient India, is thrown back from the I into the search for the I, the obsession with it. Such a person, in particular, will cultivate egoism. This is why books of this kind make such a self-seeking impression on us today, strike us as addressed to those who withdraw from the world and do not wish to seek the immortal, spiritual heart of reality, who take flight from reality instead and selfishly seek knowledge in their dreams. This is a self-seeking knowledge, one which fails to discern its own nature and is therefore the worst selfishness of all. This is why the whole book is selfish and self-obsessed. As long as the I had not yet entered humanity's evolution—that is, prior to the Mystery of Golgotha—the quest for the I was inevitably a lofty undertaking, and oriental wisdom was called for. To speak in this way today means seemingly to push the I away before you while behind Lucifer takes a hold of you and really, properly, shoves you down into selfishness. And you don't even notice!

And then the book continues: 'Whoever seeks his salvation in this world, will succumb to it and remain in its clutches.'

But since the Mystery of Golgotha we should say that whoever does not seek his salvation in the spiritual nature of the world but instead takes fright and flees it will succumb to the world even more. That is, he succumbs to the world that dreams in him!

And then the author continues: 'He will not escape by harbouring unsatisfied longing.'

He means that such a person will succumb again and again to unsatisfied longing. But the one who says this has succumbed to a longing for the I and does not notice this because he flees it.

'He will not escape through worthless play.'

Instead of accepting reality, or instead of facing it and seeking within it for what is spiritual, flight is taken from it. And because of this a person will fall back still more so into reality and fully succumb to it.

'He will not escape the tight chains of the I.'

But the very finding of this I is what enables us to wrest ourselves free of these chains!

'He who does not raise himself from this world of his will live and pass away with it.'

But if we speak in accordance with the Mystery of Golgotha, we will say this: 'Whoever binds himself to the eternal nature of this world, and seeks the eternal within the temporal, will not pass away with this world.'

Almost every sentence in the book can be turned on its head to discover what is right for our time. I myself wrote in its margin: 'He who flees the I succumbs to obsession with it, for obsession with the I makes the I into an I only for oneself; finding the I liberates one from obsession with the I, liberates us from selfishness.' The world is won through someone who penetrates the world with perception and understands it. The original says: 'He who does not raise himself from this world of his will live and pass away with it.'

Today, after the Mystery of Golgotha, we say instead: 'The world is won through someone who penetrates the world with perception and understands it.'

Thus you can see from this that what we call 'luciferic' in a fully technical sense of the word also has its profound importance in our more immediate historical development. To propound as valid for our time something that was taught millennia ago means to teach a luciferic doctrine. Seers, though, who embrace reality, are all too easily ignored today because people do not consider it important enough to concern themselves with the content of their seership. Wisdom such as that in *The High Goal of Knowledge* very much addresses what we can call higher human selfishness. To concern oneself with reality, to understand and embrace it, is of less interest. Nor do we have much talent for acknowledging and esteeming those who do so when they live amongst us, as the Oriental of past ages acknowledged and revered his Buddha.

Robert Hamerling[88] is one such figure, and in certain respects is indeed a seer or visionary, and the greatest modern poet of central Europe. I do not wish to speak about Robert Hamerling's poetry or philosophy in general here. You can read more about this in the book I referred to, which is soon to be published. I would just like to highlight how Hamerling's gift of vision has proven its worth in a thorough perception of what is happening in the world today. He demonstrated his seership, his visionary gift, in a great satirical epic, *Homunculus*, that was published shortly before he died. What kind of poem is this? Well, I won't read it to you today—you can of course read it for yourself. I wish only to show how we can understand the idea of the homunculus, homunculism, in modern terms. We have amongst us—I don't mean specifically here but in society in general, and if they were here then naturally those present would be exceptions!—people who believe that the scientific mode of thinking is the only valid one and all our views should be founded on it, that everything must or can be explained in scientific terms. Accordingly they reject everything that is either not explained or cannot be explained scientifically, regarding it as phantasm and dream, mysticism, occultism! Such people exist of course, and they assume that everything is subject to mechanistic and material laws, including all mental and spiritual phenomena and experiences. They too are subject to material, mechanistic laws of matter and energy. Well, naturally one can conceive such a thing. But the world as pictured by a materialistic thinker cannot be real, and in such a world even the smallest plant would not develop, let alone an animal or human being. But still, we could ask what kind of a human being would arise if the world was as believed to be by those who acknowledge and admit only scientific ideas. What would such a person be like? He would of course have been engendered by a world of purely mechanistic laws, and there would be no mysteries involved. Hamerling answers this question with authentically artistic, poetic power, presenting in his homunculus a person who would inevitably exist if there were only a materialistic world: a little man, a homunculus! And this homunculus achieves a good deal. If you recall various things I have said in recent lectures, you will see that the brain is in some respects a mechanical instrument, and could arise from mere mechanisms. The brain could therefore engender cleverness—such a person could be terribly clever and could place himself with extreme adroitness into this mechanistic world order. Hamerling's homunculus is very clever, and well able to handle and combine all the things that arise in the world. He launches a global newspaper, which is possible of course in a world in which the homunculus thrives—where one can be a great newspaper magnate. The homunculus also becomes a billionaire. Not just a millionaire but a billionaire! That is also perfectly feasible in a world devoid of spirit. Thus things continue. He founds a school for monkeys because, based on materialistic Darwinism, he naturally believes that human beings are descended from apes. And therefore, if you teach apes properly, give them formal schooling, they will naturally turn into human beings—their evolutionary journey is shortened by this means. The section about the ape school in Hamerling's *Homunculus* is really excellent. He also shows the position adopted by people such as journalists. All this can happen in a world of homunculism. We can really say that Hamerling wrote with visionary insight in the 80s of the last century; for naturally there would also be airships in the homunculist world—much better ones perhaps than we have so far, since our old views still hamper things somewhat, or do so at least in the opinion of some. Hamerling's homunculus builds himself an airship—he was writing in the 80s as I said—but unfortunately, when he sets out into the cosmos in it, he is caught up by the universe's powers of attraction, by cosmic gravity, and drawn by mechanical forces into space. And so when you go out in the evening and look up very carefully you may spot a tiny wreck in the far distance—and that is homunculus on his shattered spaceship. He is still clinging to its last few spars, slowly merging with the mechanical forces.

Hamerling's *Homunculus* is founded on reality and is written with a real visionary gift. Of course the world that the homunculus imagines does not exist, but people can allow their thinking to conform to it and, at least for a while, for an era, can establish homunculistic thinking. In Hamerling's view, homunculism is making headway and taking hold of people. People cannot make nature soulless, for it retains its soul; but they can make themselves soulless. And homunculus, the man without a soul, also finds a soulless wife. His perception and knowledge, to which soul and spirit find no entry, make him a soulless man.

Hamerling sensed that people would celebrate the idea that they had overcome Goethean classicism and everything connected with it. Goethean classicism still retains its complete faith in *homo sapiens*, the knowing or wise human being who could discover within his mind and spirit something that can establish a human-scale society. Such people are certain that all human society is dependent on merely economic circumstances, that these condition and create human nature and that therefore the old classicism that regarded the human being as *homo sapiens* is now outmoded. Hamerling sensed the advent of such an outlook. You may laugh at me for suggesting that anyone could be so misguided as to think that the old classicism, with its belief in *homo sapiens*, might be dismissed as a thing of the past, and that increasingly people will believe in a *homo economicus* instead. You might think it ridiculous that ideas and ideals will no longer be considered important in human society, but that the latter will be governed only by mechanistic principles, by scientific and economic laws in which *homo economicus* is but a cog in society's machine and the dull-witted idea of *homo sapiens* has been consigned to oblivion.

You may think that such a crazy idea cannot be thought intelligent. But let me relate to you, my dear friends, something I read a little while ago in the *Berliner Tageblatt*, an article by my old friend Engelbert Pernerstorfer,[89] who is now the vice-president of the Austrian Imperial Council. In many respects he is a very intelligent man. In this article he was celebrating a book by a certain Dr Renner,[90] entitled *Austria's Renewal*. I had every reason to attend to this book since in his review of it my old friend Pernerstorfer said it was a work that all our contemporaries should pay heed to. He said it showed there were still people who know how the world should be organized once this war has ended—that people with very fruitful, creative ideas still existed. Naturally, since one should keep abreast of developments, I ordered the book. And in it I read this:

> Other forces have become visible in many ways in this war. Most noticeably, one sees how the economic maturity of nations testifies to their dominance. Hindenburg's victories were rightly called 'railway victories' since the good state of roads, railways and routes in the country is a pledge of military success, albeit a sign only of more advanced economic organization.

Not to be disputed. But let us read on:

> The greatest re-evaluation brought about by this world war relates to our economic, social, political and military assessments of industry and thus of the industrialized nation as such and its labour force. Here a real revolution has occurred in public awareness.
>
> And now comes the war; and high and low, here and abroad, the cry has gone out unceasingly and ultimately indisputably

> that the victory belongs to industry! Germany's industry has saved the Fatherland and has proven itself the indestructible and irresistible impetus of the nation! The industrialized nation here conquers the trading state, the welfare state and the agrarian state. Industry is the core of our nation!
>
> Only an industrialized nation can, at one fell swoop, turn cavalrymen to infantrymen, reservists to well-armed battalions, and home guardsmen into soldiers at the Front. This is the achievement of an industrialized nation whose workers must often in their lives change company, sector and job, and repeatedly find their feet again in new circumstances if the economy is not to founder.

The author writes that the prevailing ideas of a former time should no longer govern the social order, but instead we should be guided by science: this, with its mechanical laws, informs and organizes industry and also incorporates the human being as a cog in the industrial machine. This, apparently, is the greatness of modern science and organization!

> Science and organization become living practice only in the industrial populace. From now on these experiences must inform and imbue our whole political practice.
>
> It is not by chance that in this war the idea of the state has proven to be more powerful than the principle of nationality. In the half-century since the historical high-point of the idea of pure nationalism, the world and human beings have undergone astonishing development. The predominant interests of those now distant decades were still literature, art and philosophy: the classical age remained an influence.
>
> Technology and economy now dominate human imagination, and from being *homo sapiens* in the classical age we have now become *homo economicus*: economic interests predominate and overshadow everything else.
>
> And thus the modern state is regarded differently and accorded a different value . . . as an economic state, both for its

> own members and in the eyes of outsiders, its value lies in its economic function.

There we have it! That is what we have come to: 'Technology and economy now dominate human imagination, and from being *homo sapiens* in the classical age, we have now become *homo economicus*: economic interests predominate and overshadow everything else.'

This is the book that was recommended as one of the most significant and radical new signs of modern thinking, as something we should pay full heed to if we wish to renew modern life. But what is it? Homunculism! What Hamerling anticipated in the 80s of the last century has become a reality. Here we have homunculism as system, as philosophical world-view! Homunculus not only becomes a billionaire, not only founds a global newspaper, but he also writes the book *Austria's Renewal. Political Essays* by Dr Karl Renner, Member of the Imperial Council! Hamerling was a visionary, and saw what was coming. And what has come could find a remedy if it would look back to what Hamerling created in his *Homunculus*. Dr Karl Renner, who probably lives in Vienna, need only to go to Graz to discover that a certain Hamerling lived three decades before him and predicted all this.

It is important for us to understand why a creation such as this 'homunculus' is such an achievement. It is outstanding because, without possessing spiritual science, Hamerling asked himself what a human being would be if he only had a physical body. Naturally he did not specifically say this, but that is how he described his creation. In his homunculus we have a person who basically brings no legacy with him from Saturn, Sun and Moon periods of evolution, but possesses only earthly evolution, thus lacking the core aspects of the I, astral body and the etheric body. Hamerling's *Homunculus* can properly be understood by drawing on the science of the spirit. And so, my dear friends, it is important that we closely examine modern realities and developments.

Last time I said that the idea of the Mystery of Golgotha, as we know it from spiritual science, brings three things together: firstly the Zarathustra Jesus as embodied in the Solomon Jesus child who brings what humanity has undergone through history, what he himself has undergone in passing from incarnation to incarnation. And then I described what the Nathan Jesus child brings: the nature of humankind predestined for the earth, but before it descended into incarnations and passed through historical development. I showed that the Qur'an fully acknowledges this Nathan Jesus child, including the fact that he spoke at the moment of birth. To these two elements we bring the third: Christ's non- and super-earthly nature, which enters the person of Jesus of Nazareth, the Solomon-Nathan Jesus, in his thirtieth year; and thus we can recognize in the Christ a connection between worlds of spirit beyond the earth with what was accomplished on earth. At the same time I highlighted the need for our age to acknowledge this grandeur of the figure of Jesus, and thus also the grandeur of the Mystery of Golgotha. Our time, in its fifth post-Atlantean epoch, has very greatly developed the power of reason, rational thinking; but this must be complemented by a spiritual comprehension of the world. And then people will understand the Mystery of Golgotha again, and do so in a more advanced way than was possible in preceding centuries. We must acquire the means to understand the Mystery of Golgotha. But before this can happen fully, everything that ahrimanic powers infuse into this view of humankind first emerges. Basically, all good spirits are waiting for human beings to understand the Mystery of Golgotha, but everything as yet opposes this human endeavour. People do not wish to approach an understanding of this Mystery of Golgotha, and therefore unconsciously traduce it, at the same time also unconsciously traducing the figure who must stand at the centre of this Mystery. If you imagine for a moment someone who really seeks to experience, to live through, all the profound feelings, the serious feelings and sentiments that can be engendered in us through the manner in which we understand the Mystery of Golgotha, and that he then encounters another who speaks of Christ Jesus as he is understood in modern culture, you may perhaps conceive how the first will experience the latter view as a terrible calumny and dismissal of what his real knowledge of the Mystery of Golgotha enables him to feel. His interlocutor may object by saying that his understanding flies in the face of rationality, that he is crazy, that he can only believe such things because he is a crazy fantasist, and that only such a dreamer can make anything of the way in which the Gospels describe Jesus Christ.

Someone might experience this. And if the person who raises such objections thinks himself a poet, and has even written good poetry to some degree, and, lacking further matter for his poems now also takes up the subject of Christ Jesus, he might well wish to portray this artistically. He might ask: 'What is the real nature of someone today who absorbs what the Gospels have to say about Christ Jesus?' Yes, he must be fantasist, a dreamer, somewhat weak-minded. A clever person after all, someone at the centre of our 'glorious cultural advances', will naturally regard the Gospels with a critical eye, will discover their contradictions, and realize that Jesus can only have been a good man who lived in Nazareth. A rational person, he will think, cannot possibly believe in what the Gospels contain, and so anyone who does must be weak-minded. Only someone who is weak-minded can think of following Jesus Christ. Someone at the forefront of our cultural progress cannot. A weak-minded fellow of this kind might, as described by the person who thinks himself 'advanced', go on his wanderings and arrive in some village, stand under a street light there and start preaching because he believes himself to be filled with the spirit of Christ. And then, because he is seen as weak-minded, he might well be locked up. It is possible to imagine a situation in which a modern Christian is locked up for his beliefs. Then let us imagine that he is interviewed by the local priest, who impresses on him that he must not preach about Christ because he is not a priest, and by a judge, who releases him finally after reading him the riot act. He is only an idiot after all and is allowed to go on his way. And so it goes on: he meets others who believe in his idiocy; and he finds he has the gift of healing, can heal them. You see, there is a belief nowadays that 'illness'—not real illness of course—can be cured if someone not quite in his right mind lays hands on those who seek this. The weak-minded fellow goes on growing more and more weak-minded, and comes to believe—because everyone tells him that Christ really is present in him—that he is Christ. In this further tale things take a turn for the worse and he is misjudged and maligned. Well, you can imagine the dreadful kind of tale that might be written if someone who embraces contemporary cleverness decided to represent Christ in this way.

But this has happened. Here is the book: *The Fool in Christ, Emanuel Quint*, a novel by Gerhart Hauptmann,[91] and it contains what I have just briefly summarized. This is not to say that Hauptmann has not in the past written some fairly good plays and other things. But it is the nature of our time that someone regarded as the greatest poet of the age resorts to an account of Christ that depicts him as an idiot. I realize of course that a great many people will retort that my critique is due to religious or philosophical objections, and that I have failed to recognize the work's purely aesthetic value. In purely aesthetic terms, in fact, the book is a sorry effort. And rather than a poor imitation of Dostoyevsky's *The Brothers Karamazov*, I would prefer to read Dostoyevsky himself, and would advise everyone else to do the same if that is the kind of thing they wish to read. Even small details of Hauptmann's book remind one of *The Brothers Karamazov*, for this fool in Christ is accused of committing a murder. He is innocent and is released; he regards himself as Christ and wanders through the world, knocking on any door he cares to: priests, cardinals, bishops and so on. He knocks on everyone's door because, naturally, he believes that all should accept the Christ. Everyone turns him away or throws him out, because he is seen as a fool. And the book ends pathetically after a description of him knocking on the door of a former teacher:

> The same thing happened a few days later in the house of a teacher where Emanuel Quint had once listened to Brother Nathanael's penitential sermon . . .

The names are all allusions.

> . . . The teacher's family were sitting at table while a cold autumn wind blustered in the darkness outside. A step was heard at the threshold. And then a knocking on the door. The teacher's wife did not wish to open the door, for she was afraid. With some anxiety himself, the pious teacher commended himself to the Lord and, opening the door a crack, asked, 'Who's there?'
>
> 'Christ!' came the quiet answer.
>
> With a force that made the whole house shake, the teacher slammed the door shut in the man's face. He returned shaken to his wife and told her there was a madman outside.

And so it continues. The whole tale ends neatly as follows:

> One week later the same nonsense again began to preoccupy the people of Frankfurt for a little while. In the intervening period hundreds and hundreds of doors had been flung shut in the face of the fool and beggar who called himself Christ. A Frankfurt resident who viewed these events ironically said that, with all the noise of slamming doors, the Lord in heaven must surely have noticed the goings-on amongst the human race.
>
> We should thank heaven . . .

And now comes the really outrageous passage.

> . . . that this wanderer was only a poor earthly fool and not Christ himself, for otherwise hundreds of Catholic and Protestant priests, labourers, officials, councillors, traders of all kind, general superintendents, bishops, nobles and citizens—in brief, numerous pious Christians—would have burdened themselves with the curse of damnation.
>
> But how was anyone to know—although we pray 'not to be led into temptation'—whether, at the end of the day, it was not the true Saviour who, in the guise of a fool, wished to see how his divine seed, the seed of his kingdom, was coming to fruition?

The back door is left open here to the possibility that Christ could have incarnated in the figure of the fool, to see how things were progressing on earth. Naturally Christ in the world of spirit is unable to do this, according to a man such as Gerhart Hauptmann who is part of our 'glorious culture'.

> In this case Christ would have continued his wanderings, as we saw, through Darmstadt, Karlsruhe, Heidelberg, Basel, Zurich, Lucerne to Goeschenen and Andermatt, and would only have had door-slamming in his face to report back to his Father in heaven. The last we heard of him, the fool who called himself Christ was sharing bread and shelter for the night with two merciful Swiss shepherds. Since then no one has seen him.

If you read the advertisements in the newspapers—which is an interesting thing to do after all—you may have seen a large announcement in most of them, spread over most of a whole page. The announcement came in various versions, but I will read you one of the many that have just been published:

> The paperback edition of the novel *The Fool in Christ, Emanuel Quint* by Gerhart Hauptmann is now available, 540 pp., paperback 3.75 Marks.
>
> It is easy to predict that this book will be reprinted countless times and translated into all the languages of the civilized world. It will gain fame as an authentic religious novel, one not only praised but avidly read for generations. It is no exaggeration to say this for the book is one of overwhelming power and worth. Its subject encompasses nothing less than the religious conflicts of our era, portrayed in the form of a dreamer, a son of the people, who credits himself with being the son of God. Every religious person will be edified and uplifted by this great avowal of our greatest living poet. Here Hauptmann has accomplished his finest work.

This review is not one written by the publisher himself, Samuel

Fischer, but comes from the pen of a very clever gentleman writing for a newspaper in Berlin!

You see, my dear friends, during the course of this winter I often found it necessary to speak of how spiritual science should render our thinking healthy, how it should shape our forms of thought in the right way. It is symptomatic of our time that someone who says the *homo sapiens* of classical times has been overcome, and that *homo economicus* must take his place, is not regarded as crazy, as he should be, but as a cultural benefactor: as someone who, in the figure of the homunculus Dr Karl Renner, is now in a position to solve life's enigmas.

But a great deal of work has been undertaken, my dear friends, a very great deal of work, to tempt humankind away from really healthy thinking in tune with reality. In the book by me that is shortly to appear you will find a clear account of thinking in accord with reality. Today we not only have the old *Critique of Pure Reason* by Immanuel Kant, which makes it clear that human beings cannot get near the 'thing-in-itself', that all is illusion, but we now also even have, as I have frequently mentioned, Fritz Mauthner's *Critique of Language*.[92] There are now ardent proponents of this *Critique of Language*, journalists especially who sing its praises and trumpet it abroad. Many now regard Mauthner's work as a monumental contribution to modern philosophy whereas in fact it is nothing but the most abject dilettantism. Mauthner is not even capable of realizing that we do not think or picture things through words alone but that, rather, the word is like a signpost, a gesture pointing towards what it designates, both in the physical and the spiritual domain. Because Mauthner has no inkling of the nature of language he begins to criticize the word, believing that people created it and then simply adhere to words which are devoid of any underlying reality. But you see we cannot criticize reality by attacking language. Let me illustrate this with a rather drastic example. Mauthner has written three heavy tomes—not only his *Critique of Language* but also *A Dictionary of Philosophy* in two thick volumes. There he collates, let us say, concepts of existence, knowledge and so on, all treated in terms of each word itself and its derivation: where the word originates, where it first appears, how it has been translated from one language to another. And he thinks that this will give us insight into the nature of reality. Here is the drastic example I wished to give you. Let us assume that Fritz Mauthner is travelling through Austria, and finds a phrase that originated there, let us say 'Bohemian privy counsellor'. The expression 'Bohemian privy counsellor' is very common in Austria. Now what would Mauthner, in his critique of language, be obliged to do if he follows his own methodology? First he would start with the 'B' in his dictionary of philosophy, and would have to fully critique the concept 'Bohemia'. Then he would look up the 'P' and the 'C', analyzing the idea of the privy counsellor, and in this way seeking to discover the nature of the reality of the 'Bohemian privy counsellor'. But in fact, in Austria, the 'Bohemian privy counsellor' need be neither a Bohemian nor a privy counsellor. In fact most 'Bohemian privy counsellors' there are neither Bohemian nor privy counsellors! If they are a privy counsellor, this is only accidental. And most of them are not; and they certainly do not need to come from Bohemia. It will be completely accidental if they do. In Austria, the phrase 'Bohemian privy counsellor' refers to a skulker with a gift for pushing his way forward to gain some advantage and elbowing others aside in the process. This has nothing to do with either 'Bohemian' or 'privy counsellor'. He could be a registry officer born in Steiermark, and yet still be a 'Bohemian privy counsellor'. Thus you can see that the way in which the word has formed *points* to a reality, and all words develop in this way. If you seek the reality in words themselves, you will often find as little of it as one will find in 'Bohemian privy counsellor' in Austria if one does not probe further than the mere content of the words themselves to find what the phrase actually means.

So you see, my dear friends, that we have reached this degree of confusion in our time, along with a very great dose of arrogance into the bargain since the confusion is seen as innovative achievement. It really is not unimportant to know that works in which human imagination is poisoned in the way Gerhart Hauptmann does this in *The Fool in Christ* are going into paperback editions and being read in huge numbers. It really is not a matter of indifference if human thinking becomes as confused as it can be through a work such as this *Critique of Language*. We can see such things as the outpouring of an arrogant rationality that opposes any real comprehension of the Mystery of Golgotha—which we so urgently need today. As Christ himself was crucified, the idea of Christ is now also being crucified in modern humanity, and is being so through a book such as *The Fool in Christ, Emanuel Quint* by Gerhart Hauptmann. Of course Hauptmann thinks himself so clever because he shows that bishops, priests, officials and so forth slammed the door in the fool Quint's face when he told them he was Christ. He even adds, in elegiac mode, that Christ might be present in this fool, and these people would therefore have cast him out too when he came to see how the world was getting on. But my dear friends, if the real Christ had, by way of a trial, entered some human being and knocked at the door of Gerhart Hauptmann while he was writing his words of wisdom in *The Fool in Christ*, Hauptmann too would have slammed the door shut and thrown him out.

A great many things prevent people today from approaching a threefold understanding of Christ: the historical Christ who entered the Christ figure through the soul of Zarathustra; the earthly Christ upon whom, however, earthly life had not yet exerted its influence, the Nathan Jesus child; and the third aspect for our understanding of Christ, the power which descended from spiritual heights and rendered all life on earth fruitful. This threefold understanding, my dear friends, is one we must seek to acquire. And it will be acquired if spiritual science penetrates all self-seeking and egotism: all the pride of those who, while saying that silence is the highest goal of knowledge, nevertheless chatter away about left and right and the one sometimes being the other; and of those who want to found new social orders in the image of the homunculus; and of those too who create blaspheming and worthless 'novels', if that is what they can be called, about the 'fool in Christ'. Despite all this, there will be human souls and minds who succeed in approaching an understanding of the threefold Christ.

NOTES

1. Friedrich Lienhard, 1865–1929.
2. Johann Friedrich Oberlin, 1740–1826, a priest at Waldersbach in Steintal (Vosges) 'whose committed endeavours to support an ailing parish, both inwardly and practically, awakened general admiration in several European countries' (G.H. von Schubert). The latter's biography of him brought him widespread recognition in the nineteenth century. Another book by Schubert, *The Symbolism of the Dream*, Leipzig 1840, contains an appendix entitled, 'Reports from a spiritual seer on the condition of the soul after death', in which, based on Oberlin's diary, his experiences and visions were reproduced.
3. Wilhelm Jordan, 1819–1904. See Rudolf Steiner, *Gesammelte Aufsätze zur Literatur 1886–1902*, GA 32. His epic *Demiurgos* was published in 3 volumes in Leipzig, 1854.
4. Most of the poems by Lienhard recited by Marie Steiner are to be found in the volume *Gedichte*, Stuttgart 1906.
5. Lecture on 8 February 1916 in GA 166.
6. Max Rheinhardt, 1873–1943, at that time director of the Deutsche Theater in Berlin.
7. Fyodor Mikhailovitch Dostoyevsky, 1821–81, *The Brothers Karamazov* (1879–80). See also Rudolf Steiner, *Gesammelte Aufsätze zur Literatur*, GA 32.
8. Emil Rasmussen, *Jesus, a Comparative Psychopathological Study*, Leipzig 1905; De Loosten (Dr G. Lomer), *Jesus Christ from a Psychiatric Perspective*, Bamberg 1905. See also Albert Schweitzer, *The Psychiatric Study of Jesus*, reprint edition Beacon Press, 1948.
9. Leo Nikolai Tolstoy, 1828–1910. See Rudolf Steiner, *Gesammelte Aufsätze zur Literatur*, GA 32.
10. Raphael Loewenfeld, 1854–1910, wrote a biography of Tolstoy and published his works (8 vols., 1891–3, new edition in 33 vols, 1910–11).
11. In his last published piece of research, *The formation of vegetable mould through the action of worms*, 1881, he showed the connection between the action of worms and soil fertility. See W. v. Wyss, *Charles Darwin*, Zurich 1958, pp. 263 f.
12. *Faust* I, lines 602–5.
13. This may have been Joseph Austen Chamberlain (1883–1937) who was Minister for India and the son of the statesman Joseph Chamberlain (1836–1914).
14. In *The Soul's Awakening*, Scene 6.
15. *The Soul's Probation*, Scene 1.
16. Master Bertram, *c.* 1345–1415. The Grabower Altarpiece of 1379, Kunsthalle, Hamburg.

17. Moriz Benedikt, 1835–1920, founder, with Lombroso, of criminal anthropology. *Anatomische Studien an Verbrechergehirnen*, 1878.
18. Swedish scientist Svante Arrhenius, often referred to by Steiner, ends the foreword to his book *Die Vorstellung vom Weltgebäude im Wandel der Zeiten* Leipzig 1908, with the words: 'In the firm hope that the future will grow better, we can say with Goethe, the great connoisseur of nature and humankind: "A joyful thing it is to enter in / to the spirit of the age and to perceive / how a wise man thought before our time / and how we then advanced it gloriously." '
19. 25 February 1916, GA 166.
20. Karl Christian Planck, 1819–80, *Testament eines Deutschen. Philosophie der Natur und der Menschheit*, Tuebingen 1881, new edition Jena 1915, p. XIV
21. Leipzig, 21 February 1916, GA 166.
22. 12 October 1905, in *Das Goetheanum*, 24th year, 1945, pp. 241 ff.
23. Helena Petrovna Blavatsky, 1831–91. Founder with Henry Steel Olcott of the Theosophical Society in New York, 1875.
24. According to the Old English saga, Hengist and Horsa came to the aid of King Vortigern in his war with the Picts and Scots. After their victory they settled with their Lower Saxon tribal comrades in Kent, Essex and Sussex.
25. Here Steiner is following comments by C.G. Harrison in his work *The Transcendental Universe*, London 1893, which was translated into German in 1897.
26. Pseudonym of the author A.A. Dudevant, 1804–76. Her novel *Le compagnon du Tour de France* was published in 1840 (2 vols).
27. 24 March 1916, GA 65.
28. Annie Besant, 1847–1933. The comments quoted appeared in *The Theosophist*, London 1914, Vol. XXXVI, no. 3, p. 196.
29. From 1899 the building of a railway was undertaken, with German involvement, from the Near East via Baghdad to the Persian Gulf, and this led to political tensions due to a fear of German influence in the Middle East.
30. After the central European movement separated from the Theosophical Society in India, Annie Besant asserted, without any foundation, that Steiner had been brought up by Jesuits.
31. J. Krishnamurti, under the name of Alcyone, was pronounced by Annie Besant and her followers to be the Christ reborn, with the support of the order 'The Star of the East' founded for this purpose.
32. Prominent member of the Theosophical Society.
33. Eliphas Lévi: the pseudonym of Abbé Alphonse Louis Constant, 1810–75, author of *Dogme et rituel de la haute magie* (1854–6); and *La clef des grands mystères* (1861).
34. Dr Encausse wrote under the pseudonym of Papus. His works include *Traité méthodique de science occulte*, Paris 1891, and *Traité élémentaire de magie pratique*, Paris 1893.
35. Jakob Boehme, 1575–1624. See Rudolf Steiner in GA 7 and GA 58.
36. Louis Claude Marquis de Saint-Martin, 1743–1803, *Des erreurs et de la vérité ou les hommes rappelés au principe universel de la science par un Ph(ilosophe) inc(onnu)*,

1775, German by Matthias Claudius 1782, new edition, Stuttgart, 2 vols, 1922–5.

37. Published Berlin, 1916.
38. E. v. Gumppenberg, *Was ist und was bewirkt geisteswissenschaftliche Schulung?* Leipzig 1916.
39. In this context Rudolf Steiner referred on other occasions to Scotus Erigena.
40. Vitruvius Pollio, b. *c.* 80–90 BC, d. after *c.* 15 BC, military architect under Caesar and Augustus. He wrote ten books, *De architectura*, between 16 and 13 BC.
41. Girolamo Savonarola, 1452–98.
42. Giovanni Pico della Mirandola, 1463–94. Quoted in *Giovanni Pico della Mirandola, Ausgewählte Schriften*, translated and introduced by Arthur Liebert, Leipzig 1905, pp. 54 ff.
43. Friedrich Eckstein, 1861–1939, *Comenius und die Böhmischen Brüder*, Austria, Insel-Verlag, undated. The quotes from Comenius appear on pp. 14 ff. and 42 ff. of this book. In relation to Eckstein, see Rudolf Steiner's *Autobiography*, GA 28, and *Letters I*.
44. Carl Ludwig Schleich, 1859–1922, *Vom Schaltwerk der Gedanken*, 5th edition Berlin 1917, pp. 256, 260 f., 261 f.
45. Thassilo von Scheffer, 1873–1951. It is not clear what this remark refers to.
46. August Strindberg, *A Dream Play*, first performed in April 1907.
47. Gustav Meyrink, 1868–1932, *Der Golem*, 4th edition Leipzig 1915, 'Der Kardinal Napellus' in *Fledermäuse*, seven stories, Leipzig 1916.
48. Lectures of 13 and 15 February 1916 in GA 65.
49. Eduard von Hartmann, 1842–1906, 'Englands politisches Interesse' in *Zwei Jahrzehnte deutscher Politik und die gegenwärtige Weltlage*, Berlin 1889, p. 351.
50. Hermann Lotze, 1817–81, was originally a physician and had taken a degree in medicine before writing his philosophical thesis in Leipzig.
51. Gustav Fechner, 1801–87, wrote, under the pseudonym of Dr Mises, the book *Beweis, dass der Mond aus Jodin bestehe*, 2nd edition Leipzig 1832.
52. See note 47.
53. Rudolf Kjellén, 1864–1922, Swedish historian and statesman, whom Steiner referred to on various occasions. Books by him which he had in his personal library included: *Die Ideen von 1914*, Leipzig 1915; *Die politischen Probleme des Weltkrieges*, Leipzig 1916; *Studien zur Weltkrise*, Munich 1917. The transcript of the lecture may be faulty at this point.
54. August Weismann, 1834–1914, zoologist: *Studien zur Deszendenztheorie* (2 vols, 1875/6); *Vorträge zur Deszendenztheorie* (2 vols, 1903).
55. 25 February 1916 in GA 65.
56. Lorenz Oken, 1779–1851.
57. Lecture of 27 November 1914, GA 64.
58. From Jesus to Christ, lecture 10, GA 131.
59. Robert Hamerling, 1830–89. See Rudolf Steiner, *Robert Hamerling, ein Dichter und ein Denker und ein Mensch*, Dornach 1939.
60. Maximilian Harden, 1861–1927, editor of the weekly journal *Die Zukunft*.
61. The *Berliner Tageblatt*, no. 72, 9 February 1916, published an article by Max Hochdorf entitled 'Dreyfus, the prophet Steiner and the refugees'.

62. Thomas Mann, 1875–1955, *Friedrich und die grosse Koalition*, Berlin 1916, p. 122.
63. Josef Kohler, 1849–1919, Professor of law at Berlin University.
64. Sir Thomas More, 1480–1535, *De optimo statu rei publicae deque nova insula Utopia*, 1516.
65. Edward Bellamy, 1850–98, American writer, author of a futuristic novel *Looking Backward*, 2000–1887.
66. See Herman Grimm, *Fragmente*, Berlin 1902, pp. 174 ff.
67. Albertus Magnus, Count Bollstaedt, 1193–1280. Doctor universalis and teacher of Thomas Aquinas.
68. See note 57.
69. Thomas Campanella, 1568–1639. He was locked up for 27 years and while imprisoned wrote *The City of the Sun*.
70. Eduard von Hartmann, *Die moderne Psychologie*, Leipzig 1901, p. 6.
71. Theodor Birt, *Die Laus im Altertum*, Preuss. Jahrbücher, vol. 164, p. 271, Berlin 1916.
72. Woodrow Wilson, 1856–1924, led the US to war against Germany in 1917 after having been re-elected as a 'president of peace'. He published *The New Freedom* in 1913.
73. 13 April 1916 in GA 65.
74. See note 63.
75. Rudolf Eucken, 1846–1926. See *Die Rätsel der Philosophie: Der moderne Mensch und seine Weltanschauung*.
76. Wilhelm Boelsche, born 1861, writer. He wrote many popular works on science and edited Goethe's scientific writings in the series *Meyers Klassiker*.
77. GA 20.
78. August von Kotzebue, 1761–1819, *Der hyperboräische Esel oder die heutige Bildung, ein klassisches Drama oder philosophisches Lustspiel*, 1799.
79. Adolf von Harnack, 1851–1930, *Das Wesen des Christentums*, Leipzig 1910, p. 102: 'Whatever may have occurred at the grave and in the appearances of Jesus, one thing is certain: in this grave originated the indestructible belief in the overcoming of death, and in eternal life.'
80. Rudolf Steiner's quoted text is based on the German translation by Max Henning, Reclam-Verlag, Leipzig, undated.
81. Quoted in R. Faerber, *Entwicklung der Sage von Salomo und dem Todesengel, zugleich als Beitrag zur Charakterisik der palästinensischen und babylonischen Haggada*, Vienna 1904.
82. This is a reference to Raymond Poincaré, 1860–1934, French President between 1913 and 1920, and the poet Maurice Maeterlinck, 1862–1949. See the lecture of 5 November 1914 in GA 64; and the lecture of 25 February 1915 in GA 65.
83. GA 146.
84. Helene Boehlau, 1859–1940. In 1886 in Constantinople she married the writer Friedrich Arndt who had converted to Islam and taken the name Omar al Rashid Bey.
85. See Rudolf Steiner, *The Riddle of Man*, New York 1990.
86. Shankaracharya, also called Shankara, 788–820. Reformer of the Vedas, he

is regarded as one of the most important representatives of Vedanta philosophy.

87. Omar al Rashid, *Das hohe Ziel der Erkenntnis. Aranada Upanischad*, Munich 1912.
88. Robert Hamerling, *Homunkulus. Modernes Epos in 10 Gesängen* (188). See Steiner's Autobiography, chapters VIII, XIII; and the lecture of 26 March 1914 in GA 63.
89. Engelbert Pernerstorfer, 1850–1918. Along with his friend Viktor Adler, he was the leader of the Austrian Social Democrats. *Autobiography*, chapter VII.
90. Karl Renner, 1870–1950, Social Democrat politician, Austrian Chancellor in 1918 and President in 1945. *Österreichs Erneuerung*, 2nd edition Vienna 1916. Quotations taken from pages 16 to 30.
91. Gerhart Hauptmann, 1862–1946, *Der Narr in Christo. Emanuel Quint*, first published 1910.
92. Fritz Mauthner, 1849–1923, *Beiträge zu einer Kritik der Sprache*, 3 vols, 1901–2; *Wörterbuch der Philosophie*, 2 vols, 1910–11.

RUDOLF STEINER'S COLLECTED WORKS

The German Edition of Rudolf Steiner's Collected Works (the *Gesamtausgabe* [GA] published by Rudolf Steiner Verlag, Dornach, Switzerland) presently runs to 354 titles, organized either by type of work (written or spoken), chronology, audience (public or other), or subject (education, art, etc.). For ease of comparison, the Collected Works in English [CW] follows the German organization exactly. A complete listing of the CWs follows with literal translations of the German titles. Other than in the case of the books published in his lifetime, titles were rarely given by Rudolf Steiner himself, and were often provided by the editors of the German editions. The titles in English are not necessarily the same as the German; and, indeed, over the past seventy-five years have frequently been different, with the same book sometimes appearing under different titles.

For ease of identification and to avoid confusion, we suggest that readers looking for a title should do so by CW number. Because the work of creating the Collected Works of Rudolf Steiner is an ongoing process, with new titles being published every year, we have not indicated in this listing which books are presently available. To find out what titles in the Collected Works are currently in print, please check our website at www.rudolfsteinerpress.com (or www.steinerbooks.org for US readers).

Written Work

CW 1	Goethe: Natural-Scientific Writings, Introduction, with Footnotes and Explanations in the text by Rudolf Steiner
CW 2	Outlines of an Epistemology of the Goethean World View, with Special Consideration of Schiller
CW 3	Truth and Science
CW 4	The Philosophy of Freedom
CW 4a	Documents to 'The Philosophy of Freedom'
CW 5	Friedrich Nietzsche, A Fighter against His Time
CW 6	Goethe's Worldview
CW 6a	Now in CW 30
CW 7	Mysticism at the Dawn of Modern Spiritual Life and Its Relationship with Modern Worldviews
CW 8	Christianity as Mystical Fact and the Mysteries of Antiquity
CW 9	Theosophy: An Introduction into Supersensible World Knowledge and Human Purpose
CW 10	How Does One Attain Knowledge of Higher Worlds?
CW 11	From the Akasha-Chronicle

CW 12	Levels of Higher Knowledge
CW 13	Occult Science in Outline
CW 14	Four Mystery Dramas
CW 15	The Spiritual Guidance of the Individual and Humanity
CW 16	A Way to Human Self-Knowledge: Eight Meditations
CW 17	The Threshold of the Spiritual World. Aphoristic Comments
CW 18	The Riddles of Philosophy in Their History, Presented as an Outline
CW 19	Contained in CW 24
CW 20	The Riddles of the Human Being: Articulated and Unarticulated in the Thinking, Views and Opinions of a Series of German and Austrian Personalities
CW 21	The Riddles of the Soul
CW 22	Goethe's Spiritual Nature And Its Revelation In 'Faust' and through the 'Fairy Tale of the Snake and the Lily'
CW 23	The Central Points of the Social Question in the Necessities of Life in the Present and the Future
CW 24	Essays Concerning the Threefold Division of the Social Organism and the Period 1915–1921
CW 25	Cosmology, Religion and Philosophy
CW 26	Anthroposophical Leading Thoughts
CW 27	Fundamentals for Expansion of the Art of Healing according to Spiritual-Scientific Insights
CW 28	The Course of My Life
CW 29	Collected Essays on Dramaturgy, 1889–1900
CW 30	Methodical Foundations of Anthroposophy: Collected Essays on Philosophy, Natural Science, Aesthetics and Psychology, 1884–1901
CW 31	Collected Essays on Culture and Current Events, 1887–1901
CW 32	Collected Essays on Literature, 1884–1902
CW 33	Biographies and Biographical Sketches, 1894–1905
CW 34	Lucifer-Gnosis: Foundational Essays on Anthroposophy and Reports from the Periodicals 'Lucifer' and 'Lucifer-Gnosis,' 1903–1908
CW 35	Philosophy and Anthroposophy: Collected Essays, 1904–1923
CW 36	The Goetheanum-Idea in the Middle of the Cultural Crisis of the Present: Collected Essays from the Periodical 'Das Goetheanum,' 1921–1925
CW 37	Now in CWs 260a and 251
CW 38	Letters, Vol. 1: 1881–1890
CW 39	Letters, Vol. 2: 1890–1925
CW 40	Truth-Wrought Words
CW 40a	Sayings, Poems and Mantras; Supplementary Volume
CW 42	Now in CWs 264–266
CW 43	Stage Adaptations
CW 44	On the Four Mystery Dramas. Sketches, Fragments and Paralipomena on the Four Mystery Dramas
CW 45	Anthroposophy: A Fragment from the Year 1910

Public Lectures

CW 51	On Philosophy, History and Literature
CW 52	Spiritual Teachings Concerning the Soul and Observation of the World
CW 53	The Origin and Goal of the Human Being
CW 54	The Riddles of the World and Anthroposophy
CW 55	Knowledge of the Supersensible in Our Times and Its Meaning for Life Today
CW 56	Knowledge of the Soul and of the Spirit
CW 57	Where and How Does One Find the Spirit?
CW 58	The Metamorphoses of the Soul Life. Paths of Soul Experiences: Part One
CW 59	The Metamorphoses of the Soul Life. Paths of Soul Experiences: Part Two
CW 60	The Answers of Spiritual Science to the Biggest Questions of Existence
CW 61	Human History in the Light of Spiritual Research
CW 62	Results of Spiritual Research
CW 63	Spiritual Science as a Treasure for Life
CW 64	Out of Destiny-Burdened Times
CW 65	Out of Central European Spiritual Life
CW 66	Spirit and Matter, Life and Death
CW 67	The Eternal in the Human Soul. Immortality and Freedom
CW 68	Public lectures in various cities, 1906–1918
CW 69	Public lectures in various cities, 1906–1918
CW 70	Public lectures in various cities, 1906–1918
CW 71	Public lectures in various cities, 1906–1918
CW 72	Freedom—Immortality—Social Life
CW 73	The Supplementing of the Modern Sciences through Anthroposophy
CW 73a	Specialized Fields of Knowledge and Anthroposophy
CW 74	The Philosophy of Thomas Aquinas
CW 75	Public lectures in various cities, 1906–1918
CW 76	The Fructifying Effect of Anthroposophy on Specialized Fields
CW 77a	The Task of Anthroposophy in Relation to Science and Life: The Darmstadt College Course
CW 77b	Art and Anthroposophy. The Goetheanum-Impulse
CW 78	Anthroposophy, Its Roots of Knowledge and Fruits for Life
CW 79	The Reality of the Higher Worlds
CW 80	Public lectures in various cities, 1922
CW 81	Renewal-Impulses for Culture and Science—Berlin College Course
CW 82	So that the Human Being Can Become a Complete Human Being
CW 83	Western and Eastern World-Contrast. Paths to Understanding It through Anthroposophy
CW 84	What Did the Goetheanum Intend and What Should Anthroposophy Do?

Lectures to the Members of the Anthroposophical Society

CW 88	Concerning the Astral World and Devachan
CW 89	Consciousness—Life—Form. Fundamental Principles of a Spiritual-Scientific Cosmology
CW 90	Participant Notes from the Lectures during the Years 1903–1905
CW 91	Participant Notes from the Lectures during the Years 1903–1905
CW 92	The Occult Truths of Ancient Myths and Sagas
CW 93	The Temple Legend and the Golden Legend
CW 93a	Fundamentals of Esotericism
CW 94	Cosmogony. Popular Occultism. The Gospel of John. The Theosophy in the Gospel of John
CW 95	At the Gates of Theosophy
CW 96	Origin-Impulses of Spiritual Science. Christian Esotericism in the Light of New Spirit-Knowledge
CW 97	The Christian Mystery
CW 98	Nature Beings and Spirit Beings—Their Effects in Our Visible World
CW 99	The Theosophy of the Rosicrucians
CW 100	Human Development and Christ-Knowledge
CW 101	Myths and Legends. Occult Signs and Symbols
CW 102	The Working into Human Beings by Spiritual Beings
CW 103	The Gospel of John
CW 104	The Apocalypse of John
CW 104a	From the Picture-Script of the Apocalypse of John
CW 105	Universe, Earth, the Human Being: Their Being and Development, as well as Their Reflection in the Connection between Egyptian Mythology and Modern Culture
CW 106	Egyptian Myths and Mysteries in Relation to the Active Spiritual Forces of the Present
CW 107	Spiritual-Scientific Knowledge of the Human Being
CW 108	Answering the Questions of Life and the World through Anthroposophy
CW 109	The Principle of Spiritual Economy in Connection with the Question of Reincarnation. An Aspect of the Spiritual Guidance of Humanity
CW 110	The Spiritual Hierarchies and Their Reflection in the Physical World. Zodiac, Planets and Cosmos
CW 111	Contained in CW 109
CW 112	The Gospel of John in Relation to the Three Other Gospels, Especially the Gospel of Luke
CW 113	The Orient in the Light of the Occident. The Children of Lucifer and the Brothers of Christ
CW 114	The Gospel of Luke
CW 115	Anthroposophy—Psychosophy—Pneumatosophy
CW 116	The Christ-Impulse and the Development of 'I'-Consciousness
CW 117	The Deeper Secrets of the Development of Humanity in Light of the Gospels

CW 118 The Event of the Christ-Appearance in the Etheric World
CW 119 Macrocosm and Microcosm. The Large World and the Small World. Soul-Questions, Life-Questions, Spirit-Questions
CW 120 The Revelation of Karma
CW 121 The Mission of Individual Folk-Souls in Connection with Germanic-Nordic Mythology
CW 122 The Secrets of the Biblical Creation-Story. The Six-Day Work in the First Book of Moses
CW 123 The Gospel of Matthew
CW 124 Excursus in the Area of the Gospel of Mark
CW 125 Paths and Goals of the Spiritual Human Being. Life Questions in the Light of Spiritual Science
CW 126 Occult History. Esoteric Observations of the Karmic Relationships of Personalities and Events of World History
CW 127 The Mission of the New Spiritual Revelation. The Christ-Event as the Middle-Point of Earth Evolution
CW 128 An Occult Physiology
CW 129 Wonders of the World, Trials of the Soul, and Revelations of the Spirit
CW 130 Esoteric Christianity and the Spiritual Guidance of Humanity
CW 131 From Jesus to Christ
CW 132 Evolution from the View Point of the Truth
CW 133 The Earthly and the Cosmic Human Being
CW 134 The World of the Senses and the World of the Spirit
CW 135 Reincarnation and Karma and their Meaning for the Culture of the Present
CW 136 The Spiritual Beings in Celestial Bodies and the Realms of Nature
CW 137 The Human Being in the Light of Occultism, Theosophy and Philosophy
CW 138 On Initiation. On Eternity and the Passing Moment. On the Light of the Spirit and the Darkness of Life
CW 139 The Gospel of Mark
CW 140 Occult Investigation into the Life between Death and New Birth. The Living Interaction between Life and Death
CW 141 Life between Death and New Birth in Relationship to Cosmic Facts
CW 142 The Bhagavad Gita and the Letters of Paul
CW 143 Experiences of the Supersensible. Three Paths of the Soul to Christ
CW 144 The Mysteries of the East and of Christianity
CW 145 What Significance Does Occult Development of the Human Being Have for the Sheaths—Physical Body, Etheric Body, Astral Body, and Self?
CW 146 The Occult Foundations of the Bhagavad Gita
CW 147 The Secrets of the Threshold
CW 148 Out of Research in the Akasha: The Fifth Gospel
CW 149 Christ and the Spiritual World. Concerning the Search for the Holy Grail

CW 150	The World of the Spirit and Its Extension into Physical Existence; The Influence of the Dead in the World of the Living
CW 151	Human Thought and Cosmic Thought
CW 152	Preliminary Stages to the Mystery of Golgotha
CW 153	The Inner Being of the Human Being and Life Between Death and New Birth
CW 154	How does One Gain an Understanding of the Spiritual World? The Flowing in of Spiritual Impulses from out of the World of the Deceased
CW 155	Christ and the Human Soul. Concerning the Meaning of Life. Theosophical Morality. Anthroposophy and Christianity
CW 156	Occult Reading and Occult Hearing
CW 157	Human Destinies and the Destiny of Peoples
CW 157a	The Formation of Destiny and the Life after Death
CW 158	The Connection Between the Human Being and the Elemental World. Kalevala—Olaf Åsteson—The Russian People—The World as the Result of the Influences of Equilibrium
CW 159	The Mystery of Death. The Nature and Significance of Middle Europe and the European Folk Spirits
CW 160	In CW 159
CW 161	Paths of Spiritual Knowledge and the Renewal of the Artistic Worldview
CW 162	Questions of Art and Life in Light of Spiritual Science
CW 163	Coincidence, Necessity and Providence. Imaginative Knowledge and the Processes after Death
CW 164	The Value of Thinking for a Knowledge That Satisfies the Human Being. The Relationship of Spiritual Science to Natural Science
CW 165	The Spiritual Unification of Humanity through the Christ-Impulse
CW 166	Necessity and Freedom in the Events of the World and in Human Action
CW 167	The Present and the Past in the Human Spirit
CW 168	The Connection between the Living and the Dead
CW 169	World-being and Selfhood
CW 170	The Riddle of the Human Being. The Spiritual Background of Human History. Cosmic and Human History, Vol. 1
CW 171	Inner Development-Impulses of Humanity. Goethe and the Crisis of the 19th Century. Cosmic and Human History, Vol. 2
CW 172	The Karma of the Vocation of the Human Being in Connection with Goethe's Life. Cosmic and Human History, Vol. 3
CW 173	Contemporary-Historical Considerations: The Karma of Untruthfulness, Part One. Cosmic and Human History, Vol. 4
CW 174	Contemporary-Historical Considerations: The Karma of Untruthfulness, Part Two. Cosmic and Human History, Vol. 5
CW 174a	Middle Europe between East and West. Cosmic and Human History, Vol. 6
CW 174b	The Spiritual Background of the First World War. Cosmic and Human History, Vol. 7

CW 175 Building Stones for an Understanding of the Mystery of Golgotha. Cosmic and Human Metamorphoses
CW 176 Truths of Evolution of the Individual and Humanity. The Karma of Materialism
CW 177 The Spiritual Background of the Outer World. The Fall of the Spirits of Darkness. Spiritual Beings and Their Effects, Vol. 1
CW 178 Individual Spiritual Beings and their Influence in the Soul of the Human Being. Spiritual Beings and their Effects, Vol. 2
CW 179 Spiritual Beings and Their Effects. Historical Necessity and Freedom. The Influences on Destiny from out of the World of the Dead. Spiritual Beings and Their Effects, Vol. 3
CW 180 Mystery Truths and Christmas Impulses. Ancient Myths and their Meaning. Spiritual Beings and Their Effects, Vol. 4
CW 181 Earthly Death and Cosmic Life. Anthroposophical Gifts for Life. Necessities of Consciousness for the Present and the Future.
CW 182 Death as Transformation of Life
CW 183 The Science of the Development of the Human Being
CW 184 The Polarity of Duration and Development in Human Life. The Cosmic Pre-History of Humanity
CW 185 Historical Symptomology
CW 185a Historical-Developmental Foundations for Forming a Social Judgement
CW 186 The Fundamental Social Demands of Our Time—In Changed Situations
CW 187 How Can Humanity Find the Christ Again? The Threefold Shadow-Existence of our Time and the New Christ-Light
CW 188 Goetheanism, a Transformation-Impulse and Resurrection-Thought. Science of the Human Being and Science of Sociology
CW 189 The Social Question as a Question of Consciousness. The Spiritual Background of the Social Question, Vol. 1
CW 190 Impulses of the Past and the Future in Social Occurrences. The Spiritual Background of the Social Question, Vol. 2
CW 191 Social Understanding from Spiritual-Scientific Cognition. The Spiritual Background of the Social Question, Vol. 3
CW 192 Spiritual-Scientific Treatment of Social and Pedagogical Questions
CW 193 The Inner Aspect of the Social Riddle. Luciferic Past and Ahrimanic Future
CW 194 The Mission of Michael. The Revelation of the Actual Mysteries of the Human Being
CW 195 Cosmic New Year and the New Year Idea
CW 196 Spiritual and Social Transformations in the Development of Humanity
CW 197 Polarities in the Development of Humanity: West and East Materialism and Mysticism Knowledge and Belief
CW 198 Healing Factors for the Social Organism
CW 199 Spiritual Science as Knowledge of the Foundational Impulses of Social Formation

CW 200 The New Spirituality and the Christ-Experience of the 20th Century
CW 201 The Correspondences Between Microcosm and Macrocosm. The Human Being—A Hieroglyph of the Universe. The Human Being in Relationship with the Cosmos: 1
CW 202 The Bridge between the World-Spirituality and the Physical Aspect of the Human Being. The Search for the New Isis, the Divine Sophia. The Human Being in Relationship with the Cosmos: 2
CW 203 The Responsibility of Human Beings for the Development of the World through their Spiritual Connection with the Planet Earth and the World of the Stars. The Human Being in Relationship with the Cosmos: 3
CW 204 Perspectives of the Development of Humanity. The Materialistic Knowledge-Impulse and the Task of Anthroposophy. The Human Being in Relationship with the Cosmos: 4
CW 205 Human Development, World-Soul, and World-Spirit. Part One: The Human Being as a Being of Body and Soul in Relationship to the World. The Human Being in Relationship with the Cosmos: 5
CW 206 Human Development, World-Soul, and World-Spirit. Part Two: The Human Being as a Spiritual Being in the Process of Historical Development. The Human Being in Relationship with the Cosmos: 6
CW 207 Anthroposophy as Cosmosophy. Part One: Characteristic Features of the Human Being in the Earthly and the Cosmic Realms. The Human Being in Relationship with the Cosmos: 7
CW 208 Anthroposophy as Cosmosophy. Part Two: The Forming of the Human Being as the Result of Cosmic Influence. The Human Being in Relationship with the Cosmos: 8
CW 209 Nordic and Central European Spiritual Impulses. The Festival of the Appearance of Christ. The Human Being in Relationship with the Cosmos: 9
CW 210 Old and New Methods of Initiation. Drama and Poetry in the Change of Consciousness in the Modern Age
CW 211 The Sun Mystery and the Mystery of Death and Resurrection. Exoteric and Esoteric Christianity
CW 212 Human Soul Life and Spiritual Striving in Connection with World and Earth Development
CW 213 Human Questions and World Answers
CW 214 The Mystery of the Trinity: The Human Being in Relationship with the Spiritual World in the Course of Time
CW 215 Philosophy, Cosmology, and Religion in Anthroposophy
CW 216 The Fundamental Impulses of the World-Historical Development of Humanity
CW 217 Spiritually Active Forces in the Coexistence of the Older and Younger Generations. Pedagogical Course for Youth

CW 217a Youth's Cognitive Task
CW 218 Spiritual Connections in the Forming of the Human Organism
CW 219 The Relationship of the World of the Stars to the Human Being, and of the Human Being to the World of the Stars. The Spiritual Communion of Humanity
CW 220 Living Knowledge of Nature. Intellectual Fall and Spiritual Redemption
CW 221 Earth-Knowing and Heaven-Insight
CW 222 The Imparting of Impulses to World-Historical Events through Spiritual Powers
CW 223 The Cycle of the Year as Breathing Process of the Earth and the Four Great Festival-Seasons. Anthroposophy and the Human Heart (Gemüt)
CW 224 The Human Soul and its Connection with Divine-Spiritual Individualities. The Internalization of the Festivals of the Year
CW 225 Three Perspectives of Anthroposophy. Cultural Phenomena observed from a Spiritual-Scientific Perspective
CW 226 Human Being, Human Destiny, and World Development
CW 227 Initiation-Knowledge
CW 228 Science of Initiation and Knowledge of the Stars. The Human Being in the Past, the Present, and the Future from the Viewpoint of the Development of Consciousness
CW 229 The Experiencing of the Course of the Year in Four Cosmic Imaginations
CW 230 The Human Being as Harmony of the Creative, Building, and Formative World-Word
CW 231 The Supersensible Human Being, Understood Anthroposophically
CW 232 The Forming of the Mysteries
CW 233 World History Illuminated by Anthroposophy and as the Foundation for Knowledge of the Human Spirit
CW 233a Mystery Sites of the Middle Ages: Rosicrucianism and the Modern Initiation-Principle. The Festival of Easter as Part of the History of the Mysteries of Humanity
CW 234 Anthroposophy. A Summary after 21 Years
CW 235 Esoteric Observations of Karmic Relationships in 6 Volumes, Vol. 1
CW 236 Esoteric Observations of Karmic Relationships in 6 Volumes, Vol. 2
CW 237 Esoteric Observations of Karmic Relationships in 6 Volumes, Vol. 3:
The Karmic Relationships of the Anthroposophical Movement
CW 238 Esoteric Observations of Karmic Relationships in 6 Volumes, Vol. 4:
The Spiritual Life of the Present in Relationship to the Anthroposophical Movement
CW 239 Esoteric Observations of Karmic Relationships in 6 Volumes, Vol. 5

CW 240	Esoteric Observations of Karmic Relationships in 6 Volumes, Vol. 6
CW 243	The Consciousness of the Initiate
CW 245	Instructions for an Esoteric Schooling
CW 250	The Building-Up of the Anthroposophical Society. From the Beginning to the Outbreak of the First World War
CW 251	The History of the Goetheanum Building-Association
CW 252	Life in the Anthroposophical Society from the First World War to the Burning of the First Goetheanum
CW 253	The Problems of Living Together in the Anthroposophical Society. On the Dornach Crisis of 1915. With Highlights on Swedenborg's Clairvoyance, the Views of Freudian Psychoanalysts, and the Concept of Love in Relation to Mysticism
CW 254	The Occult Movement in the 19th Century and Its Relationship to World Culture. Significant Points from the Exoteric Cultural Life around the Middle of the 19th Century
CW 255	Rudolf Steiner during the First World War
CW 255a	Anthroposophy and the Reformation of Society. On the History of the Threefold Movement
CW 255b	Anthroposophy and Its Opponents, 1919–1921
CW 256	How Can the Anthroposophical Movement Be Financed?
CW 256a	Futurum, Inc. / International Laboratories, Inc.
CW 256b	The Coming Day, Inc.
CW 257	Anthroposophical Community-Building
CW 258	The History of and Conditions for the Anthroposophical Movement in Relationship to the Anthroposophical Society. A Stimulus to Self-Contemplation
CW 259	The Year of Destiny 1923 in the History of the Anthroposophical Society. From the Burning of the Goetheanum to the Christmas Conference
CW 260	The Christmas Conference for the Founding of the General Anthroposophical Society
CW 260a	The Constitution of the General Anthroposophical Society and the School for Spiritual Science. The Rebuilding of the Goetheanum
CW 261	Our Dead. Addresses, Words of Remembrance, and Meditative Verses, 1906–1924
CW 262	Rudolf Steiner and Marie Steiner-von Sivers: Correspondence and Documents, 1901–1925
CW 263/1	Rudolf Steiner and Edith Maryon: Correspondence: Letters, Verses, Sketches, 1912–1924
CW 264	On the History and the Contents of the First Section of the Esoteric School from 1904 to 1914. Letters, Newsletters, Documents, Lectures
CW 265	On the History and from the Contents of the Ritual-Knowledge Section of the Esoteric School from 1904 to 1914. Documents, and Lectures from the Years 1906 to 1914, as well as on New Approaches to Ritual-Knowledge Work in the Years 1921–1924

CW 266/1 From the Contents of the Esoteric Lessons. Volume 1: 1904–1909. Notes from Memory of Participants. Meditation texts from the notes of Rudolf Steiner
CW 266/2 From the Contents of the Esoteric Lessons. Volume 2: 1910–1912. Notes from Memory of Participants
CW 266/3 From the Contents of the Esoteric Lessons. Volume 3: 1913, 1914 and 1920–1923. Notes from Memory of Participants. Meditation texts from the notes of Rudolf Steiner
CW 267 Soul-Exercises: Vol. 1: Exercises with Word and Image Meditations for the Methodological Development of Higher Powers of Knowledge, 1904–1924
CW 268 Soul-Exercises: Vol. 2: Mantric Verses, 1903–1925
CW 269 Ritual Texts for the Celebration of the Free Christian Religious Instruction. The Collected Verses for Teachers and Students of the Waldorf School
CW 270 Esoteric Instructions for the First Class of the School for Spiritual Science at the Goetheanum 1924, 4 Volumes
CW 271 Art and Knowledge of Art. Foundations of a New Aesthetic
CW 272 Spiritual-Scientific Commentary on Goethe's 'Faust' in Two Volumes. Vol. 1: Faust, the Striving Human Being
CW 273 Spiritual-Scientific Commentary on Goethe's 'Faust' in Two Volumes. Vol. 2: The Faust-Problem
CW 274 Addresses for the Christmas Plays from the Old Folk Traditions
CW 275 Art in the Light of Mystery-Wisdom
CW 276 The Artistic in Its Mission in the World. The Genius of Language. The World of Self-Revealing Radiant Appearances—Anthroposophy and Art. Anthroposophy and Poetry
CW 277 Eurythmy. The Revelation of the Speaking Soul
CW 277a The Origin and Development of Eurythmy
CW 278 Eurythmy as Visible Song
CW 279 Eurythmy as Visible Speech
CW 280 The Method and Nature of Speech Formation
CW 281 The Art of Recitation and Declamation
CW 282 Speech Formation and Dramatic Art
CW 283 The Nature of Things Musical and the Experience of Tone in the Human Being
CW 284/285 Images of Occult Seals and Pillars. The Munich Congress of Whitsun 1907 and Its Consequences
CW 286 Paths to a New Style of Architecture. 'And the Building Becomes Human'
CW 287 The Building at Dornach as a Symbol of Historical Becoming and an Artistic Transformation Impulse
CW 288 Style-Forms in the Living Organic
CW 289 The Building-Idea of the Goetheanum: Lectures with Slides from the Years 1920–1921
CW 290 The Building-Idea of the Goetheanum: Lectures with Slides from the Years 1920–1921

CW 291	The Nature of Colours
CW 291a	Knowledge of Colours. Supplementary Volume to 'The Nature of Colours'
CW 292	Art History as Image of Inner Spiritual Impulses
CW 293	General Knowledge of the Human Being as the Foundation of Pedagogy
CW 294	The Art of Education, Methodology and Didactics
CW 295	The Art of Education: Seminar Discussions and Lectures on Lesson Planning
CW 296	The Question of Education as a Social Question
CW 297	The Idea and Practice of the Waldorf School
CW 297a	Education for Life: Self-Education and the Practice of Pedagogy
CW 298	Rudolf Steiner in the Waldorf School
CW 299	Spiritual-Scientific Observations on Speech
CW 300a	Conferences with the Teachers of the Free Waldorf School in Stuttgart, 1919 to 1924, in 3 Volumes, Vol. 1
CW 300b	Conferences with the Teachers of the Free Waldorf School in Stuttgart, 1919 to 1924, in 3 Volumes, Vol. 2
CW 300c	Conferences with the Teachers of the Free Waldorf School in Stuttgart, 1919 to 1924, in 3 Volumes, Vol. 3
CW 301	The Renewal of Pedagogical-Didactical Art through Spiritual Science
CW 302	Knowledge of the Human Being and the Forming of Class Lessons
CW 302a	Education and Teaching from a Knowledge of the Human Being
CW 303	The Healthy Development of the Human Being
CW 304	Methods of Education and Teaching Based on Anthroposophy
CW 304a	Anthroposophical Knowledge of the Human Being and Pedagogy
CW 305	The Soul-Spiritual Foundational Forces of the Art of Education. Spiritual Values in Education and Social Life
CW 306	Pedagogical Praxis from the Viewpoint of a Spiritual-Scientific Knowledge of the Human Being. The Education of the Child and Young Human Beings
CW 307	The Spiritual Life of the Present and Education
CW 308	The Method of Teaching and the Life-Requirements for Teaching
CW 309	Anthroposophical Pedagogy and Its Prerequisites
CW 310	The Pedagogical Value of a Knowledge of the Human Being and the Cultural Value of Pedagogy
CW 311	The Art of Education from an Understanding of the Being of Humanity
CW 312	Spiritual Science and Medicine
CW 313	Spiritual-Scientific Viewpoints on Therapy
CW 314	Physiology and Therapy Based on Spiritual Science
CW 315	Curative Eurythmy
CW 316	Meditative Observations and Instructions for a Deepening of the Art of Healing
CW 317	The Curative Education Course

CW 318 The Working Together of Doctors and Pastors
CW 319 Anthroposophical Knowledge of the Human Being and Medicine
CW 320 Spiritual-Scientific Impulses for the Development of Physics 1: The First Natural-Scientific Course: Light, Colour, Tone, Mass, Electricity, Magnetism
CW 321 Spiritual-Scientific Impulses for the Development of Physics 2: The Second Natural-Scientific Course: Warmth at the Border of Positive and Negative Materiality
CW 322 The Borders of the Knowledge of Nature
CW 323 The Relationship of the various Natural-Scientific Fields to Astronomy
CW 324 Nature Observation, Mathematics, and Scientific Experimentation and Results from the Viewpoint of Anthroposophy
CW 324a The Fourth Dimension in Mathematics and Reality
CW 325 Natural Science and the World-Historical Development of Humanity since Ancient Times
CW 326 The Moment of the Coming Into Being of Natural Science in World History and Its Development Since Then
CW 327 Spiritual-Scientific Foundations for Success in Farming. The Agricultural Course
CW 328 The Social Question
CW 329 The Liberation of the Human Being as the Foundation for a New Social Form
CW 330 The Renewal of the Social Organism
CW 331 Work-Council and Socialization
CW 332 The Alliance for Threefolding and the Total Reform of Society. The Council on Culture and the Liberation of the Spiritual Life
CW 332a The Social Future
CW 333 Freedom of Thought and Social Forces
CW 334 From the Unified State to the Threefold Social Organism
CW 335 The Crisis of the Present and the Path to Healthy Thinking
CW 336 The Great Questions of the Times and Anthroposophical Spiritual Knowledge
CW 337a Social Ideas, Social Reality, Social Practice, Vol. 1: Question-and-Answer Evenings and Study Evenings of the Alliance for the Threefold Social Organism in Stuttgart, 1919–1920
CW 337b Social Ideas, Social Realities, Social Practice, Vol. 2: Discussion Evenings of the Swiss Alliance for the Threefold Social Organism
CW 338 How Does One Work on Behalf of the Impulse for the Threefold Social Organism?
CW 339 Anthroposophy, Threefold Social Organism, and the Art of Public Speaking
CW 340 The National-Economics Course. The Tasks of a New Science of Economics, Volume 1
CW 341 The National-Economics Seminar. The Tasks of a New Science of Economics, Volume 2

CW 342	Lectures and Courses on Christian Religious Work, Vol. 1: Anthroposophical Foundations for a Renewed Christian Religious Working
CW 343	Lectures and Courses on Christian Religious Work, Vol. 2: Spiritual Knowledge—Religious Feeling—Cultic Doing
CW 344	Lectures and Courses on Christian Religious Work, Vol. 3: Lectures at the Founding of the Christian Community
CW 345	Lectures and Courses on Christian Religious Work, Vol. 4: Concerning the Nature of the Working Word
CW 346	Lectures and Courses on Christian Religious Work, Vol. 5: The Apocalypse and the Work of the Priest
CW 347	The Knowledge of the Nature of the Human Being According to Body, Soul and Spirit. On Earlier Conditions of the Earth
CW 348	On Health and Illness. Foundations of a Spiritual-Scientific Doctrine of the Senses
CW 349	On the Life of the Human Being and of the Earth. On the Nature of Christianity
CW 350	Rhythms in the Cosmos and in the Human Being. How Does One Come To See the Spiritual World?
CW 351	The Human Being and the World. The Influence of the Spirit in Nature. On the Nature of Bees
CW 352	Nature and the Human Being Observed Spiritual-Scientifically
CW 353	The History of Humanity and the World-Views of the Folk Cultures
CW 354	The Creation of the World and the Human Being. Life on Earth and the Influence of the Stars

SIGNIFICANT EVENTS IN THE LIFE OF RUDOLF STEINER

1829: June 23: birth of Johann Steiner (1829–1910)—Rudolf Steiner's father—in Geras, Lower Austria.

1834: May 8: birth of Franciska Blie (1834–1918)—Rudolf Steiner's mother—in Horn, Lower Austria. 'My father and mother were both children of the glorious Lower Austrian forest district north of the Danube.'

1860: May 16: marriage of Johann Steiner and Franciska Blie.

1861: February 25: birth of *Rudolf Joseph Lorenz Steiner* in Kraljevec, Croatia, near the border with Hungary, where Johann Steiner works as a telegrapher for the South Austria Railroad. Rudolf Steiner is baptized two days later, February 27, the date usually given as his birthday.

1862: Summer: the family moves to Mödling, Lower Austria.

1863: The family moves to Pottschach, Lower Austria, near the Styrian border, where Johann Steiner becomes stationmaster. 'The view stretched to the mountains ... majestic peaks in the distance and the sweet charm of nature in the immediate surroundings.'

1864: November 15: birth of Rudolf Steiner's sister, Leopoldine (d. November 1, 1927). She will become a seamstress and live with her parents for the rest of her life.

1866: July 28: birth of Rudolf Steiner's deaf-mute brother, Gustav (d. May 1, 1941).

1867: Rudolf Steiner enters the village school. Following a disagreement between his father and the schoolmaster, whose wife falsely accused the boy of causing a commotion, Rudolf Steiner is taken out of school and taught at home.

1868: A critical experience. Unknown to the family, an aunt dies in a distant town. Sitting in the station waiting room, Rudolf Steiner sees her 'form,' which speaks to him, asking for help. 'Beginning with this experience, a new soul life began in the boy, one in which not only the outer trees and mountains spoke to him, but also the worlds that lay behind them. From this moment on, the boy began to live with the spirits of nature ...'

1869: The family moves to the peaceful, rural village of Neudörfl, near Wiener-Neustadt in present-day Austria. Rudolf Steiner attends the village school. Because of the 'unorthodoxy' of his writing and spelling, he has to do 'extra lessons.'

1870: Through a book lent to him by his tutor, he discovers geometry: 'To grasp something purely in the spirit brought me inner happiness. I know that I first learned happiness through geometry.' The same tutor allows him to draw, while other students still struggle with their reading and writing. 'An artistic element' thus enters his education.

1871: Though his parents are not religious, Rudolf Steiner becomes a 'church child,' a favourite of the priest, who was 'an exceptional character.' 'Up to the age of ten or eleven, among those I came to know, he was far and away the most significant.' Among other things, he introduces Steiner to Copernican, heliocentric cosmology. As an altar boy, Rudolf Steiner serves at Masses, funerals, and Corpus Christi processions. At year's end, after an incident in which he escapes a thrashing, his father forbids him to go to church.

1872: Rudolf Steiner transfers to grammar school in Wiener-Neustadt, a five-mile walk from home, which must be done in all weathers.

1873–75: Through his teachers and on his own, Rudolf Steiner has many wonderful experiences with science and mathematics. Outside school, he teaches himself analytic geometry, trigonometry, differential equations, and calculus.

1876: Rudolf Steiner begins tutoring other students. He learns bookbinding from his father. He also teaches himself stenography.

1877: Rudolf Steiner discovers Kant's *Critique of Pure Reason*, which he reads and rereads. He also discovers and reads von Rotteck's *World History*.

1878: He studies extensively in contemporary psychology and philosophy.

1879: Rudolf Steiner graduates from high school with honours. His father is transferred to Inzersdorf, near Vienna. He uses his first visit to Vienna 'to purchase a great number of philosophy books'—Kant, Fichte, Schelling, and Hegel, as well as numerous histories of philosophy. His aim: to find a path from the 'I' to nature.

October 1879–1883: Rudolf Steiner attends the Technical College in Vienna—to study mathematics, chemistry, physics, mineralogy, botany, zoology, biology, geology, and mechanics—with a scholarship. He also attends lectures in history and literature, while avidly reading philosophy on his own. His two favourite professors are Karl Julius Schröer (German language and literature) and Edmund Reitlinger (physics). He also audits lectures by Robert Zimmermann on aesthetics and Franz Brentano on philosophy. During this year he begins his friendship with Moritz Zitter (1861–1921), who will help support him financially when he is in Berlin.

1880: Rudolf Steiner attends lectures on Schiller and Goethe by Karl Julius Schröer, who becomes his mentor. Also 'through a remarkable combination of circumstances,' he meets Felix Koguzki, a 'herb gatherer' and healer, who could 'see deeply into the secrets of nature.' Rudolf Steiner will meet and study with this 'emissary of the Master' throughout his time in Vienna.

1881: January: '... I didn't sleep a wink. I was busy with philosophical problems until about 12:30 a.m. Then, finally, I threw myself down on my couch. All my striving during the previous year had been to research whether the following statement by Schelling was true or not: *Within everyone dwells a secret, marvelous capacity to draw back from the stream of time—out of the self clothed in all that comes to us from outside—into our innermost being and there, in the immutable form of the Eternal, to look into ourselves*. I believe, and I am still quite certain of it, that I discovered this capacity in myself; I had long had an inkling of it. Now the whole of idealist philosophy stood before me in modified form. What's a sleepless night compared to that!'

Rudolf Steiner begins communicating with leading thinkers of the day, who send him books in return, which he reads eagerly.

July: 'I am not one of those who dives into the day like an animal in human form. I pursue a quite specific goal, an idealistic aim—knowledge of the truth! This cannot be done offhandedly. It requires the greatest striving in the world, free of all egotism, and equally of all resignation.'

August: Steiner puts down on paper for the first time thoughts for a 'Philosophy of Freedom.' 'The striving for the absolute: this human yearning is freedom.' He also seeks to outline a 'peasant philosophy,' describing what the worldview of a 'peasant'—one who lives close to the earth and the old ways—really is.

1881–1882: Felix Koguzki, the herb gatherer, reveals himself to be the envoy of another, higher initiatory personality, who instructs Rudolf Steiner to penetrate Fichte's philosophy and to master modern scientific thinking as a preparation for right entry into the spirit. This 'Master' also teaches him the double (evolutionary and involutionary) nature of time.

1882: Through the offices of Karl Julius Schröer, Rudolf Steiner is asked by Joseph Kürschner to edit Goethe's scientific works for the *Deutschen National-Literatur* edition. He writes 'A Possible Critique of Atomistic Concepts' and sends it to Friedrich Theodor Vischer.

1883: Rudolf Steiner completes his college studies and begins work on the Goethe project.

1884: First volume of Goethe's *Scientific Writings* (CW 1) appears (March). He lectures on Goethe and Lessing, and Goethe's approach to science. In July, he enters the household of Ladislaus and Pauline Specht as tutor to the four Specht boys. He will live there until 1890. At this time, he meets Josef Breuer (1842–1925), the co-author with Sigmund Freud of *Studies in Hysteria*, who is the Specht family doctor.

1885: While continuing to edit Goethe's writings, Rudolf Steiner reads deeply in contemporary philosophy (Eduard von Hartmann, Johannes Volkelt, and Richard Wahle, among others).

1886: May: Rudolf Steiner sends Kürschner the manuscript of *Outlines of Goethe's Theory of Knowledge* (CW 2), which appears in October, and which he sends out widely. He also meets the poet Marie Eugenie Delle Grazie and writes 'Nature and Our Ideals' for her. He attends her salon, where he meets many priests, theologians, and philosophers, who will become his friends. Meanwhile, the director of the Goethe Archive in Weimar requests his collaboration with the *Sophien* edition of Goethe's works, particularly the writings on colour.

1887: At the beginning of the year, Rudolf Steiner is very sick. As the year progresses and his health improves, he becomes increasingly 'a man of letters,' lecturing, writing essays, and taking part in Austrian cultural life. In August–September, the second volume of Goethe's *Scientific Writings* appears.

1888: January–July: Rudolf Steiner assumes editorship of the 'German Weekly' (*Deutsche Wochenschrift*). He begins lecturing more intensively, giving, for example, a lecture titled 'Goethe as Father of a New Aesthetics.' He meets and becomes soul friends with Friedrich Eckstein (1861–1939), a vegetarian, philosopher of symbolism, alchemist, and musician, who will introduce him to various spiritual currents (including Theosophy) and with whom he will meditate and interpret esoteric and alchemical texts.

1889: Rudolf Steiner first reads Nietzsche (*Beyond Good and Evil*). He encounters Theosophy again and learns of Madame Blavatsky in the Theosophical circle around Marie Lang (1858–1934). Here he also meets well-known figures of Austrian life, as well as esoteric figures like the occultist Franz Hartmann and Karl Leinigen-Billigen (translator of C.G. Harrison's *The Transcendental Universe*). During this period, Steiner first reads A.P. Sinnett's *Esoteric Buddhism* and Mabel Collins's *Light on the Path*. He also begins travelling, visiting Budapest, Weimar, and Berlin (where he meets philosopher Eduard von Hartmann).

1890: Rudolf Steiner finishes volume 3 of Goethe's scientific writings. He begins his doctoral dissertation, which will become *Truth and Science* (CW 3). He also meets the poet and feminist Rosa Mayreder (1858–1938), with whom he can exchange his most intimate thoughts. In September, Rudolf Steiner moves to Weimar to work in the Goethe-Schiller Archive.

1891: Volume 3 of the Kürschner edition of Goethe appears. Meanwhile, Rudolf Steiner edits Goethe's studies in mineralogy and scientific writings for the *Sophien* edition. He meets Ludwig Laistner of the Cotta Publishing Company, who asks for a book on the basic question of metaphysics. From this will result, ultimately, *The Philosophy of Freedom* (CW 4), which will be published not by Cotta but by Emil Felber. In October, Rudolf Steiner takes the oral exam for a doctorate in philosophy, mathematics, and mechanics at Rostock University, receiving his doctorate on the twenty-sixth. In November, he gives his first lecture on Goethe's 'Fairy Tale' in Vienna.

1892: Rudolf Steiner continues work at the Goethe-Schiller Archive and on his *Philosophy of Freedom*. *Truth and Science*, his doctoral dissertation, is published. Steiner undertakes to write introductions to books on Schopenhauer and Jean Paul for Cotta. At year's end, he finds lodging with Anna Eunike, née Schulz (1853–1911), a widow with four daughters and a son. He also develops a friendship with Otto Erich Hartleben (1864–1905) with whom he shares literary interests.

1893: Rudolf Steiner begins his habit of producing many reviews and articles. In March, he gives a lecture titled 'Hypnotism, with Reference to Spiritism.' In September, volume 4 of the Kürschner edition is completed. In November, *The Philosophy of Freedom* appears. This year, too, he meets John Henry Mackay (1864–1933), the anarchist, and Max Stirner, a scholar and biographer.

1894: Rudolf Steiner meets Elisabeth Förster Nietzsche, the philosopher's sister, and begins to read Nietzsche in earnest, beginning with the as yet unpublished *Antichrist*. He also meets Ernst Haeckel (1834–1919). In the fall, he begins to write *Nietzsche, A Fighter against His Time* (CW 5).

1895: May, *Nietzsche, A Fighter against His Time* appears.

1896: January 22: Rudolf Steiner sees Friedrich Nietzsche for the first and only time. Moves between the Nietzsche and the Goethe-Schiller Archives, where he completes his work before year's end. He falls out with Elisabeth Förster Nietzsche, thus ending his association with the Nietzsche Archive.

1897: Rudolf Steiner finishes the manuscript of *Goethe's Worldview* (CW 6). He moves to Berlin with Anna Eunike and begins editorship of the *Magazin für Literatur*. From now on, Steiner will write countless reviews, literary and philosophical articles, and so on. He begins lecturing at the 'Free Literary Society.' In September, he attends the Zionist Congress in Basel. He sides with Dreyfus in the Dreyfus affair.

1898: Rudolf Steiner is very active as an editor in the political, artistic, and theatrical life of Berlin. He becomes friendly with John Henry Mackay and poet Ludwig Jacobowski (1868–1900). He joins Jacobowski's circle of writers, artists, and scientists—'The Coming Ones' (*Die Kommenden*)—and contributes lectures to the group until 1903. He also lectures at the 'League for College Pedagogy.' He writes an article for Goethe's sesquicentennial, 'Goethe's Secret Revelation,' on the 'Fairy Tale of the Green Snake and the Beautiful Lily.'

1898–99: 'This was a trying time for my soul as I looked at Christianity. . . . I was able to progress only by contemplating, by means of spiritual perception, the evolution of Christianity. . . . Conscious knowledge of real Christianity began to dawn in me around the turn of the century. This seed continued to develop. My soul trial occurred shortly before the beginning of the twentieth century. It was decisive for my soul's development that I stood spiritually before the Mystery of Golgotha in a deep and solemn celebration of knowledge.'

1899: Rudolf Steiner begins teaching and giving lectures and lecture cycles at the Workers' College, founded by Wilhelm Liebknecht (1826–1900). He will continue to do so until 1904. Writes: *Literature and Spiritual Life in the Nineteenth Century; Individualism in Philosophy*; *Haeckel and His Opponents; Poetry in the Present;* and begins what will become (fifteen years later) *The Riddles of Philosophy* (CW 18). He also meets many artists and writers, including Käthe Kollwitz, Stefan Zweig, and Rainer Maria Rilke. On October 31, he marries Anna Eunike.

1900: 'I thought that the turn of the century must bring humanity a new light. It seemed to me that the separation of human thinking and willing from the spirit had peaked. A turn or reversal of direction in human evolution seemed to me a necessity.' Rudolf Steiner finishes *World and Life Views in the Nineteenth Century* (the second part of what will become *The Riddles of Philosophy*) and dedicates it to Ernst Haeckel. It is published in March. He continues lecturing at *Die Kommenden*, whose leadership he assumes after the death of Jacobowski. Also, he gives the Gutenberg Jubilee lecture before 7,000 typesetters and printers. In September, Rudolf Steiner is invited by Count and Countess Brockdorff to lecture in the Theosophical Library. His first lecture is on Nietzsche. His second lecture is titled 'Goethe's Secret Revelation.' October 6, he begins a lecture cycle on the mystics that will become *Mystics after Modernism* (CW 7). November-December: 'Marie von Sivers appears in the audience....' Also in November, Steiner gives his first lecture at the Giordano Bruno Bund (where he will continue to lecture until May, 1905). He speaks on Bruno and modern Rome, focusing on the importance of the philosophy of Thomas Aquinas as monism.

1901: In continual financial straits, Rudolf Steiner's early friends Moritz Zitter and Rosa Mayreder help support him. In October, he begins the lecture cycle *Christianity as Mystical Fact* (CW 8) at the Theosophical Library. In November, he gives his first 'Theosophical lecture' on Goethe's 'Fairy Tale' in Hamburg at the invitation of Wilhelm Hubbe-Schleiden. He also attends a gathering to celebrate the founding of the Theosophical Society at Count and Countess Brockdorff's. He gives a lecture cycle, 'From Buddha to Christ,' for the circle of the *Kommenden*. November 17, Marie von Sivers asks Rudolf Steiner if Theosophy needs a Western-Christian spiritual movement (to complement Theosophy's Eastern emphasis). 'The question was posed. Now, following spiritual laws, I could begin to give an answer....' In December, Rudolf Steiner writes his first article for a Theosophical publication. At year's end, the Brockdorffs and possibly Wilhelm Hubbe-Schleiden ask Rudolf Steiner to join the Theosophical Society and undertake the leadership of the German section. Rudolf Steiner agrees, on the condition that Marie von Sivers (then in Italy) work with him.

1902: Beginning in January, Rudolf Steiner attends the opening of the Workers' School in Spandau with Rosa Luxemberg (1870–1919). January 17, Rudolf Steiner joins the Theosophical Society. In April, he is asked to become general secretary of the German Section of the Theosophical Society, and works on preparations for its founding. In July, he visits London for a Theosophical congress. He meets Bertram Keightly, G.R.S. Mead, A.P. Sinnett, and Annie Besant, among others. In September, *Christianity as Mystical Fact* appears. In October, Rudolf Steiner gives his first public lecture on Theosophy ('Monism and Theosophy') to about three hundred people at the Giordano Bruno Bund. On October 19–21, the German Section of the Theosophical Society has its first meeting; Rudolf Steiner is the general secretary, and Annie Besant attends. Steiner lectures on practical karma studies. On October 23, Annie Besant inducts Rudolf Steiner into the Esoteric School of the Theosophical Society. On October 25, Steiner begins a weekly series of lectures: 'The Field of Theosophy.' During this year, Rudolf Steiner also first meets Ita Wegman (1876–1943), who will become his close collaborator in his final years.

1903: Rudolf Steiner holds about 300 lectures and seminars. In May, the first issue of the periodical *Luzifer* appears. In June, Rudolf Steiner visits

London for the first meeting of the Federation of the European Sections of the Theosophical Society, where he meets Colonel Olcott. He begins to write *Theosophy* (CW 9).

1904: Rudolf Steiner continues lecturing at the Workers' College and elsewhere (about 90 lectures), while lecturing intensively all over Germany among Theosophists (about 140 lectures). In February, he meets Carl Unger (1878–1929), who will become a member of the board of the Anthroposophical Society (1913). In March, he meets Michael Bauer (1871–1929), a Christian mystic, who will also be on the board. In May, *Theosophy* appears, with the dedication: 'To the spirit of Giordano Bruno.' Rudolf Steiner and Marie von Sivers visit London for meetings with Annie Besant. June: Rudolf Steiner and Marie von Sivers attend the meeting of the Federation of European Sections of the Theosophical Society in Amsterdam. In July, Steiner begins the articles in *Luzifer-Gnosis* that will become *How to Know Higher Worlds* (CW 10) and *Cosmic Memory* (CW 11). In September, Annie Besant visits Germany. In December, Steiner lectures on Freemasonry. He mentions the High Grade Masonry derived from John Yarker and represented by Theodore Reuss and Karl Kellner as a blank slate 'into which a good image could be placed.'

1905: This year, Steiner ends his non-Theosophical lecturing activity. Supported by Marie von Sivers, his Theosophical lecturing—both in public and in the Theosophical Society—increases significantly: 'The German Theosophical Movement is of exceptional importance.' Steiner recommends reading, among others, Fichte, Jacob Boehme, and Angelus Silesius. He begins to introduce Christian themes into Theosophy. He also begins to work with doctors (Felix Peipers and Ludwig Noll). In July, he is in London for the Federation of European Sections, where he attends a lecture by Annie Besant: 'I have seldom seen Mrs. Besant speak in so inward and heartfelt a manner. . . .' 'Through Mrs. Besant I have found the way to H.P. Blavatsky.' September to October, he gives a course of thirty-one lectures for a small group of esoteric students. In October, the annual meeting of the German Section of the Theosophical Society, which still remains very small, takes place. Rudolf Steiner reports membership has risen from 121 to 377 members. In November, seeking to establish esoteric 'continuity,' Rudolf Steiner and Marie von Sivers participate in a 'Memphis-Misraim' Masonic ceremony. They pay forty-five marks for membership. 'Yesterday, you saw how little remains of former esoteric institutions.' 'We are dealing only with a "framework". . . for the present, nothing lies behind it. The occult powers have completely withdrawn.'

1906: Expansion of Theosophical work. Rudolf Steiner gives about 245 lectures, only 44 of which take place in Berlin. Cycles are given in Paris, Leipzig, Stuttgart, and Munich. Esoteric work also intensifies. Rudolf Steiner begins writing *An Outline of Esoteric Science* (CW 13). In January, Rudolf Steiner receives permission (a patent) from the Great Orient of the Scottish A & A Thirty-Three Degree Rite of the Order of the Ancient

Freemasons of the Memphis-Misraim Rite to direct a chapter under the name 'Mystica Aeterna.' This will become the 'Cognitive-Ritual Section' (also called 'Misraim Service') of the Esoteric School. (See: *Freemasonry and Ritual Work: The Misraim Service*, CW 265). During this time, Steiner also meets Albert Schweitzer. In May, he is in Paris, where he visits Edouard Schuré. Many Russians attend his lectures (including Konstantin Balmont, Dimitri Mereszkovski, Zinaida Hippius, and Maximilian Woloshin). He attends the General Meeting of the European Federation of the Theosophical Society, at which Col. Olcott is present for the last time. He spends the year's end in Venice and Rome, where he writes and works on his translation of H.P. Blavatsky's *Key to Theosophy*.

1907: Further expansion of the German Theosophical Movement according to the Rosicrucian directive to 'introduce spirit into the world'—in education, in social questions, in art, and in science. In February, Col. Olcott dies in Adyar. Before he dies, Olcott indicates that 'the Masters' wish Annie Besant to succeed him: much politicking ensues. Rudolf Steiner supports Besant's candidacy. April-May: preparations for the Congress of the Federation of European Sections of the Theosophical Society—the great, watershed Whitsun 'Munich Congress,' attended by Annie Besant and others. Steiner decides to separate Eastern and Western (Christian-Rosicrucian) esoteric schools. He takes his esoteric school out of the Theosophical Society (Besant and Rudolf Steiner are 'in harmony' on this). Steiner makes his first lecture tours to Austria and Hungary. That summer, he is in Italy. In September, he visits Edouard Schuré, who will write the introduction to the French edition of *Christianity as Mystical Fact* in Barr, Alsace. Rudolf Steiner writes the autobiographical statement known as the 'Barr Document.' In *Luzifer-Gnosis*, 'The Education of the Child' appears.

1908: The movement grows (membership: 1,150). Lecturing expands. Steiner makes his first extended lecture tour to Holland and Scandinavia, as well as visits to Naples and Sicily. Themes: St. John's Gospel, the Apocalypse, Egypt, science, philosophy, and logic. *Luzifer-Gnosis* ceases publication. In Berlin, Marie von Sivers (with Johanna Mücke (1864–1949) forms the *Philosophisch-Theosophisch* (after 1915 *Philosophisch-Anthroposophisch*) *Verlag* to publish Steiner's work. Steiner gives lecture cycles titled *The Gospel of St. John* (CW 103) and *The Apocalypse* (104).

1909: *An Outline of Esoteric Science* appears. Lecturing and travel continues. Rudolf Steiner's spiritual research expands to include the polarity of Lucifer and Ahriman; the work of great individualities in history; the Maitreya Buddha and the Bodhisattvas; spiritual economy (CW 109); the work of the spiritual hierarchies in heaven and on earth (CW 110). He also deepens and intensifies his research into the Gospels, giving lectures on the Gospel of St. Luke (CW 114) with the first mention of two Jesus children. Meets and becomes friends with Christian Morgenstern (1871–1914). In April, he lays the foundation stone for the Malsch model—the building that will lead to the first Goetheanum. In May, the International Congress of the Federation of European Sections of the

Theosophical Society takes place in Budapest. Rudolf Steiner receives the Subba Row medal for *How to Know Higher Worlds*. During this time, Charles W. Leadbeater discovers Jiddu Krishnamurti (1895–1986) and proclaims him the future 'world teacher,' the bearer of the Maitreya Buddha and the 'reappearing Christ.' In October, Steiner delivers seminal lectures on 'anthroposophy,' which he will try, unsuccessfully, to rework over the next years into the unfinished work, *Anthroposophy (A Fragment)* (CW 45).

1910: New themes: *The Reappearance of Christ in the Etheric* (CW 118); *The Fifth Gospel; The Mission of Folk Souls* (CW 121); *Occult History* (CW 126); the evolving development of etheric cognitive capacities. Rudolf Steiner continues his Gospel research with *The Gospel of St. Matthew* (CW 123). In January, his father dies. In April, he takes a month-long trip to Italy, including Rome, Monte Cassino, and Sicily. He also visits Scandinavia again. July–August, he writes the first mystery drama, *The Portal of Initiation* (CW 14). In November, he gives 'psychosophy' lectures. In December, he submits 'On the Psychological Foundations and Epistemological Framework of Theosophy' to the International Philosophical Congress in Bologna.

1911: The crisis in the Theosophical Society deepens. In January, 'The Order of the Rising Sun,' which will soon become 'The Order of the Star in the East,' is founded for the coming world teacher, Krishnamurti. At the same time, Marie von Sivers, Rudolf Steiner's co-worker, falls ill. Fewer lectures are given, but important new ground is broken. In Prague, in March, Steiner meets Franz Kafka (1883–1924) and Hugo Bergmann (1883-1975). In April, he delivers his paper to the Philosophical Congress. He writes the second mystery drama, *The Soul's Probation* (CW 14). Also, while Marie von Sivers is convalescing, Rudolf Steiner begins work on *Calendar 1912/1913*, which will contain the 'Calendar of the Soul' meditations. On March 19, Anna (Eunike) Steiner dies. In September, Rudolf Steiner visits Einsiedeln, birthplace of Paracelsus. In December, Friedrich Rittelmeyer, future founder of the Christian Community, meets Rudolf Steiner. The *Johannes-Bauverein*, the 'building committee,' which would lead to the first Goetheanum (first planned for Munich), is also founded, and a preliminary committee for the founding of an independent association is created that, in the following year, will become the Anthroposophical Society. Important lecture cycles include *Occult Physiology* (CW 128); *Wonders of the World* (CW 129); *From Jesus to Christ* (CW 131). Other themes: esoteric Christianity; Christian Rosenkreutz; the spiritual guidance of humanity; the sense world and the world of the spirit.

1912: Despite the ongoing, now increasing crisis in the Theosophical Society, much is accomplished: *Calendar 1912/1913* is published; eurythmy is created; both the third mystery drama, *The Guardian of the Threshold* (CW 14) and *A Way of Self-Knowledge* (CW 16) are written. New (or renewed) themes included life between death and rebirth and karma and reincarnation. Other lecture cycles: *Spiritual Beings in the Heavenly Bodies and in the Kingdoms of Nature* (CW 136); *The Human Being in the Light of Occultism, Theosophy, and Philosophy* (CW 137); *The Gospel of St. Mark* (CW 139); and *The Bhagavad Gita and the Epistles of Paul* (CW 142). On May 8, Rudolf Steiner celebrates White Lotus Day, H.P. Blavatsky's death day, which he had faithfully observed for the past decade, for the last time. In August, Rudolf Steiner suggests the 'independent association' be called the 'Anthroposophical Society.' In September, the first eurythmy course takes place. In October, Rudolf Steiner declines recognition of a Theosophical Society lodge dedicated to the Star of the East and decides to expel all Theosophical Society members belonging to the order. Also, with Marie von Sivers, he first visits Dornach, near Basel, Switzerland, and they stand on the hill where the Goetheanum will be built. In November, a Theosophical Society lodge is opened by direct mandate from Adyar (Annie Besant). In December, a meeting of the German section occurs at which it is decided that belonging to the Order of the Star of the East is incompatible with membership in the Theosophical Society. December 28: informal founding of the Anthroposophical Society in Berlin.

1913: Expulsion of the German section from the Theosophical Society. February 2–3: Foundation meeting of the Anthroposophical Society. Board members include: Marie von Sivers, Michael Bauer, and Carl Unger. September 20: Laying of the foundation stone for the *Johannes Bau* (Goetheanum) in Dornach. Building begins immediately. The third mystery drama, *The Soul's Awakening* (CW 14), is completed. Also: *The Threshold of the Spiritual World* (CW 147). Lecture cycles include: *The Bhagavad Gita and the Epistles of Paul* and *The Esoteric Meaning of the Bhagavad Gita* (CW 146), which the Russian philosopher Nikolai Berdyaev attends; *The Mysteries of the East and of Christianity* (CW 144); *The Effects of Esoteric Development* (CW 145); and *The Fifth Gospel* (CW 148). In May, Rudolf Steiner is in London and Paris, where anthroposophical work continues.

1914: Building continues on the *Johannes Bau* (Goetheanum) in Dornach, with artists and co-workers from seventeen nations. The general assembly of the Anthroposophical Society takes place. In May, Rudolf Steiner visits Paris, as well as Chartres Cathedral. June 28: assassination in Sarajevo ('Now the catastrophe has happened!'). August 1: War is declared. Rudolf Steiner returns to Germany from Dornach—he will travel back and forth. He writes the last chapter of *The Riddles of Philosophy*. Lecture cycles include: *Human and Cosmic Thought* (CW 151); *Inner Being of Humanity between Death and a New Birth* (CW 153); *Occult Reading and Occult Hearing* (CW 156). December 24: marriage of Rudolf Steiner and Marie von Sivers.

1915: Building continues. Life after death becomes a major theme, also art. Writes: *Thoughts during a Time of War* (CW 24). Lectures include: *The Secret of Death* (CW 159); *The Uniting of Humanity through the Christ Impulse* (CW 165).

1916: Rudolf Steiner begins work with Edith Maryon (1872–1924) on the sculpture 'The Representative of Humanity' ('The Group'—Christ, Lucifer, and Ahriman). He also works with the alchemist Alexander von Bernus on the quarterly *Das Reich*. He writes *The Riddle of Humanity* (CW 20). Lectures include: *Necessity and Freedom in World History and Human Action* (CW 166); *Past and Present in the Human Spirit* (CW 167); *The Karma of Vocation* (CW 172); *The Karma of Untruthfulness* (CW 173).

1917: Russian Revolution. The U.S. enters the war. Building continues. Rudolf Steiner delineates the idea of the 'threefold nature of the human being' (in a public lecture March 15) and the 'threefold nature of the social organism' (hammered out in May-June with the help of Otto von Lerchenfeld and Ludwig Polzer-Hoditz in the form of two documents titled *Memoranda*, which were distributed in high places). August–September: Rudolf Steiner writes *The Riddles of the Soul* (CW 20). Also: commentary on 'The Chymical Wedding of Christian Rosenkreutz' for Alexander Bernus (*Das Reich*). Lectures include: *The Karma of Materialism* (CW 176); *The Spiritual Background of the Outer World: The Fall of the Spirits of Darkness* (CW 177).

1918: March 18: peace treaty of Brest-Litovsk—'Now everything will truly enter chaos! What is needed is cultural renewal.' June: Rudolf Steiner visits Karlstein (Grail) Castle outside Prague. Lecture cycle: *From Symptom to Reality in Modern History* (CW 185). In mid-November, Emil Molt, of the Waldorf-Astoria Cigarette Company, has the idea of founding a school for his workers' children.

1919: Focus on the threefold social organism: tireless travel, countless lectures, meetings, and publications. At the same time, a new public stage of Anthroposophy emerges as cultural renewal begins. The coming years will see initiatives in pedagogy, medicine, pharmacology, and agriculture. January 27: threefold meeting: ' We must first of all, with the money we have, found free schools that can bring people what they need.' February: first public eurythmy performance in Zurich. Also: 'Appeal to the German People' (CW 24), circulated March 6 as a newspaper insert. In April, *Towards Social Renewal* (CW 23) appears—'perhaps the most widely read of all books on politics appearing since the war.' Rudolf Steiner is asked to undertake the 'direction and leadership' of the school founded by the Waldorf-Astoria Company. Rudolf Steiner begins to talk about the 'renewal' of education. May 30: a building is selected and purchased for the future Waldorf School. August–September, Rudolf Steiner gives a lecture course for Waldorf teachers, *The Foundations of Human Experience (Study of Man)* (CW 293). September 7: Opening of the first Waldorf School. December (into January): first science course, the *Light Course* (CW 320).

1920: The Waldorf School flourishes. New threefold initiatives. Founding of limited companies *Der Kommende Tag* and *Futurum A.G.* to infuse spiritual values into the economic realm. Rudolf Steiner also focuses on the sciences. Lectures: *Introducing Anthroposophical Medicine* (CW 312); *The Warmth Course* (CW 321); *The Boundaries of Natural Science* (CW 322); *The Redemption of Thinking* (CW 74). February: Johannes Werner

Klein—later a co-founder of the Christian Community—asks Rudolf Steiner about the possibility of a 'religious renewal,' a 'Johannine church.' In March, Rudolf Steiner gives the first course for doctors and medical students. In April, a divinity student asks Rudolf Steiner a second time about the possibility of religious renewal. September 27–October 16: anthroposophical 'university course.' December: lectures titled *The Search for the New Isis* (CW 202).

1921: Rudolf Steiner continues his intensive work on cultural renewal, including the uphill battle for the threefold social order. 'University' arts, scientific, theological, and medical courses include: *The Astronomy Course* (CW 323); *Observation, Mathematics, and Scientific Experiment* (CW 324); the *Second Medical Course* (CW 313); *Colour*. In June and September-October, Rudolf Steiner also gives the first two 'priests' courses' (CW 342 and 343). The 'youth movement' gains momentum. Magazines are founded: *Die Drei* (January), and—under the editorship of Albert Steffen (1884–1963)—the weekly, *Das Goetheanum* (August). In February–March, Rudolf Steiner takes his first trip outside Germany since the war (Holland). On April 7, Steiner receives a letter regarding 'religious renewal,' and May 22–23, he agrees to address the question in a practical way. In June, the Klinical-Therapeutic Institute opens in Arlesheim under the direction of Dr. Ita Wegman. In August, the Chemical-Pharmaceutical Laboratory opens in Arlesheim (Oskar Schmiedel and Ita Wegman are directors). The Clinical Therapeutic Institute is inaugurated in Stuttgart (Dr. Ludwig Noll is director); also the Research Laboratory in Dornach (Ehrenfried Pfeiffer and Günther Wachsmuth are directors). In November–December, Rudolf Steiner visits Norway.

1922: The first half of the year involves very active public lecturing (thousands attend); in the second half, Rudolf Steiner begins to withdraw and turn toward the Society—'The Society is asleep.' It is 'too weak' to do what is asked of it. The businesses—*Der Kommende Tag* and *Futurum A.G.*—fail. In January, with the help of an agent, Steiner undertakes a twelve-city German lecture tour, accompanied by eurythmy performances. In two weeks he speaks to more than 2,000 people. In April, he gives a 'university course' in The Hague. He also visits England. In June, he is in Vienna for the East–West Congress. In August–September, he is back in England for the Oxford Conference on Education. Returning to Dornach, he gives the lectures *Philosophy, Cosmology, and Religion* (CW 215), and gives the third priests' course (CW 344). On September 16, The Christian Community is founded. In October–November, Steiner is in Holland and England. He also speaks to the youth: *The Youth Course* (CW 217). In December, Steiner gives lectures titled *The Origins of Natural Science* (CW 326), and *Humanity and the World of Stars: The Spiritual Communion of Humanity* (CW 219). December 31: Fire at the Goetheanum, which is destroyed.

1923: Despite the fire, Rudolf Steiner continues his work unabated. A very hard year. Internal dispersion, dissension, and apathy abound. There is conflict—between old and new visions—within the Society. A wake-up call is needed, and Rudolf Steiner responds with renewed lecturing vitality. His focus: the spiritual context of human life; initiation science; the course of the year; and community building. As a foundation for an artistic school, he creates a series of pastel sketches. Lecture cycles: *The Anthroposophical Movement; Initiation Science* (CW 227) (in England at the Penmaenmawr Summer School); *The Four Seasons and the Archangels* (CW 229); *Harmony of the Creative Word* (CW 230); *The Supersensible Human* (CW 231), given in Holland for the founding of the Dutch society. On November 10, in response to the failed Hitler-Ludendorff putsch in Munich, Steiner closes his Berlin residence and moves the *Philosophisch-Anthroposophisch Verlag* (Press) to Dornach. On December 9, Steiner begins the serialization of his *Autobiography: The Course of My Life* (CW 28) in *Das Goetheanum*. It will continue to appear weekly, without a break, until his death. Late December–early January: Rudolf Steiner re-founds the Anthroposophical Society (about 12,000 members internationally) and takes over its leadership. The new board members are: Marie Steiner, Ita Wegman, Albert Steffen, Elisabeth Vreede, and Günther Wachsmuth. (See *The Christmas Meeting for the Founding of the General Anthroposophical Society*, CW 260). Accompanying lectures: *Mystery Knowledge and Mystery Centres* (CW 232); *World History in the Light of Anthroposophy* (CW 233). December 25: the Foundation Stone is laid (in the hearts of members) in the form of the 'Foundation Stone Meditation.'

1924: January 1: having founded the Anthroposophical Society and taken over its leadership, Rudolf Steiner has the task of 'reforming' it. The process begins with a weekly newssheet ('What's Happening in the Anthroposophical Society') in which Rudolf Steiner's 'Letters to Members' and 'Anthroposophical Leading Thoughts' appear (CW 26). The next step is the creation of a new esoteric class, the 'first class' of the 'University of Spiritual Science' (which was to have been followed, had Rudolf Steiner lived longer, by two more advanced classes). Then comes a new language for Anthroposophy—practical, phenomenological, and direct; and Rudolf Steiner creates the model for the second Goetheanum. He begins the series of extensive 'karma' lectures (CW 235–40); and finally, responding to needs, he creates two new initiatives: biodynamic agriculture and curative education. After the middle of the year, rumours begin to circulate regarding Steiner's health. Lectures: January–February, *Anthroposophy* (CW 234); February: *Tone Eurythmy* (CW 278); June: *The Agriculture Course* (CW 327); June–July: *Speech Eurythmy* (CW 279); *Curative Education* (CW 317); August: (England, 'Second International Summer School'), *Initiation Consciousness: True and False Paths in Spiritual Investigation* (CW 243); September: *Pastoral Medicine* (CW 318). On September 26, for the first time, Rudolf Steiner cancels a lecture. On September 28, he gives his last lecture. On September 29, he withdraws to his studio in the carpenter's shop; now he is definitively ill. Cared for by Ita Wegman, he continues working, however, and writing the weekly installments of his *Autobiography* and *Letters to the Members/Leading Thoughts* (CW 26).

1925: Rudolf Steiner, while continuing to work, continues to weaken. He finishes *Extending Practical Medicine* (CW 27) with Ita Wegman.
On March 30, around ten in the morning, Rudolf Steiner dies

INDEX